Goliath

BEATRIX CAMPBELL is a print and television journalist, whose *Wigan Pier Re-Visited*, her rendezvous with George Orwell's classic, was the winner of the 1984 Cheltenham Festival Prize for Literature. In 1987 her book about the success of the Conservative Party among women, *The Iron Ladies*, was the winner of the Fawcett Prize; in 1988 she published *Unofficial Secrets: The Cleveland Case*; and in 1989 she was awarded the 300 Committee's Nancy Astor Campaigning Journalist of the Year award. She lives in Newcastle-upon-Tyne.

This book is dedicated to
A Good Woman

GOLIATH

Britain's Dangerous Places

Beatrix Campbell

Methuen

First published in Great Britain in 1993
by Methuen London
an imprint of Reed Consumer Books Ltd
Michelin House, 81 Fulham Road, London SW3 6RB
and Auckland, Melbourne, Singapore and Toronto

Reprinted 1993 (twice)

A CIP catalogue record for this book
is available at the British Library
ISBN 0 413 45411 8

Typeset by Falcon Graphic Art Ltd
Wallington, Surrey
Printed in England
by Clays Ltd, St Ives plc

Contents

Acknowledgements

Elsbeth Lindner commissioned this book as a text about *fin de siècle* Britain, and then accepted its reincarnation as a local window on a larger landscape. It owes its existence to her. I owe my own well-being during its production to my friends Inez and Vincent McCormack and Judith Jones, who kept me going.

Most of the material is based on interviews with the protagonists and on court proceedings, unless otherwise footnoted. Thanks to Joe Hamill, the lads and West Belfast Concerned Parents Support Group, Extern, and Sally McErleane, from Divis, who first got me thinking about joyriders. West Belfast had much to teach mainland Britain about the periphery's challenge to the centre, not least the robust passion for dangerous driving among young men whose addiction defied the most retaliatory punishment in these islands.

I am grateful for the cooperation and candour of Northumbria Police, South Wales Police, Thames Valley Police and West Yorkshire Police. Thanks, for ideas and information, to South Glamorgan County Council Research and Information, Cardiff Juvenile Offenders' Panel, South Glamorgan Racial Equality Council, the Chapter, Nina Edge, Ely Youth Club, Clare Hudson, Malika Kabba, Barnardos, Jean and George Crabbe, the Peace Shop, Alfie and John Osmond, Community Education; Blackbird Leys youth and community workers, Oxford Probation Service, Robert Metcalfe, Debbie McAlvine, Sister Ettie, the Watersons; North Tyneside Council, Meadowell Resource Centre, Scotswood Project, the Council for Racial Equality, Newcastle City Council, Social Services Director Brian Roycroft, Social Services Area 4, Roshni Asian

Women's Centre, Asian Girls' Group, Clifton Mount Interpreters' Group, Northumbria Probation Service, Juvenile Justice, Newcastle Tenants' Federation and Credit Unions, Architecture Workshop; Bristol Racial Equality Council, Peter Courtier, Dan Lloyd, Colin Thomas; Kirklees Council; Statewatch; Pam Trevithick, Raphael Samuel, Elaine Snaith, Kate Howie, Doreen Massey, Walter Easey, Fred Robinson, Peter Wells, Barbara Hudson, my sister and brother Tina Webb and Jimmy Barnes, and finally all the children in Cardiff, Oxford and Tyneside whose experience enlightened this book.

Introduction

At the end of the summer of 1991 riots exploded in Britain. Fires and fighting bled across municipal suburbs in Cardiff, Oxford and Tyneside and angry young men made their mark on history. Nearly five hundred of them were arrested during street spectacles which cost their communities an estimated £12 million.

Crowds gathered for three days around a parade of shops in Ely, an airy estate in Cardiff, to 'purge' the estate of a Pakistani shopkeeper. There were seventy-five arrests. Oxford riot police threw a cordon around the main square of Blackbird Leys, another municipal homestead on the edge of town, to put an end to the illicit sport of 'joyriding'. Police occupied the estate for almost a week. There were eighty-three arrests.

A week later the Meadowell housing estate in Tyneside, a few miles from the point where the River Tyne meets the North Sea, was besieged for five hours when a criminal fraternity, having failed to lure the police into its territory for a beating, was joined by crowds who laid waste to community buildings and shops. The Asian shopkeepers feared for their lives that night; some found sanctuary, some escaped. By the next morning they had all fled, never to return. Over the next four days riots spread west to the city of Newcastle, the heart of the Tyneside conurbation. There were two hundred calls to the firefighters. Hundreds of young men took to the streets in Elswick and Scotswood, two neighbourhoods which are emblematic of the city's industrial rise and fall, to challenge the police. More than three hundred people were arrested.

These extravagant events were an enigma. They made

worldwide news and yet they seemed to be powered by no particular protest, no just cause, no fantasy of the future. However, even in their political emptiness they were telling us something about what Britain had become; the message in the medium of riotous assemblies showed us how the authorities and the angry young men were communicating with each other. The riots were the young men's way of speaking to their world.

This book is about those events, but its intention is not simply to describe or analyse the riots, it is also to hold up a window through which we can look at locales that tell us something more important than themselves. They show us something about the country in which we live, what people do with their troubles and their anger, who gets hurt and who gets heard.

There have been riotous outbreaks for most of Britain's history, from the Peasants' Revolt in 1381 when thousands of people, pauperised by the economic aftermath of the Black Death, marched on London to a fatal encounter with King Richard II. A new word, Peterloo, entered the national vocabulary in 1819, when yeomen and cavalry charged at thousands of desperate weavers meeting in Manchester's St Peter's Fields, and caused hundreds of injuries and eleven deaths. Riots, known as Captain Swing in England and Rebecca in Wales, were the form of rural resistance to machinery and cheap labour on and off for nearly fifteen years after 1830. There were 'police riots' and 'race riots' in Liverpool and Cardiff in 1919. The last two centuries in Britain have been punctuated by race riots against the Irish, Africans and Caribbeans, riots against Catholics, riots between fascists and socialists, between police and workers, between police and 'protestors'.

But in the popular ideology of Englishness they have been consigned to a rowdy past which has been put behind the peace of the present. Postwar Britain's sense of itself has included the image of a national temperament cleansed of tumult. Of course, there were exceptions. There were Belfast and Derry, where official British brutalism was practised and made perfect. Whatever the Loyalists want to think, the British really believe that Northern Ireland is another country, over the water to the west where protest and punishment are generic. There was the Notting Hill race riot in the Fifties. But that was black people. There was Grosvenor Square in the Sixties, Red Lion Square and Grunwick in the Seventies, but that was the reds. There was the Stonehenge rout in the Eighties, but they were hippies. There was the poll tax riot in 1990, but that was anarchists. There was Strangeways, too, but that was prisoners. Thus was the riot purged from the mainstream of modern Britain. Rioters were *others*.

What was new in the Eighties and Nineties was that riot became routine. Its persistent resurgence demands that we ask new questions about community, solidarity, law and disorder among men and women living with desperate local economies. Fissured by gender and generation, race and class, the riots of the Nineties are as much *against* the community as they are *about* it; indeed, they render the very concept of 'community' problematic.

All the neighbourhoods which spontaneously combusted in 1991 are communicating a new kind of crisis, the ordinary 'state of emergency' which is symbolic of an era: they are the effect of Britain's bitter but becalmed political culture. After Margaret Thatcher's new economic order was inaugurated in 1979, these neighbourhoods were doomed. They were evacuated by British business and the economic discipline of the New Right left them unable to make a legitimate living. They were largely abandoned by the main parliamentary political parties, left without representation. 'Poverty', 'despair', 'alienation' – none of these terms exhaust a description of the life of these communities, however. Nor do the purportedly self-evident terms like 'unemployment' or 'hooligans', slung around like slogans in 1991, explain them away.

These neighbourhoods exist everywhere. They are often the size of a small town, not exotic exceptions: they are not that geographical other – the ghettos. They are simply the places where people live; they shape the character of the national landscape no less than chimneys, the post office, gardens, shopping parades or motorways. They are part of where we are and who we are. However, as Britain teeters towards the end of the century, it is hard to imagine that anyone, other than the inhabitants themselves, will reinvest in these domestic disaster areas. That is why they, and those who live somewhere else but are members of the same society, need to know and understand what happened in the summer of 1991, if for no other reason than that we need to know what the future holds.

PART I

THE BOYS GO INTO BATTLE

The 1991 riots

T he confrontation between incendiary young bucks and the Boys in Blue in 1991 confirmed Britain's reputation as the most riotous country in Europe. Bombed, blazing neighbourhoods and automobile acrobatics, much of it the work of young masked men, appeared on nationwide television. The stars of the riots were boys. Lads who rarely travelled more than a mile or so from home were suddenly globalised, became international icons, were seen on television screens from Toulouse to Tokyo. They achieved not just Andy Warhol's fifteen minutes of fame, but a fortnight of it.

On the ground, boys who could barely read became the stars of the schoolyard; hopeless terrestrials who did not talk much made their presence felt through the eloquence of arson. They preserved their activities on homemade videos of stolen cars doing pirouettes around suburban streets.

Their show came a decade after the spectacular destruction during the 1981 riots in Brixton and Toxteth, in a symmetry that was irresistibly suggestive. The years between 1981 and 1991 were like no other decade since the Second World War. They saw the demise of the disciplined disorders that had characterised postwar politics in Britain. The national tone of what had always been a quarrelsome country was now reckless, butch and dangerous.

The 1991 riot season was detonated in Ely, a municipal homeland on the edge of Cardiff. At the end of August, three days' fighting between young men and the police outside a parade of local shops were reported as 'a bread riot'. That, of course, gave it a subliminal legitimacy: bread is basic, one of the West's elemental commodities, an ancient emblem of survival, a code in politics. Bread riots are embedded in Europe's radical history, and that granted Ely the sanction of a long and heroic past.

Ely was soon followed by Blackbird Leys in Oxford, where the riot was occasioned by illicit public pleasure in the quintessential product of affluent modernity, the motorcar. There the riots were confrontations between the police and the virtuoso drivers of stolen, high-performance cars. The public – the community – were the audience: the drivers needed to be seen and the police needed to stop people watching.

Stolen cars were also the ignition for the Meadowell riot in Tyneside, when the death of two young drivers, Dale Robson and Colin Atkins, who were followed by the police while speeding along the A19 near the Northumbria coast, was misinterpreted by their friends as martyrdom and avenged by a siege. The Meadowell estate, where the boys lived, was torched and looted by rioters who kept it cut off from the outside world by challenging police and firefighters when they responded to calls for help. A few days later the revenge haemorrhaged westward into Elswick, way up in the West End of Newcastle, one of the poorest places in Britain, overlooking what was once one of its greatest shipbuilding rivers. A local landmark, the empty Dodds Arms public house, was burned down. A day later, petrol bombers set light to cars and community buildings in Scotswood, a couple of miles further along the Tyne. Scotswood, too, was once one of the iconic industrial landscapes of England, now a very poor old place.

So these local collisions appeared to be about bread, automobiles, honour and revenge. The appearance of chaos and coercion, and spontaneity and solidarity, gave the events the allure of 'riot' as a moment of collective transgression – when a crowd became a mob, and when a mob became a riot.

CHAPTER 1

Encounter Ely

The splash on the *Wales on Sunday* newspaper's front page on 1 September 1991 explained that 'more than one hundred police in riot gear fought to control a mob' outside a grocer's shop. The shop had been run for seven years by Abdul Waheed, who lived with his family upstairs. The paper said police were moving people on when onlookers started attacking the shop. 'All of a sudden things started flying. It was getting really violent with large stones being thrown at the police and people were on rooftops hurling slate tiles. The police charged at the crowds to move them.' What had brought the people to the streets was a dispute between two shopkeepers. 'Resentment had been simmering since Tuesday when shopkeeper Abdul Waheed won a court injunction banning the shop next door from selling bread.'

Before the riots, the attrition between neighbouring traders in the Wilson Road shopping parade in Ely hovered on the raw edge of race. The relationship between Abdul Waheed, the grocer, and his newsagent neighbours, Sue and Carl Agius, was rough but not unusual – it had all the elements of irascible competition, bad manners and luck-pushing that might be found between many small businesses surviving through hard times. The grocer was doing well, the newsagent was failing. Mr Waheed was a successful businessman – his capital investment in the shop enabled him to install chilling and freezing equipment; he carried a large stock and sold it swiftly. He had also fortified his shop because of racially motivated incidents: he had shutters, an alarm, and an anti-theft device which enabled him to detain a shoplifter by throwing a switch under the counter, which locked the door. The grocer was abiding by the restrictive covenant imposed by the original owner of the shops, which controlled their stock and trade. The newsagent had contravened it. Carl and Sue Agius, after buying the newsagent's business next door in 1989, broke the covenant by selling food as well as newspapers, cigarettes and sweets.

Ethnicity haunted the newsagent's campaign. Carl Agius had, in fact, taken his case to the South Glamorgan Racial Equality Council in Cardiff. He always denied racism, and yet, as if to pre-empt such criticism, he had taken his complaints about *competition* to the city's racial equality forum.

Always anxious to ensure that white citizens did not feel unheeded in their complaints of racial discrimination, the REC paid attention to Agius and, using its informal networking, began to unearth some of the history of bad blood over the covenant. Prominent Pakistanis who were made aware of the long-running dispute counselled Mr Waheed to make sure he did not, by his own behaviour, expose himself to criticism.

The REC's director in South Wales was Dr Rita Austin, an Indian whose former academic career had included pioneering research on racial harassment. She was to become a significant character in the Ely events. She was a daughter of the Indian intelligentsia: her father had been India's Attorney General during Indira Ghandi's premiership. She had studied in Britain and was a long-time Labour Party member who later became both active and ambitious. When, in the Eighties, she became South Glamorgan County Council's first black woman councillor and soon the chair of Finance, she seemed set for a political trajectory to Parliament. Labourism's predilection for sectarian self-destruction secured her defeat in an inner-party scrum, however, and she was deselected by the party. In 1989 she became director of the REC. Tribunal cases that had seemed hopeless were taken up and through the labyrinth of labour laws; proactive promotion of the rights of ethnic minorities began to have an impact on the region's culture of complacency.

When the newsagent had brought himself to the REC she

had guided him to the City Solicitor and advised him that if he wanted to challenge the covenant he should make a counter-claim in court. Carl Agius continued to dispatch his complaints to the REC, however, though they were always about his economic grievances and about competitiveness. Agius always denied any racial motivation, but his war of attrition with his neighbour was shadowed by race and racism and he had kith and kin in Ely who did not deny their racism: the police were already aware of several incidents and were being kept informed of the dispute by the REC. Asian traders in the city were the regular victims of attacks that went way beyond the normal aggravation they would expect as shop-keepers providing services late at night. Ten days before the riot two other Asian shopkeepers had trouble, one of them involving a gun, and in the week of the riots police recorded the racially motivated firebombing of another Asian trader.

On 27 August the conflict between Agius and Waheed went to court. The court confirmed the covenant and thus the con-ditions under which Mr Waheed had bought his business. He was vindicated. He was also granted an injunction preventing his newsagent neighbour from selling groceries. The newsagent was ordered to pay £3,000 compensation to the grocer for lost trade. That Tuesday a very angry Carl Agius stuck a cardboard notice in his shop window which announced that 'because of our good neighbours' he could no longer sell bread and milk and other food. One of his relatives on the estate, Sue Davies, began collecting local signatures to a petition against Waheed's efforts to enforce the covenant.

On Wednesday, 28 August, Mr Waheed caught a thief. He locked the door by flicking the switch under the counter and waited for the police to come. The man, who was in his twenties, shouted racial abuse and then sprung himself from the shop by throwing himself through the window.

By the time the police arrived the man had fled, but while they were interviewing the shopkeeper the police themselves came under attack. Their car was being stoned and a gang out-side was shouting at Waheed. The police radioed for reinforcements. There were no arrests. A gang of young men gathered again outside Waheed's shop the next day. Minutes before 8 p.m. that night his windows were smashed. A crowd was hanging around outside and Abdul Waheed called the police. 'They smashed my windows last night and they are doing the same tonight,' he reported. A police patrol stationed itself outside the shop and at 11.16 p.m. people began throwing bottles at the officers. Again, there were no arrests. Two days of abuse and criminal damage, including injury to a sacred object, a police car – attacks on police cars were often seen as tension indicators – were met with no legal sanction.

On Friday the police urged Mr Agius to remove his cardboard protest from his window. Although it did not constitute an offence under the Public Order Act, it was felt to be provocative. The police had also checked out whether it was incitement to racial hatred, and concluded that it was not. However, they believed that the campaign against the shopkeeper was serious enough to warrant their permanent presence. People had been going into Waheed's shop, spitting at him, complaining about 'greedy Paki bastards' and demanding to know 'Why can't white men sell bread when you can?'

When the shop's closing time arrived, at 10 p.m., Waheed's assistant Abu Nakeeb needed a police escort to get out and Waheed himself felt forced to leave his home above the shop and stay in a hotel for the night. A crowd of about thirty people was hanging around outside and the police expected an explosion. They had been warned all day that there would be trouble and the crowd was providing plenty of clues: 'Bomb the Pakis!' they shouted.[1] An inspector took position up the road; at least one officer was posted inside the shop. Beyond that, according to one officer, the police at first made no move: 'They were just standing about.' But after the pubs' closing time the police decided to take action: they called in the Central Area Response Team, who brought a dog handler and riot gear.

[1] *Western Mail*, 29 February 1992.

Once the police van arrived on the estate it attracted raucous abuse and its inhabitants reckoned they would be safer
outside. They charged the crowd: 'Without hesitation I ran
towards the group,' the dog handler, PC Peter Thomas, later
told the Crown Court. He set his dog on the young men, who
scattered into the streets, running towards the northern edge
of the estate. Seven young men were arrested. Two, who were
later convicted, complained of rough treatment by the police.
One of them, who had been sitting on the wall by the shop
when the crowd was charged, said he was handcuffed before
being loaded into a police van. Another found himself in the
van and later complained that he was kept down by an officer
who put his foot on his neck.[2] The police denied allegations
of brutality but their tactics provoked a great debate about
the genesis of the violence that night. Were the young men
responsible, or the police who, according to defence counsel
Greg Taylor in one of the subsequent Ely trials, 'jumped the
gun' and provoked the violence by charging the crowd?[3]

Whatever the cause, the result was a riot, and it was the
biggest thing that had happened in Ely. It was the talk of the
taverns on Saturday, and the young men who had missed it
made sure they were there outside the shops that night. One
of them was Craig Raisis, who lived in Caerau, the newer,
southern end of the estate. He was a pretty, stoical young
man. He had missed Friday's drama, but when he went to the
Highfields pub early in the afternoon he and his friends heard
about what had been going on around the shop and decided
to go up there to have a look. He had no views one way or
another about the traders' troubles or Waheed's demeanour as
a shopkeeper. 'I used the shop myself, so I had no views about
the dispute,' he said. Neither did his friends. 'We just went up
there to see what was going on.' After a while he left and went
home.

The sun was shining that Saturday. It was the kind of

[2] *South Wales Echo*, 8 January 1992.
[3] *South Wales Echo*, 10 January 1992.

hot day that Europeanised the British, bringing them out
of the shadows and into the streets. The off-licence and the
fish and chip shop were doing brisk business while a crowd
gathered on a grass patch nearby.

REC director Rita Austin telephoned contacts in the Pakistani community to make sure Waheed was safe. He had
friends and family in Birmingham and rumours began cir-
culating that young Pakistani men would be travelling down
to South Wales to do what the police had failed to do enough
about, safeguarding Waheed's business.

'This is the part of my job I hate most,' she said. 'The
very moment I feel impelled to exert control upon the black
communities – the phrase I use is "cooling out" – I know I
am acting as an agent of control on behalf of white agencies. I
was keen that our young Pakistanis did not mobilise and fight
back; I did not want to see them ending up in court! It seemed
sensible, but I hated doing it, telling Pakistani groups, "Thank
you, but don't come. Stay off the streets, don't put yourselves
in the wrong." At least I was able to reassure them that the
police had recorded the incidents as racially motivated and
were giving protection.'

She then mobilised REC members. 'We set up a variety of
informal helplines among members of the organisation so that
people in the community who might not like talking to the
police could talk instead to me and other members of the REC
who were known to the network as friends.' Asian shopkeepers
in Cardiff were thus reassured that if they needed help, it was
waiting at the end of a telephone. The Pakistani community
in Swansea, Wales' second city, feared that the attacks would
spread and they, too, were reassured that the police were on
the case.

That weekend, Pakistan's hockey team was in Cardiff as
part of an international goodwill tour and since the city
was, therefore, host to many Asians arriving to watch the
world champions, the constabulary's ethnic affairs unit was
on duty to make sure that no one got involved in Waheed's
troubles. The unit and the REC did what their brief seemed

to require: to circulate within a black orbit, to create calm, and to maintain a commitment to 'law and order'.

So, the black community was calmed. The white community was not. No one seemed to know how to manage its angry young men gathering outside Waheed's shop. On Saturday senior police officers briefed themselves on the expected eruptions in Ely. The plan was to do nothing to excite the intemperate. But, as if in anticipation of failure, they kept two special response groups – riot squads, trained in the management of public disorder – in the shadows a few hundred yards away from the shops. Indeed, the situation was deemed so serious that the constabulary booked a helicopter from neighbouring West Mercia police to monitor the terrain.

Officers were posted around the Wilson Road shops all day. However, during the preceding three days the police could not prevent all of Waheed's windows being broken. He had had to get away for his own safety.

That day angry young men among the crowd and among the police faced each other outside the shops. As the day wore on, so the argument about Abdul Waheed's business receded as the focus of the disturbances: it became a gladiatorial contest between the lads and the police. Shirt-sleeved officers mingling with the crowd watched its mood metamorphose into menace. The man in charge, Superintendent Michael Milton, reckoned that during the evening the mood was 'generally calm' but the crowd's intention was clear: it would not allow Abdul Waheed to stay. PC Russell Gardiner, who knew the area very well, felt that the hostility did not yet amount to violent disorder, but that the crowd's talk, punctuated by threats to torch the 'Paki bastards', was threatening, and everyone had Friday night's police charge in their minds. Ely was set for a storm. Among the crowd was a young man who told PC Gardiner, 'There's going to be a barbecue tonight and there's pork on the menu. You're going to burn, man.' Whether this was meant seriously or was just lighthearted banter, no arrests were made at that time for threatening behaviour or incitement.

At 6 p.m. Abdul Waheed shut his shop and the police

escorted him away from Ely, his home. 'A lot of people were in the area waiting for something to happen,' explained the Crown Prosecutor later. Superintendent Milton, the divisional police commander, and his deputy, Chief Inspector Roy Morgan, were in charge of the police operation, watching and waiting. About thirty officers were stationed in Ely, but the police presence swelled to a peak of about a hundred and seventy later that night. After Waheed's departure, Superintendent Milton himself left Ely for a couple of hours. When he relieved Inspector Morgan at 9.30 p.m., police were still chatting to residents while everyone waited for something to happen. The plan was to keep a minimal profile, with back-up support nearby. Inspector Morgan had been keeping a close eye on the crowd to identify 'troublemakers' and 'ringleaders'.

An hour later the crowd outside the row of shops had grown to over two hundred. There were men, women and children among them, waiting, waiting, while some of the men, laced with lager and bearing no goodwill toward the police, were becoming reckless. Superintendent Milton's thirty officers, some of them riot squads, waited in vans nesting in nearby streets. Milton was a worried man, doubtful that he had enough men to manage the crisis. So he enrolled the local councillor, the Reverend Bob Morgan, who was in the year of his chairmanship of the County Council, to come and calm the situation. They did not contact the Tenants' Association leader, Maureen Roach, who also lived nearby. She had been back and forth to the shops during the day, but kept away from the scene at night. Apparently, neither she herself nor anyone else thought she might be useful.

The Reverend Bob was the dominant figure in Ely politics. His church, the Resurrection, was much more than a place of worship – it was one of the best-known public places on the estate. It belonged to the Community of the Resurrection, known for its liberal and even socialist theology. In the mid-Seventies the Reverend Bob had united the functions of parish priest and politician when he joined the Labour Party after he had been a curate for ten years. He got himself elected to the County Council. Politics was in the patrician tradition: it was not about empowerment, it was a medium for lobbying for resources.

The Reverend Bob arrived at about 10 p.m., mingled in his winning, whimsical way with his constituents and quickly caught the drift of the crowd's intentions: to burn out Waheed. Superintendent Milton had been hearing the same thing all day. His placid patrol became very nervous towards 11 p.m., the major moment of public disorder in British streets, when men tumble out of the pubs at closing time. But the police had not attempted to close the off-licence selling liquor in the same parade as Waheed's shop. They did not want to do anything provocative, Superintendent Milton explained.

At 10.20 p.m. John Davies, a constable attached to the Criminal Investigation Department, the CID, arrived with a message for the senior officer. He had policed the estate for about twelve years and therefore knew many of the men standing outside the off-licence. He recognised a young man sitting on the wall by the shops; he knew him because he had arrested him many times before. The policeman and the young man both gave the court a different account of what happened next: the officer says that the lad was amidst an aggressive crowd chanting 'CID, CID' at him. He 'seemed to be orchestrating this' and then came towards the car, opened the door and said to Davies, 'Why don't you fuck off like the Pakis?' The young man says that Davies beckoned to him, that he went over to the car and said, 'Don't talk to me, I don't want to know you.' What happened then was not disputed. The young man walked back to the wall. PC Davies followed him and tried to arrest him for an offence under the Public Order Act, and when he took hold of the young man's arm the latter clung to the wall and refused to let go. The crowd was angry. Davies' colleague, Detective Sergeant Kemp, intervened and advised PC Davies to withdraw.

With the crowd tense and twitchy, a police constable tried to arrest a man with whom he had a long and well-known history. It was an intervention that could not be sustained, as things turned out. It was perceived by the crowd as provocative. It was believed by his colleague to pose enough danger to him to demand that he be rescued.

Just before closing time, Superintendent Milton appealed to the Cardiff central command for reinforcements to be brought in from the nearby Fairwater police station where they were ready and waiting, and he sought authority from Assistant Chief Constable Bob Evans to move into riot mode. At 10.58 p.m. a rock was thrown at the police; then came bottles, cans, bricks and abuse. He shouted at the crowd over a loudhailer and told them to go home. The crowd did not move – this was their home. The crowd outside the shops was not going to give up now, and the hundreds of people watching from their gardens were not going to close their doors on the action.

More insults echoed from the crowd at the shops and from others standing around nearby junctions. An exasperated Superintendent Milton asked Inspector Morgan to call up the riot squads waiting nearby. To local people there appeared to have been no *strategic* crowd management. No cordons had been deployed, for example. At 11.15 p.m. they charged into the street, and for the next hour they were running and shouting at the crowd, who were scattering and re-grouping.

That night the police entered the South Wales community wearing armour, as they were to do again the following night. Supported from behind by local officers who knew the terrain, riot squads drafted in from the region charged, wearing NATO-style helmets, their eyes covered by visors, their right arms gripping circular shields, targeting those identified earlier as 'ringleaders'. As the police rushed the crowd, a squad leapt out from behind the front line and seized individuals.

One of the officers who knew the area and its people well was PC Russell Gardiner, who had worked in Ely for three years. 'I was used as a spotter of people. I was to run up from behind the line to apprehend people concerned. Sometimes we were called a snatch squad.' After screaming for more men and equipment, Superintendent Milton got both, and for the next couple of hours he moved in men armed with long shields, flame-proof overalls and heavy-duty helmets to go around the estate making arrests.

The street in front of the shops was soon cleared. The riot squads turned their attention to the other crowds getting away and clustering around roads running into the hinterland of the estate. They re-formed in their stiff, straight lines, supported by spotters behind them, guiding them to familiar faces. One of the targets had returned home for the afternoon and joined his friends up on Wilson Road later in the evening. They had spent a couple of hours watching the police charges from the vantage point of a friend's front garden.

'All of a sudden they started coming real close to us and one of the officers grabbed me round the neck and just dragged me off. I was saying, "Leave me alone, I haven't done anything." He punched me. When we got to the riot van he put handcuffs on me, behind my back, pushed me onto the ground and kicked me, once in the eye, once in my side. He took hold of my hair and started scraping my head on the ground. Then they put me in the van.' His injuries were photographed after he was released.

During one of the charges, a second young man was knocked down by a shield and arrested. At 11.45 p.m. he was charged with a minor offence under the Public Order Act. Another man was thrown to the ground by a shield-wielding young police officer.

PC Andrew Morgan was a member of the area response group based at Bridgend who had arrived at Ely at 10.40 p.m. and watched a crowd of about fifty people 'chanting abuse – they seemed to be happy doing that.' A resolute, firm-faced young officer, he gave passionate evidence to the Crown Court trial of the men arrested that night. His team moved toward the crowd and, as he later told the court, he noticed half a dozen men. 'My fear was that they had instruments that might harm us. My intention was to disperse them.' One of the men who, he said, menaced him was thirty-seven-year-old Martin Cole, who lived in a neighbourhood several miles away from Ely. 'He was there the whole time, inciting other members of the crowd to join in the chanting,' the officer told the trial in March 1992. 'As I approached him, he adopted a karate stance and raised his right leg towards me and shouted, "Come on, pig, and fucking get some!" I continued to move towards him; he continued to adopt an aggressive, fighting stance. Then he said, "Come on, wanker." I ran towards him, raised my shield to protect myself. I hit him to the ground.' Martin Cole was a disabled man who had, like many others joined friends to watch the big event in Ely. He could walk, though he had a slow, shaky step, and could only move with the aid of a stick. He could have mounted a karate attack on no one. He rejected the police officer's story. He was believed by the jury and acquitted.

A distinctive-looking man with a ponytail and arms decorated with tattoos had spent the evening with his friends and family outside the shops. When the crowd there was surrounded by police, he felt besieged and told the police angrily that he wanted to get home. He was arrested and charged with a minor public order offence. He was mentioned many times during the trial as the man with the ponytail, though no evidence was offered that he had thrown anything at anyone. His presence in the threatening crowd was enough, it seemed, to secure his conviction for violent disorder. A young man whose hobby was angling and who had joined the crowd on his way home from a fishing expedition, had taken the fish home and returned to the crowd later. Police saw him sharing out sandwiches, crisps and shiny objects among his friends. Police said the shiny objects were weapons, 'metal instruments'. He said they were biscuits wrapped in silver paper. The police conceded during the trial that no weapons or 'metal instruments' were ever found in the debris left after the riots. His presence in the crowd led to his conviction for violent disorder. All these men were represented in the trial as having been 'ringleaders' on the Saturday night.

The Revered Bob Morgan was surprised by the riot strategy adopted by the police that night. 'They foolishly put on the whole armour of God: helmets of salvation and the breastplates of self-righteousness. They had the shield, but not the sword of the spirit. They set themselves up as a target.' He reckoned that the police should have sealed off the street much earlier, rather than letting a crowd, committed to destroying Waheed's business, gather outside his shop.

People scattered in the panicky aftermath of these manoeuvres. The sound of the crowd's shouting and of truncheons clattering on shields ricocheted around the night. Two men had climbed up onto the roof over the shops and straddled the coping stones at the top. One of them was Frank Pritchard, who was well acquainted with the local bobbies on the beat, but who was alarmed by the 'strangers with the shields making funny noises'. His ascent was something of a surprise – a little earlier local PC Russell Gardiner had been talking to him while he was walking away from the crowd with his son on their way home. In the mêlée, Pritchard had lost sight of his son and hoped to find him from his vantage point above it all. It was a daft plan. He 'had a wobbly' on the roof and refused to come down. The other man on the roof was James Gauci, who had climbed up there after the police charge. 'I didn't go up because of Frank's son, I just jumped up to get away,' he said.

Their presence on the roof was represented later as marking a new episode of escalation, though what exactly its status was in the story depended on the storyteller's disposition. The Reverend Bob Morgan had gone home at midnight when it looked as if the police had claimed control of the territory in front of the shops. But he was called out again by the police to help them with the men on the roof, whose families had already tried, and failed, to talk them down. He believed that after their initial 'bad tactics', 'the police then behaved in an exemplary manner.' He was happy to try to persuade the men to come down. 'They said that the police would beat them up. I said, "No they won't, I'll come with you." Then they asked us to get their solicitors. So we did.'

The borrowed police helicopter arrived at 12.15 a.m. and hovered over the crowd for about five minutes, ferocious and yet feeble, throwing a great light across them but unable to get anywhere near them because the turbulence might have blown the men off the roof.

What it did do, however, was create a new spectacle for a neighbourhood that had been ordered to its bed but, since midnight, had been given no chance to sleep by the shouting riot squads, the mercurial crowd, and now the raucous helicopter. The log kept by the police command headquarters of reports coming in from officers on the estate showed that by 1 a.m. the operational officers felt that it was almost all over. Their big problem was the residents whose interest in the drama on the roof was excited by the presence of the helicopter and the police. The situation had been 'dealt with', said the log, and, although many of the people were still out on the streets, officers believed they were 'just residents watching'. At 1.14 a.m. the police log recorded, 'Situation calm, one of the main problems is residents watching.' And fifteen minutes later the log added, 'Problem with residents, won't leave.'

Well into the small hours, residents were out in their gardens drinking coffee and eating sandwiches. It was reminiscent of an ancient battle, with the great and the good assembled with their comestibles at a safe distance to observe the sport of war. Actually it was simply a neighbourhood bearing witness to something that belonged to it. There was no record suggesting that the police felt that the men on the roof were dangerous – their difficulty was that they could not get them down and that the neighbours were staying out on the street to see what happened at the end of the story. At about 3 a.m. Frank Pritchard's solicitor, Roy Morgan, arrived and immediately the men on the roof came down. Solicitor Morgan and Reverend Morgan insisted on accompanying the two men to Fairwater police station and went to the cells with them where the two men were locked up together.

They had been scared, stranded men stuck on a roof, not wanting to get down again because they feared the police. When they were given protection they knew they could trust, they gave themselves up. These men were retrospectively reincarnated as 'ringleaders', daredevils whose bravado inspired a riot, who kept the law at bay by throwing missiles. However, their long sojourn on the roof came *after* the great confrontations at the shops had already happened. It was well away from the other arenas on the estate where police fought with residents, and, according to police records, the problem was not so much the men on the roof as the stamina of the spectators.

Throughout the night another building was under constant attack – the housing office nearby. At 11.25 p.m. the police called the senior housing officer, Mrs Asra Ali, and asked her to come to Ely to deal with the building's alarm. When she arrived she was stopped by a police cordon and someone shouted, 'It's a riot! Get out!' She did. She returned at 2 a.m., but the place was still in the throes of the drama surrounding the men on the roof and so she went home. After another call from the police at 4.55 a.m., she returned at dawn to find every window of her office smashed. Inside, rocks and bricks lay on the floor and there was a dark, scorched patch on the carpet – evidence of a petrol bomb.

Before everything erupted on Saturday night, Reverend Bob Morgan had telephoned Rhodri Morgan, the Labour MP whose constituency included Ely. The MP did not get the message until late and expected to catch up with the Reverend Bob on Sunday. The last thing he envisaged was another riot. By coincidence, the command structure of the police underwent a long-planned management restructuring overnight, which eliminated many senior and middle managers in the division. It could not have happened on a worse weekend. Sunday, 1 September, was the first day in Chief Superintendent A'herne's new command. At lunchtime A'herne telephoned Rhodri Morgan, and 'he told me, "The riot isn't just a night-time thing. It is a hot, sticky Sunday and do you think you could possibly come up because the crowd are refusing to leave the little green by the shops. We think it would be useful to have the politicians there."' The MP readily agreed. He went down to the police station where he was briefed about the history of the disturbances: the legal dispute between the shopkeepers.

A'herne suggested to the MP that they go to Ely together. 'That was a mistake. I just did not realise how tense the community had become, and how it would appear if we turned up together,' said Morgan with the regret of hindsight. They walked up toward the shops where they saw a line of police vans on the right, outside Waheed's shop. 'On the left there was a group of about twenty women sitting on the low wall. Some had prams. They were quite young, probably teenage brides, and beyond them there was a group of aggressive young men, teenagers, on a patch of grass, and media people, all with microphones at the ready. The men were jeering at me and the police.'

It seemed to the MP to be 'like some kind of Greek tragedy, media in the middle, housewives to the left, young men to the right, Pakistani shopkeeper cowering inside.' A'herne called over another officer and while they were all having a conversation on the edge of the green, 'all of a sudden, there was a whoosh past my ear. It was an egg. It landed on the officer and a bit of it on A'herne – two inches this way and it would have landed on my nose.'

The crowd were very angry that their MP was talking not to them but to the police. 'We voted for you and what do you do? You just come up, siding with the police. Why don't you come and talk to these people?' his constituents told him. The women seemed to have a grievance he knew he should hear. 'The housewives said, "We want you to get him out." They meant Waheed. I had a chat with them and they explained that Agius was undercutting Waheed by about five pence for a loaf of bread, and that the price of bread meant a lot to them.' They were also furious about the police tactics the previous night. 'They made lots of complaints about police brutality on Saturday night; they were very bitter about that.' The MP chatted with some of the younger people. 'The kids, they were having the time of their lives shouting various anti-police and anti-shopkeeper slogans, like "Paki Out!"' But Rhodri Morgan decided not to talk to the young men. 'They looked too aggressive.' It was as if they made themselves the untouchables, impregnable, beyond reach. 'I just didn't have any feeling that I could go up to these lads and talk to them. I just didn't know how they'd react, whether they'd thump you or whether they'd be nice to you; it felt like putting your head in the lion's den.' It seemed that the most powerful men around could not engage the angry young men.

The MP began to feel he was doing no good by sticking around the green so he went home. After conferring with the Reverend Morgan and other Ely councillors, he returned later that evening. This time he went in his own car, parked at the Resurrection Church and walked up to the shops where there was still a large crowd. Councillors were wandering around talking to people, if for no other reason than to show that they were not all part of a single bloc of public authority. Constituents all around made it plain to their MP that they were frightened and they were furious with the police for keeping them awake at night with their helicopter.

What vexed all the 'authorities' was what to do about a crowd that thought it was simply claiming the right of congregation, the right to own its space. Rhodri Morgan remembered the atmosphere as being like 'a rave, a scene'. For all the sense of festivity, people were throwing bottles at Waheed's shop and singing 'Old Macdonald Had a Farm' at the police. It was also a crowd whose presence had a purpose – it wanted to torch a neighbour.

That was made plain again that evening by one of Carl Agius' relatives standing in front of Abdul Waheed's shop, facing the crowd, clattering her heels against the shutters, shouting, 'Pakis out . . . Kill the pigs . . . Fuck off back to Fairwater!' Rhodri Morgan remembered the incident well. The woman did not appear to have been challenged and 'All the teenage boys thought this was wonderful; she was shouting and the teenagers were egging her on,' said the MP.

What did the police do? 'They watched and did nothing,' said one of the onlookers. Though the police were close to her and although, to the people watching, she seemed to be defying them to arrest her, the police were in difficulty. It was another of those paralysing moments. 'They let her carry on,' said the MP. 'They couldn't think of what to do.'

It was another hot, sticky night; the helicopter was out, the crowds were out, parents couldn't keep their children in. People with jobs dreaded another sleepless night. 'Even people who weren't nearby the actual disturbances couldn't sleep,' said Maureen Roach. 'That got a lot of people's backs up. Those who had to get up in the morning were totally bushwacked after two or three nights being kept awake.' People tackled their MP on his way home close to midnight. 'I said, "Well, it's pretty difficult." Apart from praying for a shower of rain, what could we do?'

At midnight the crowd was still outside the shops, swearing, drinking, throwing the occasional lager can. They would not go home. So the police decided to force them. Riot squads arrived, scattering people and spreading through the streets radiating away from Wilson Road. Sue Davies and her husband, Chris, were arrested. They were later convicted of Public Order Act offences. There was another large crowd on the green in what was known as the 'bullring', a circular road at the top end of Wilson Road. Riot squads were dispatched there, too, to clear the crowd. They were watched by an Ely ice-cream vendor. 'I was just down there being nosy. When the riot police came, people started running. A police officer approached me and said, "Fuck off home" – those were his exact words.' He tried to oblige, but the direct route to his home on the northern edge of Ely, only a few streets away, was blocked. However, there was another way home; he could skirt round the boundary of the estate, through some fields which had been given one of those unmistakably municipal titles, the Recreation Ground, known as 'the rec'. He had one problem; he suffered from a disability in his knees, could walk well enough but could not run. So he started walking.

Stuck in the same area was another young man who, like the ice-cream vendor, lived in the northern corner of the estate. After missing Saturday's riots, he had gone to watch at about

10 p.m. He, too, felt he had no stake in the shopkeepers' dispute. 'I didn't agree with the riot.' Indeed, he was disposed to be sympathetic to Waheed's predicament. A white Welshman, he happened to be a good-looking young man with a bronze complexion and a reputation for being hard. People often saw him through a white filter and *accused* him of being black. He watched the stones and bottles being thrown, saw the riot squads rush at the crowd, then re-form in a straight line and rush at the crowd again. He was part of the crowd on the bullring at the top of Wilson Road. Junctions were cordoned off, people were cornered, some of them were running around throwing bricks at the police. One group around the bullring was urging a young man in a car to drive straight at one of the police cordons to drive a wedge through it. 'He picked up speed and drove into them. Youths were hurling bricks as well,' said one of the bystanders.

Suddenly a police line opened up. Two vans shot through and dispatched riot police into the crowd, who scattered, making for 'the rec', up the gulleys, across the gardens. The Welshman was picked up and put into a police van where he says a police officer inside started hitting him. 'He was shouting, "Get back you nigger, get back!" and every time he said that he punched me.'

The ice-cream vendor had managed to get himself over a wall into someone's garden, but he got no further. He was arrested under the Public Order Act and taken to a police van where what he saw terrified him. 'A man was being punched in the face by a police officer. I thought, Oh shit, I'm going to get the same treatment. The police officer grabbed me round the throat and started choking me. He pushed my face onto a chair and started elbowing me in the face. He pushed his fingers up my nose and pulled my head back. They took us off in the van and then they stopped – they opened the doors outside the chip shop and the driver said, "Fucking close the doors, there's cameras out there! Let's go, let's go."' The Welshman said later that he was already in the van when he saw 'one of the police officers had his fingers up a man's nose and he was pulling his head backwards, pushing him and slapping him.' They were taken with several other arrested men to Fairwater police station where a police surgeon noted his injured nose and lip. Three of the arrested men made complaints about ill-treatment.

Ely was exhausted. It could not go through another such night. On Monday, his second day as commander of the Ely area, Superintendent A'herne called a meeting of community leaders and residents. He was a big, brusque man, with a contra-dictory reputation among police officers for being progressive and yet rude and capricious. 'Sometimes you are talking to him and you feel as though you might as well not be there,' said one officer. He nonetheless seemed to believe that Ely deserved a better police service and a commitment to consultation with the community. When the residents met him they had one priority: to get that helicopter down. They wanted a night's sleep, and they were also worried that sightseers, descending on their estate, might have a stake in 'stirring it'. The police agreed to ground the helicopter and throw a curfew around Ely from 7 p.m. that evening. There was no trouble on Monday, nor for the rest of that week.

Now was the time for the argument about the meaning of the 'disturbances'. Was it a race riot, as it had been dubbed in the local press on Saturday? That was the question that preoccupied the public debate. It was profoundly resisted by the residents and their representatives as well as by police managers. The first press reports in the *South Wales Echo* on Saturday dubbed these events 'race riots'. The newspaper reported that Mr Waheed had been warned that his shop would be burned down during the weekend, and that there were more threats of petrol bombs. The *Echo* said that 'bricks and stones shattered the doubled-glazed windows of his flat above the cor-ner shop in Wilson Road as the rioters shouted racist taunts.' Thereafter, in the representation of this and the later riots the precise function of racism became unintelligible, a muddle.

After that first report all the press claimed that race was not a factor in the attack on Mr Waheed's shop. 'You can't pin that one on us,' one woman told the *Wales on Sunday*.

'There were people of all colours out there.' The *South Wales Echo* changed its mind and concluded, 'There is general agreement that race had nothing to do with the trouble.' The police told the *Echo* on Monday, 2 September, 'There are no racist undertones.' However, the newspaper's editorial on the same day said, 'It is difficult to accept that there is no racial side to the disturbances, however subconscious that may be.' That same day the *Western Mail* reported, 'Residents denied there was any racist motive to the riots.' A couple of days later the Reverend Bob Morgan, the irreverent and popular vicar, wrote in his regular column in the *Echo*, 'The public reads "race riot", which couldn't be further from the truth. Ely people, regardless of colour, intermarry and live harmoniously together.' That view was shared by Maureen Roach, the tenants' leader, Rhodri Morgan, and many of the people who had been arrested. The police had also muffled the race factor in their public pronouncements. The national newspaper reporters, who roamed across the riot territories over the next two weeks, repeated the denials.

There were several sources which suggested otherwise, apart from the crowd itself, whose 'racist taunts' had been recorded in the first press report of the riot. These were the police, the Racial Equality Council, and the Crown Prosecutor in the three trials in spring 1992 which followed the arrests made during the three nights of fighting.

It was the modernisation of police procedures which created the archives that clinched the argument. South Wales Constabulary was one of the first police forces in Britain to create a specialist department to liaise with ethnic minority communities and to monitor racially motivated incidents. The police station in Butetown is a small, scruffy, Sixties office block, a brick coffin amidst the relics of Cardiff's once wealthy coal port. Butetown is home to one of Britain's stalwart black neighbourhoods – thirty-six per cent of the population belong to an ethnic minority. This is the highest local proportion anywhere in the city, although the actual number of ethnic minority citizens in other districts, like Grangetown and Riverside, is

greater. Butetown, like many of the country's nineteenth-
century port neighbourhoods, has declined with the demise
of the docks. As in most port cities, Cardiff's developers have
lately recognised the pleasures of water and warehouses. What
had been wastelands metamorphosed as heritage quaysides in
the Eighties. But in all of them, London, Liverpool, Bristol,
Tyneside, Glasgow and Cardiff, their sanitised histories were
cleansed of ethnicity: they were purged of their cosmopolitan cultures. Dockland areas, rising like phoenixes from the
wastelands of urban shorelines in the Eighties, became rich and
white. The redevelopment of Cardiff Bay could not have been
more open in its intentions – the route into the bay became a
big new road, the Butetown *bypass*. The city's black presence
was being planned out of the place.

The aim to cultivate good relations between Cardiff's many
nationalities and the police might have motivated the location of South Glamorgan Constabulary's ethnic affairs unit at
Butetown, whose cultural history has been a black history.
The unit was set up in 1981, just after the 1981 riots, to pre-
empt Lord Scarman's report and recommendations that police
forces reform their relations with communities and with black
citizens. From 1981 the unit monitored racially motivated
incidents. After 1986 monitoring had to be guided not only by
the interpretations of police officers but also by the perception
of the victims. This followed a definition introduced by the
Association of Chief Police Officers that an incident could be
deemed to be racially motivated by the police, the victim, or
anyone else. In 1989 police obligations toward black people,
being victimised because they were black, were further clarified by the Home Office report, *Response to Racial Attacks
and Harassment*, published in 1989. This report helped to concentrate the collective mind of many constabularies, including
South Wales. In 1990, REC director Rita Austin encouraged the
police to sponsor a multi-agency forum, as the Home Office
report had recommended. This prompted the police to revise
their procedures and their response to racial attacks. The South
Wales ethnic affairs unit's officers had come not from the

community relations corner, often derided as 'soft' in macho canteen culture, but from 'hard' operations. After modernising their procedures, there was an increase of two hundred per cent in the racially motivated incidents *recorded* by the ethnic affairs unit, bringing the total in 1990 to over three hundred.

Though Butetown was home to the unit and to a higher proportion of ethnic minority residents than anywhere else in the city, it had a lower proportion of racial attacks than Ely, where the ethnic minority presence was four per cent, less than Cardiff's overall figure of five and a half per cent. In the year before the riots, ten per cent of Cardiff's racially motivated incidents happened in Ely. Butetown was part of a police subdivision which included the city centre and together these wards had almost the same number of racially motivated incidents as Ely.

Several of these were endured by Abdul Waheed. Five years before the 1991 riot, the police began recording racist elements in the many minor and major misdemeanours he had to put up with. Apart from the ordinary, everyday crime that his shop attracted (like many others), the number of racially motivated attacks increased steadily. This is what the police records showed:

1987:   Waheed's van was set alight.
        He was abused by young men.
1988:   He was abused by a drunken customer.
1989:   Annoyance caused by youths.
        Waheed's car set alight.
        Waheed's arm was broken.
        The shop's lock superglued.
1990:   Eggs thrown at the shop.
1991:   1 January – Windows broken.
        3 January – Annoyance by youths, calling names,
        causing aggravation in the shop.
        17 May – Petrol bomb thrown at the shop after
        it had closed, at 11.15 p.m.

The 6 p.m BBC radio news on Monday evening carried Rita

Austin reminding listeners that since the police had recorded racially motivated incidents at Ely, the constabulary was
wrong not to make that clear in public pronouncements. Senior
officers' anxiety not to emphasise racism had led them into a
denial of it. That denial left an empty space – where there
needed to be an argument, an explanation, there was instead
reassurance. That was directed primarily at black people and
was intended to pre-empt panic and vigilante initiatives. As
a proactive tactic it was directed at the only people any
agency, including the REC and the police ethnic affairs unit,
felt able to influence: *black people*. As a reactive response
to what had happened, it removed responsibility from the
white participants and assigned it instead to acts of God and
government: the weather and unemployment. Insofar as they
apportioned blame, the collective wisdom and the newspaper
editors invoked booze and boredom. These responses were
indicative of a political crisis – a profound pessimism about
anyone's ability to influence the majority population, the
white people, and a resort to the myths about the working
class: rough, rude, drunk, idle, doing the devil's work. The
white participants' alleged degeneracy was also given an alibi:
it was represented a response to a real problem, reasonable
citizens rebelling against an unreasonable trader in a dispute
over bread. Only thus could it be dignified by history.

CHAPTER 2

High Performance

Oxfordshire is home to one of Britain's great motor racing tracks, Silverstone, where the annual Grand Prix in July attracts one of the biggest crowds of spectators assembling for any sport in Britain. Motor sports had always enthralled and enraged the neighbourhood of Blackbird Leys on the periphery of Oxford, but there they had their own motor shows, illicit rodeos, known as *hotting* displays. They had taken over the night life of the estate's main square, dubbed the Arena, or the Manor, where the night boys came out to play when their ownership of the public domain was unchallenged. There was a long, nightly prelude to the performances, when the young men gathered around the chip shop, posing, gossiping, trading bulletins about the location of stolen cars waiting for a driver to take them out to do a turn. They seemed like awkward, argumentative shadows whose conversation around the shops was brittle banter. But their demeanour seemed to become brave eloquence once they sat behind the wheel of a car and threw it around the square before an audience of adolescent admirers and irritated neighbours. They were not driving any old cars, they were high performers in high-performance motors which could gather enough speed in a small space to go screaming into a swerve created by, and controlled by, the handbrake.

The night boys defied the definition of a passive underclass: these young men weren't *under* anyone. Economically they were spare, surplus; personally they were dependent on someone else for their upkeep, usually their mothers; socially they were fugitives, whose lawlessness kept them inside and yet outside their own community. They had no jobs, no incomes, no property, no cars, no responsibilities. But that is not to say they weren't busy, with their 'own business'. And what they did have was a reputation.

In many ways, they were the 'invisibles', their reputation derived nonetheless from being seen, from performing. Their vanity powered their valour. They planned, primed and tuned a local drama that took place nightly in a small square. It was a show that the police decided, suddenly that summer, had to be stopped. They began arresting a handful of the serious drivers during July and August 1991. On Sunday night, 1 September, the police mobilised a massive public order operation and aroused considerable public ire by imposing, in effect, a curfew. It was designed to disperse audiences gathering in the square. There were nine arrests on Sunday night, and sixteen arrests on Tuesday when another attempt by the police to cordon off the centre of the estate provoked running skirmishes, interrupted by a masked joyrider who swept into the square in a two-litre red Maestro – watched by the national press and television. He was introduced at 2 a.m. by a young man, described by the *Daily Mail* as a 'ringmaster', 'who announced that he would be doing "a real burn".' The man in the Maestro had become a star.

Several times that night, police lines, disciplined by their shouting senior officers, were filmed by Central Television sweeping around the square. When riot police stormed the balcony of a block of flats, a black resident came out, shouting in fury at the police, 'I've got my kids sleeping . . . fuck off . . . you lot! Get out, I've had enough!' He was followed by his wife in her dressing gown, trying to get him back into their flat. Why had riot police been drafted into a suburb to deal with car crime? The displays had dominated the nightlife of the square on and off for eighteen months. There had been no effective investigation or intervention, but suddenly, now, there was a public order crisis.

Blackbird Leys was an acclaimed municipal homestead, with few of the tower blocks or deck walkways which brought disgrace to public housing. The estate was made up mainly of houses and gardens. It had a reputation for being a place where the encounter between black and white was peaceable and pleasurable. That is not to say that black people from Blackbird Leys didn't have a different experience of the white city from their neighbours, however.

Among older residents who arrived in the late Fifties and Sixties to work in the city's factories, there is a collective memory of economic partition. However respectable themselves, these residents have stories of the suspicious white gaze that still greets them in public places, and of their children's tribulations, not with their neighbours, but with the law.

The Black Elderly Group, a vigorous association of black pensioners in East Oxford, found themselves being stopped in their mini-van by police. They were well used to their children being arrested and released without apology, but not themselves. 'I felt it so much,' said one of them. 'All these wrongful things going on.' Dedicatedly law-abiding, they saw justice through their children's experience – they saw salespeople shuffle suspiciously as they entered stores with their children, they suffered separation from their children when they left the city just 'because the police are always interrogating the black youth.'

'The police behaviour to black people is horrible,' said a retired factory worker active among the elderly. His generation arrived in Oxford in the late Fifties and the men found work in Pressed Steel or in the Morris car factories. 'When I started they would only give us cleaning jobs, they wouldn't give us a responsible job. Only sweeping. I was cleaning for the first ten years. I would have liked to go on the production line – it was more money. The management told me plainly that this was all they could offer me. They didn't say why. But I knew why.'

Blackbird Leys was a terminus, the end of the road eastwards out of Oxford, past the Rover motor car factory at Cowley. Cowley and Blackbird Leys are the *alter ego* of Oxford, a city synonymous with intellectual industry and tradition. It was a topography corrugated by brick factories, steel chimneys and pleasant, suburban estates. The Leys was a major supplier of labour, both black and white, for the car industry, the industry associated for much of the twentieth century with a popular experience of modernity, mass production and mobility.

It was also an industry associated with masculinity – cars were mainly made by men and for men. In the early Seventies the Cowley car factories employed nearly thirty thousand people, ninety per cent of them men. By the Nineties, Cowley employed only five thousand and the proportion of Oxford's workers employed in manufacturing had dropped to only twenty per cent, even lower than the national average of twenty-three per cent.[1] The McCarthy report on Rover's proposals for closures at Cowley in 1990 warned that there would be 'a collective cultural price to pay' in neighbourhoods which had been sending their people to work there for generations. 'The history of families and communities is written on the tracks at Cowley. Ways of life have established themselves around the factories. As a result, the working-class culture of Oxford bears the stamp of the works, perhaps more than any other single influence.'[2] Within a single generation a major tradition of employment, political alignment, income and identity for working-class men, indeed a tradition that formed cultures of masculinity, was all but extinguished. In 1991 there were two hundred and seventy young men aged between seventeen and twenty-nine without a job in Blackbird Leys alone. A Youth Service report to Oxford City Council in 1991 noted that throughout the city there were only ten vacancies for eighteen-year-olds.

The lads may have stopped making cars, but that did not prevent them stealing them. The collapse of manufacturing work for men was succeeded in Oxford by the rise in car theft, a crime that was emblematic of the Eighties and Nineties. Oxfordshire, together with Berkshire and Buckinghamshire,

---

[1] Lord McCarthy *et al.*, *The Future of Cowley: Report of the Independent Inquiry into the Rover Cowley Works Closure Proposals*, Oxford City Council, 1990.
[2] *Ibid.*

comprised the area controlled by the Thames Valley Police. It came second only to Northumbria in the national league of car crime. According to a report in August 1991 by Chief Superintendent David Lindley, Oxford Police area commander, in the year before the riots 2,395 cars were stolen and 2,934 cars were burgled. In the first half of 1991 car theft rose by ten per cent and thefts from cars rose by twenty-nine per cent. Car theft in Oxford was running at about four thefts a day.

Car crime on the estate was about much more than trade, however. It was about a relationship between young men and power, machinery, speed and transcendence. Blackbird Leys figured in Oxford's statistics as a theatre of car crime. It was the spectacle of the displays which vexed and humiliated the police. Christmas 1990 was celebrated by a display in the estate's central square, and residents remember the howl of a handbrake-turn right on midnight on New Year's Eve.

The displays united thieves, drivers and audiences in an alliance against the authorities. The performances were witnessed by people whose participation amounted only to watching, but whose gaze gave endorsement to the drivers' audacity and, more than that, afforded them protection. The audience enjoyed an ambiguous status. 'I didn't do anything, I was only watching,' was its protest. Its innocence was entirely tactical, a conceit designed to cause confusion to the enemy. Passivity conferred a certain innocence on the audience – after all, it was not stealing cars. But by giving protection to the performers and by bearing witness to illicit performance, the audience was entirely necessary to the show. In the summer of 1990 the displays of 'auto acrobatics' were regularly being watched at 3 a.m. by an audience of thirty or forty people. What made the displays problematic for the police was what sustained them, the combustion of power and pleasure in public space.

The Nineties saw the emergence of a generation of young men to whom the notion of 'going equipped' acquired a new meaning. They would be found with a screwdriver and a scanner, tools to steal cars and taunt the police. A radio scanner the size of a portable telephone and easily bought in

High Street electrics stores enabled them to trace the enemy and torment him by laying false trails. The boys could tap into the police communications systems, discover their response to a car theft, telephone the police station and deflect or disorient the police by offering false information. They could even draw them in by giving accurate information – as time had gone on it was the police whom the boys needed to attract, to bear witness to their performances. The scanners provided a form of technological control that gave the boys a sense of mastery over public space – they controlled the Leys square, they could take control of almost any car they wanted, and they knew exactly where the police were.

Scanners became the bad boys' accessories. The domestication of video technology also transformed their relationship to visibility and to posterity: the joyriders recorded their displays with video cameras and circulated their cassettes around a samizdat network. They could watch themselves being watched, endlessly, in a serial of uninterrupted narcissism. These marginal young men were now the centre of attention. These were men who *loved*, and *lived for*, dangerous displays.

Clearly the displays divided the community between those who wanted to watch and those who felt tormented by the night noise. Several complaints against the displays had been lodged by Councillor Tony Stockford, a Blackbird Leys member of the city council. A burly, affable, former firefighter, he was also a Labour member of the police authority who challenged its convivial camaraderie, which so often silenced political criticism, more than many councillors. But Stockford's complaints did not penetrate the paralysis of the police, which showed a classic breach between community policing, regarded as soft, and hard investigation, which had a privileged status in corporate culture within the constabulary. The community beat officer's reports had had no impact on the police management of Blackbird Leys and had not initiated serious intervention. Nor had the community beat developed strong links with the bad lads, and thus there was little contact with the community's streetwise. Blackbird Leys was a case of the failure of community policing – local bobbies on the beat were aware of the neighbourhood's conflicting imperatives but the bobbies did not penetrate the police management, they were used neither as a *source of intelligence* nor as *mediation*.

Senior officers did not confront the problem with consistency. They were indifferent to it, afraid of it or defeated by it. A senior officer later admitted that the inertia 'was down to poor leadership and management at senior officer level locally. Police officers down at Blackbird Leys felt that the extent of the problem was not appreciated, and that they were unsupported.'

In autumn 1990, Councillor Stockford, utterly frustrated with the lack of police action, told the Chief Constable at a police authority meeting, 'The people of Blackbird Leys are coming to the conclusion that the Chief Constable has lost the ability to maintain law and order on the estate.' Clearly there was a difficulty. Here were public events which had escaped police control – the police could not catch the joyriders. After Stockford's outburst there was a swift change in attitude. The police did not *develop* a strategy, but they were seen to be *doing* something when they regularly dispatched police transit vans to the square and started arresting youngsters under the Public Order Act, to purge people from the public space. This response did not appear to have included a calculation of its effects, however. It created a new crisis in the relations between the police and the community. Blackbird Leys carried an echo of the explosions in areas of Bristol, London, Liverpool and Birmingham during the 1980s. These were the very confrontations which had provoked pressure to reform the Public Order law. But now Oxford police reliance on the Public Order Act provoked complaints about police harassment by young citizens in Blackbird Leys. A fifth of all boys between the ages of ten and sixteen had been apprehended by the police at some time. There were echoes of the protests against the 'sus' (suspected persons) law, repeated under the Public Order Act in 1981, which had criminalised young people on the streets.

The police had no plan to deal with the joyriding phenomenon itself, its addictive character, its pleasures, its public
protection, and its dangerousness. An instinctive response – to
enter the chase – was also constrained by a no-pursuit policy
introduced in police forces by 1990. Dangerous and sometimes deadly car chases through city streets had aroused great
public criticism, not least because they had killed innocent
pedestrians. So, the chase was not encouraged. That meant,
however, that unless the police caught the joyriders in the
act, in mid-performance, they were unable to apprehend either
the performers or the thieves, technically known as TWOCers
(from the offence of Taking Without the Owner's Consent). If
the police managed to intervene in a display, or if a car 'over-
cooked' and tumbled over, there was always an audience to
fight them and rescue the drivers. If the police did go for a
chase – the most dangerous option – they always risked defeat
or even greater public disorder.

So the police responded to the problem of the audience by
trying to stop the young people hanging around. That in turn
generated low-grade public order offences and bad feeling. By
the autumn of 1990 many people were becoming seriously
worried not only that 'law and order' had broken down –
in that the police had, effectively, admitted defeat about the
displays – but also that relations between the police and the
mainly male, mainly young people, both black and white, had
reached crisis point.

The probation service was becoming worried by persistent
local clamour for 'something to be done' about the nightly displays and the signs that police action was creating a new slate
of offences and a new wave of public criticism. The chip shop,
the video hire shop, the pub and the youth club were around
the square. They were the sites of social life on the estate,
they were where people would hang around *doing nothing* –
the term described the most potent focus for young people's
social life in that square. Its significance had been identified
in the Seventies as 'the largest and most complex youth sub-
culture' by the radical sociologist, Paul Corrigan, in his 1975

study of Sunderland, *The Smash Street Kids*. Doing nothing was, in fact, full of incident, intensity and activity: eating chips, talking, smashing something, riding stolen cars. But in Blackbird Leys it had become not just a way of passing the time, it was a public order problem, and young people might find themselves being stopped and searched or questioned.

In the winter of 1990 the probation service covering Blackbird Leys was so worried about the crisis in relations between the youth and the police that in November it approached Cowley police station, which happened to be next door to their own office in Oxford Road, and invited the police to a meeting with young people from the estate. Word went out across the bush telegraph and a group who called themselves the Posse, who socialised around the chip shop, who were black and white, male and female, mostly without a criminal record, turned up and complained fiercely about being harassed. The police explained that they could not just let the young men race their cars around, that the displays were connected with car theft, and that they were under pressure from residents, councillors and the local Labour MP, Andrew Smith. The Posse complained that people were being pushed around and some were being searched in the street. People were being arrested for making petty comments to the police, that younger rather than older people were being moved on, that the police were picking on 'known' individuals, and that they were not bothering to explain what they were doing. '*We* live here, it is *our* estate, but *you* come in and grab us and search us. You've no right,' they insisted.

During deepest winter, the combination of weather and police presence diminished the displays. But by springtime the night boys came out of hibernation and the long, slow escalation to September's riots began. Other peripheral estates, like Barton to the north and Littlemore to the east, began to see displays, 'but the Leys was still the Mecca,' said Councillor Stockford.

By the summer a crowd of a hundred, with deckchairs and refreshments, could be drawn to watch a display. The Leys became an alternative Silverstone. Sometimes it was wild: 'Some of these cars were spinning round and smashing into walls,' recalled one resident. That summer, after the police had been challenged by the joyriders for a year and a half, two things happened to change the city's perspective on the phenomen: the probation service set up TRAX, a specialist team to work with the drivers; and the police acquired a new commander interested in the problem.

TRAX ran pilot schemes with young offenders to find an approach to help them avoid future offending. Of course, most of them did not want to stop. 'For some, illegality was part of the pleasure, for some it was the profit, for others it was the status of being seen with a great car,' said Patsy Townsend, the project leader. They didn't want to be given old bangers to fling around a field in the hope that legitimacy would cure them. 'Some didn't want to be seen driving a dirty old car in a dirty old field.' Others were simply possessed by a passion for wild driving or by control over the object of their desire, a car. But what this work began to clarify was that the joyriders were animated by precisely that – joy. TRAX provided the first context in which they could both exercise their passion for cars, and be challenged about their offences.

At the same time police attention and energy was suddenly engaged when Oxford acquired a new operational commander, Superintendent Ralph Perry, on 1 July 1991. A dynastic policeman, his father had been a police sergeant, and he had joined the force when he was nineteen years old. Perry was a member of the élite targeted for the promotion fast track. He had been a sergeant at Bristol Central on 2 April 1980 when the first calls for assistance came through from officers whose raid on the Black and White Café, a sacred black hostelry in St Paul's – home to a third of Bristol's twelve thousand black people – ignited the Bristol riot. There had been a hundred and thirty-two arrests in the operation, which created wreckage costing £500,000. The police and the prosecution had fared ill in the courts – all the defendants had been discharged or acquitted. Police practice had provoked firm criticism by the Home Office.[3]

Perry recalled that, of the four sergeants who had gone out to give assistance to police in St Paul's that night, he had been the only one to turn up for work in one piece the following morning. 'I remember feeling something that wasn't exactly excitement, though the challenge of it was a thrill, and I remember thinking that people in war must have this feeling of enhancement.' Superintendent Perry hung on to the memory that the force had been totally unprepared. 'That level of violence was totally unexpected. There were all sorts of fashionable explanations, but I don't think anybody could have foreseen the level of violence. It was because we weren't able to stifle it, so it got a grip.'

Perry was more impressed by Bristol's drugs strategy, costing the force £900,000 and named Operation Delivery, launched in the mid-Eighties. Until then, he believed, some police managers were not confronting street robberies and drug dealing 'for fear that the police would be blamed for any subsequent disorder. They did not have the will to deal with it until Operation Delivery. Then we had to take control of the streets, literally.'[4]

Superintendent Perry's personal and professional experience in the Eighties had made him a complex police officer, a thoughtful man who had confronted some hard questions about himself and his chosen profession. His training made him nothing if not a public order man. After the St Paul's riot he studied for a university degree, and after more promotion he had a spell in charge of a specialist public order team, Task Force. He was not frightened.

[3] Home Secretary's Memorandum, 28 April 1980, on *Serious Disturbances in St Paul's, Bristol, on 2 April 1980*, following the Avon and Somerset Chief Constable's report on the riots, House of Commons Library.
[4] The police and the prosecution fared not much better in the courts than in 1980 – of the twenty initial drug arrests, only one defendant received a custodial sentence. Others faced charges of affray which were later reduced to obstruction. A later wave of arrests produced forty-four people found guilty of minor charges and sixty-three against whom there were no charges.

When, in July, he was posted to Oxford, Perry brought with him a history that was to embolden his approach to Blackbird Leys: practical experience of public order management; those potent memories of April 1980; and some scepticism about the impact of Lord Scarman's report on the Brixton riots a year after St Paul's. 'Scarman sent us some wrong signals. He sent powerful messages about consultation that were right and I've no problem with that: I see a very strong role for consultative committees, even when they're not adversarial. But Scarman could also be interpreted as saying that if dealing with a problem was going to cause confrontation, you should avoid confronting the problem. Scarman said, "Do not do saturation policing," so everybody was terrified that we, the police, would be seen to be the cause of the problem.'

Superintendent Perry and Chief Superintendent David Lindley looked at policing priorities and problems. 'Car crime,' they agreed. An auto-crime unit had already been set up. Lindley and Perry initiated an offensive, first against known TWOCers and then against their audience. Between July and August, half a dozen offenders were arrested and in August the police were able to go to the press and announce a drop of twenty-five per cent in car crime. That was immediately answered by a public challenge from the joyriders, a display in Blackbird Leys.

TWOCing is not, in itself, a 'hanging' offence. The police could not keep these boys locked up forever, and neither did half a dozen arrests exhaust the reservoir of drivers and their apprentices. There were boys waiting in the shadows for stardom, and others supplying them with vehicles. The police were still not getting close to the major perpetrators, nor to the displays. 'Their efforts were hampered by the associates of the car thieves and the displayers, who followed the stolen cars and picked up the thieves when they decamped,' said Councillor Stockford – lookouts with scanners were posted along their routes, stoning any officers on their trail. Cars could simply be torched to destroy any evidence that might lead a forensic detective to a joyrider.

Superintendent Perry and Chief Superintendent Lindley believed that, as Perry put it, 'The audience needed to be tackled, because if there was no crowd then there was no kudos, no status, no danger to the public. If there was no crowd, there was no context and therefore no destruction of the quality of life.' But the importance of 'quality of life' here only referred to some citizens; it could not describe the pride of others, the performers. By now the night boys had acquired their own moral creed, based entirely on their own experience, on their own pleasure and on their sense of innocence in the face of victimisation. Taking cars was mitigated, in their minds, by the existence of insurance – the very fact that the car was smart and on the road meant that the owner was covered. To them, the injured parties were not the owners, but themselves: people ill-treated by the authorities, which, of course, they were. Their creed stripped away impediments, like ownership, theft, loss, grief and consequences. It was a commitment to pure pleasure, pride in the performance and their own celebration of conspicious consumption; their relationship to the world was one realised through the medium of a motorcar. 'We spent days and weeks trying to explain our moral dilemma,' said Perry, 'but we had no impact.'

The night boys and the police were not even talking the same moral language, and yet they were mesmerised by each other, utterly interested in each other. After Superintendent Perry's arrival the police had a sense of the joyriders' need for news and their readiness to take them on. They would talk to police patrols cruising around their territory with a confidence that communicated 'a feeling that they had the upper hand, as if they were thinking, "You're afraid to come round here," and "What do you think you're going to do anyway?"' said one senior officer. 'They'd try to elicit information from us. They knew a new superintendent had arrived from Bristol and they attached a significance to it that we didn't know was there. They thought there was going to be a massive change of tactics.' The joyriders seemed to know which officers were assigned to what shifts, and 'the excitement of confronting us was part of it. They were certainly up to any challenge from us,' said the officer.

Both sides had the other under a sort of surveillance. They were watching, listening, tracking, waiting for each other, angry with each other. It was a relationship which came to dominate not just the drama of the displays, but the time and place of public congregation around the square. Everyone's freedom of movement and freedom of assembly was disrupted. Towards the end of August it seemed that the escalation was such that anything was likely to light the fuse. One night residents watched two police officers turn up outside the Blackbird Leys pub on the edge of the square, to arrest someone. 'They dragged him out and one of them had a long stick, like they use in South Africa,' said one man. 'They were knocking hell out of him, and instead of handcuffing him they were just hitting him. I saw them doing it, time and time again, across his back. They did that in front of everybody out-side the pub. We saw it, my wife and I, and we thought, Well, there's going to be trouble! If that's what you call community policing, well . . .!'

The incident that ignited the riots happened later, on Thursday, 29 August, when police officers, led by Superin-tendent Perry, went to Barton estate where there had been a display. Actually there had been simultaneous displays at both Barton and Blackbird Leys. When he got to Barton, Superintendent Perry saw a young man in his late teens pull something up towards his shoulder. It was a catapult, which fired a piece of flint at the police car. With stunning accuracy it went through his window and hit another officer. Later that night a police car in Blackbird Leys was rammed.

That was it. For the next couple of days police moved in and tried to disperse the crowd. By Sunday, aware of increasing risk of a clash, they brought protective clothing. One resident described it as an 'invasion'. Another found himself thinking what many people came to wonder that night: 'Why this now? The joyriding has been happening for years!'

When the police arrived they were able to control movement

around the estate without much difficulty – there were only two main roads and they lined up across them to block all movement in or out of the square. There was no display, but groups of people were hanging around, doing nothing, as usual. Nineteen people were arrested. Although there was widespread support for police action to prevent displays, there were also protests at overreaction.

On Sunday there were rumours of petrol bombs being gathered and stored outside the pub for retaliation, to reassert the right of assembly. Bottles had been spotted by residents, lined up along the wall of the pub, while young men in balaclavas were patrolling the pavements. Houses were searched, young men were picked up and some were detained overnight on suspicion of preparing petrol bombs. No petrol bombs were found, no one was charged. Just after 10 p.m. police arrived but could get nowhere near the pub and retreated. An hour later they arrived *en masse* and made a second attempt to stride across the square and straddle the roads amidst dozens of young people milling around, mocking them. This time the police were dressed in riot gear, and after the crowd showed no sign of going home, they lined up and, guided by a senior officer shouting through a loudhailer, charged across the square, scattering the crowd who ran on to the grass verges and into the surrounding streets. The police occupied the square overnight and maintained a strong presence during Monday. A furious resident was wounded during a fracas that rekindled the frisson. Riot police moved in again that night and took up their positions across the roads converging on the square. Everyone moving in to the estate, whether by foot, by car or by bus, was checked.

By Tuesday a massive media corps had gathered. The police were watching – and listening to – the movements of the main protagonists, who were in turn monitoring the police. Joyriders were being offered payment to perform by some people in the press. Young residents were wandering around waiting for something to happen. The media had now become the audience and, like the crowd, they *needed* a show. They were not at this point fixated on a confrontation between the police and the people; what the media wanted was the forbidden exhibition, a display. 'My lad was approached to do a display that night,' said one of the mothers. 'The press were offering to pay. All they were doing was throwing their money around.' Display was what the police presence for four nights had been designed to prevent. The media thus became the joyriders' accomplices.

Senior police officers had heard about money changing hands for a day or so. They suspected a symbiotic relationship developing between the joyriders and the media, and they feared that there was going to be some action. Missiles were being thrown from behind the media lines and the police reckoned the press were being used as cover. Late that Tuesday evening, the officers stationed in the square in their shirt-sleeves were withdrawn and replaced by riot squads. That was their moment of weakness, when the square became the Manor again, when the joyriders seized the moment and a red MG Maestro swept into vision and danced across the stage, driven by one of Blackbird Leys' master drivers, a suave performer in disguise, wearing 'working' clothes, an inconspicuous old jacket and a black balaclava, watched by the world's media. Then he disappeared back to where he came from, the darkness.

This *coup de théâtre* was, of course, a great embarrassment to the police. 'On the other hand, it did show the world what we were up against,' said Superintendent Perry. The police then gave the media a thirty-seconds' warning to leave. They did, for a while. The police cleared the square and retreated. The audience were hanging around the edges when the Maestro swept back on to the stage and the driver and car repeated their *pas de deux*, an encore for the scattered spectators. At 2 a.m. one of the joyrider's crew appeared before the dedicated fans as a master of ceremonies and with panache announced 'a real burn'. Immediately the man in the Maestro filled the air with burning rubber, swept the car into half a dozen handbrake-turns and disappeared. 'Thank you gentlemen, the performance is over,' said the master of ceremonies.

It was night-time on Wednesday when the tournaments between police and the joyriders again took over the estate and riot squads returned and sealed off the square at about 10 p.m. There were no displays that night, but enterprising young men were doing a swift trade among journalists, promoting a political prospectus, which was probably the *only* document to appear during the disturbances that summer which resembled a traditional manifesto. For £20, journalists could buy a copy of a letter which could be conceived as a joyrider's manifesto. It said, 'In taking performance cars and making them perform, the joyriders demonstrate the only proper use of all technology – its use for fun. To live as we choose we must suppress those who choose how we live.'

As a text it slithered between the political rhetoric of the Right and the Left. It belonged to neither; it said what no one wanted to hear. The riders refused to be victimised by their lack of economic power: it was not a complaint or a lament. The text positioned the joyrider in the same place as the men with more money than sense, the men who enjoy the conspicuous fetishism of an expensive car, one of the few commodities that men have allowed themselves to consume with impunity. In Blackbird Leys, where men's employment in making cars had given way to young men's enjoyment in stealing them, the car was the fetish, *par excellence*, that encouraged men to be represented in the same way as women often are, to see themselves shamelessly as consumers rather than producers.

The text also echoed a political rhetoric of the Sixties and Seventies that it simultaneously repudiated. It expressed Sixties Situationism, a model of modern society as spectacle and individuals as spectators, the world as only the world of the commodity.[5] Its challenge to the police implied an anti-authoritarianism that was, in practice, undermined by the

[5] Sadie Plant, *The Most Radical Gesture: The Situationist International in a Postmodern Age*, Routledge, London, 1992.

boys' authoritative appropriation of public space, their demand to be seen, their demand for attention. The text challenged an earlier puritanism that was anti-commodity, anti-materialist, and anti-property. In that sense this manifesto positioned the night boys and the police closer to each other than either might have imagined. What was known about their shared culture was the passion for fast cars.

At the end of an expensive, week-long occupation of the estate, eighty-three people had been arrested, mostly for breach of the peace and other minor public order offences. The displays diminished, the estate was subdued. Within two weeks, traffic planners were modifying the roads around the estate. Without the riots, a traffic-calming project for Blackbird Leys would never have been such a priority among the three-hundred-odd schemes demanding attention from the county engineers. A traffic island was built in the square within a few months, and bumps were constructed on the surface of the main roads circling the estate. The joyriders liked driving over the bumps.

Then the debate began. Had the estate been protected or had it been punished? 'The question is, when does defending the estate become harassment of the estate?' Councillor Stockford asked himself. The residents were divided. Some welcomed the police because they wanted something to be seen to be done to stop the displays. 'There's lots of elderly people who live round here and they couldn't get a night's sleep,' said one. Others felt fed up with the police because 'one day they're not here, the next day they're here *en masse*. It was frightening. They were everywhere, you couldn't breathe.' That kind of feeling supported another: that to describe the confrontation as a riot was to misrepresent the events and the estate. 'It wasn't a riot, there wasn't a window broken!' said a resident who had to get through the mêlée every night on her way home from work.

The local community's perceptions of the police, the joy-riders and the 'problem' – the displays – seemed to be ambivalent. 'There's nothing else for the kids to do!' Even residents described as 'fossils' by some of the young bucks were agnostic. 'The kids were just interested in cars, they weren't breaking into houses,' said one who lived near the square. 'When it happens we go out and watch! It's the curiosity of watching Nigel Mansell driving at ninety miles an hour. This estate isn't dangerous, it's a nice estate.' One of the TWOCer's parents expressed a widely-held tolerance: 'He doesn't rob banks, he doesn't hurt old people, and he doesn't do it for profit.'

The public perception of the problem, then, was pragmatic rather than moral: it was the noise and nuisance – *order* rather than *law* – which bothered them. The residents felt that their home was given a bad name, their territory was invaded by an occupying force, and all for what? Councillor Stockford embodied the difficulty: 'I would go down to the police station and say what the hell were they doing, and maybe I even got a forlock touched, but I got bugger all done.' Ultimately something was done, of course. 'But I honestly believe it was a no-win situation. The only way the displays were going to stop was if we had serious disorder, a riot, or a high-profile accident. Well, we had a serious public disorder, and it hasn't stopped it.'

CHAPTER 3

A Poor Place

Meadowell was one of the demonised domains of the North East. It was a thrown-away place, imagined as akin to Botany Bay, a place to which folks had been transported. Politicians representing the agreeable townships dotted along the Northumbria coast saw it as a blot, a place where people didn't pay their rates and didn't give them their votes, and therefore, didn't deserve their attention. Pigsville, the Bronx, Vietnam: that was how it was known in its reputation as a war zone. Policing priorities had been set decades earlier by a Conservative authority, and had survived various political incarnations. The estate had been built by the Tynemouth Tories in the Thirties to rehouse the poor of the North Shields Quayside. It was always unloved, a poor old place, arranged as if it was a village of airy avenues and crescents marooned in the Tyneside conurbation.

Despite Northumbria's pioneering presence in the national crime prevention debates of the late Eighties, little or nothing was being done to prevent crime against Meadowell's two thousand dwellings, nor to protect its citizens and what little property they possessed. Crime was part of its economy, and part of what it had to put up with. It endured an epidemic of poverty. Every one of the children at one of the estate's primary schools depended on clothing grants and three-quarters depended on free school meals. A quarter of young men up to the age of twenty-four were unemployed and long-term unemployment among males was the highest in the North East. Thirty years before the riots of 1991, nearly eighty-five per cent of all crime in the borough occurred in this one housing estate. In the period between the Sixties and the Nineties, the region lost most of its staple jobs for men in the shipyards. In the year before the riots, it had the highest crime rate in the country. Residents perceived the police as 'uncaring and indifferent'.

The Meadowell community's complaints were: the mobile panda control seemed neither visible nor mobile; police response times were in excess of half an hour, while they were only a matter of minutes in middle-class areas like Whitley Bay and Gosforth; there was alarming juvenile crime but no coherent response – young men roared into the estate in stolen cars, dumped them and set fire to them daily.

Here was a community overwhelmed by crime, a term that sanitised what people had to put up with. Ram-raiding warehouses and large stores had become a local speciality, while everyday domestic existence was not just lawless but often dangerous. Houses were set on fire, roofs were cleared of tiles, walls were stripped of radiators. Houses were ram-raided, too. Residents were robbed, threatened and pestered by gangs of lads who seemed beyond society's reach. Victimisation was a way of life. When citizens tried to cooperate with the police they became the victims of harassment and abuse who were offered no protection plan. Anyone who was vulnerable, who was challenging, or who excited the criminals' paranoia, could be tormented.

An elderly couple who lived opposite a known criminal barricaded themselves inside their home – that was their only defence – when the neighbour felled a tree and used the trunk as a battering ram against their front door one Sunday afternoon. Just because he could be *seen* the neighbour had apparently assumed that he was being *watched*. The police were called. They arrived four hours later. Such scenarios were information to everyone about where power and protection lay.

Meadowell was an accusation. Its entire edifice had 'failure' grafitti-ed all over it. One police manager described it as a 'boil on the bum of the organisation. Nobody was prepared to take penicillin or go to the doctor about it. It was astounding.' Meadowell was a paradigm of the crisis candidly aired by the Home Office principal adviser and Chief Inspector of Constabulary, Sir John Woodcock, when he said the service faced challenges that brought it 'close to disaster'. Constabulary culture and 'the workplace values of the police have not fully cut free of the past'. It was time for the police to 're-invent themselves'. For those police officers in North Shields who did not feel contempt for the citizens of Meadowell, and especially for those who had themselves grown up on estates like it, it represented a secret shame. 'Some people's attitude was to build a wall round it and throw raw meat over.' Police paralysis was cemented by an authoritarian attitude that could not admit defeat, would not forgive mistakes, and did not encourage innovation. Doing something meant breaking out, taking risks, thinking afresh. Above all it meant doing two difficult things: *confronting* a frightening, fearless fraternity of criminals, hard men (several of them belonging to a coterie of well-known families whose culture wrapped an awesome web around the estate); and *creating* an alliance with the active citizens, diligent women who organised all the informal networks sustaining Meadowell's social integrity: play groups, play campaigns, pensioners' evenings, a credit union, a tenants' movement, welfare advocacy, a mental health campaign. These opposing groups were the two axes in Meadowell's civil society.

But the police and the local authority shrank from the place and consequently conceded ground to the criminal fraternity. Economic retreat had starved community facilities of resources and thus devastated the only groups who were *organising*, who were *creating community* and solidarity, who were trying to make life liveable by reforming relations with the local authority landlord, tackling the panic of debt, providing public pleasures for children and old people. The retreat of the law enforcers left both the active – and passive – citizens the prisoners of the criminal fraternity. There was no protection.

*

At the beginning of the Nineties the ecology of everyday life on Meadowell declined dramatically. Everything was worse after North Tyneside Council, the major agency in the life of the estate, was punished by the Government for 'over-spending' and compelled to introduce cuts in services.[1] But the organised criminal fraternity began to be challenged during the spring of 1991. Superintendent John Broughton arrived in May and was promoted the new chief at North Shields subdivision. Broughton and his colleagues were keen to take on crime in Meadowell. But the first problem he encountered was police estrangement from the estate, which had been seen hitherto as undeserving and difficult. Not surprisingly, 'We weren't welcome,' said Superintendent Broughton. 'That produced a situation where the very people we needed to give us help to do our job – the public – weren't helping us in any way, because of the fear of retribution. We would get reports of incidents and go in but nobody was prepared to talk to us. So we investigated everything cold, from the bottom level: we weren't starting from the first rung, we were starting on the floor. That tends to be resource-intensive and it is not very productive.'

The police were confronted by a fraternity that knew more about them than they could reciprocate. Offences ranging from 'survival' crime to 'serious' crime seemed beyond reach. 'The problem in Meadowell was a fraternity of criminals who classed themselves as professionals,' said Chief Inspector Heath Waddington, the detective who ultimately began to penetrate their system in the months before the riot.

The fraternity seemed omnipotent. The ram-raid was a speciality. A core of organisers seemed to be surrounded by young satellites, many of whom took responsibility for acquiring and disposing of stolen cars. The fraternity knew how the police were going about their business. They knew

---

[1] Its excess was exemplified in the provision of a nursery school place for every three-year-old. Its commitment to children made it second to only one other council in the national nursery provision league table.

who was on duty and who was chasing whom. The key was the fraternity's easy access to technology that took them inside police communications – the portable radio scanner. 'For two years before the riots a group of ram-raiders roamed around the North East. And in the year before the riot it was not unusual to have a ram-raid a night,' said Chief Inspector Waddington. Trading estates where premises had been fortified by barriers, designed to block the ram-raiders, found that they resorted instead to a battering ram mounted on a truck. The raiders would operate in daylight and they would escape, in stolen getaway cars. 'They would go home, sit back and have a cup of tea and listen to the scanners. They loved the scanners,' said the Inspector. 'They loved listening to the police racing around and thinking, "We're the boys and nothing can stop us!"'

It was many months before the police infiltrated the raiders' networks. Their informants' intelligence revealed a system that was militaristic, organised around a cell structure, in which information was passed by word of mouth. Participants would gather at agreed locations and only then would the final team be selected. The destination was not disclosed until the convoy was *en route*.

With great good fortune, in the spring of 1991 North Shields police discovered the time and place of a major raid. In May the ram-raiders found themselves challenged for the first time. Police officers were stationed inside the warehouse of Curry's, the electrical retailers, on the Silverlink industrial estate in North Tyneside when eight masked men arrived in two cars at about 7 p.m. All accessorised with scanners tuned into police frequencies, they smashed through the shutters and through the pitch darkness could be heard the screech of a portable, petrol-driven circular saw designed to cut through concrete. When the raiders cut through the cage containing all the valuable property, the police pounced. There was a violent fight. The police had truncheons, the raiders had baseball bats, crowbars and, of course, the circular saw. There were three arrests.

During the summer masked raiders attacked the same Curry's warehouse in daylight and got away with a haul of camcorders. Police turned up that evening at a house where they arrested five men, although only one was ultimately convicted and gaoled. The stolen camcorders were recovered at a house nearby.

One summer night, on his way home from a football match, Chief Inspector Waddington spotted two stolen Cosworths – formidably powerful cars – packed with masked passengers, in an audacious convoy with another stolen Golf GTI and a stolen excavator, slowly trundling past Meadowell. 'They were moving along slowly, heading towards a trading estate,' recalled the Inspector. Two things were obvious to him – they could not be recognised, and they could mow down anyone who tried to stop them.

The Inspector was off duty, he had no car phone and in any case any telephone communication with his station would have been overheard by the raiders and any action would have been aborted. The only option was to alert his colleagues and hope they could flood the area. The convoy scattered, leaving the excavator to trundle along.

All of this communicated a potent message to the community and to the criminals and their disciples. The fraternity reacted by punishing the police – they targeted individual officers, followed them home and attacked their houses and cars.

Between May and August the fraternity suffered fifty-seven arrests. The police were piling on the pressure, which was a new experience for men who had hitherto moved around with complete freedom. At the same time, a small squad of community police officers was assigned to the estate with a tough brief: whatever else they did, they had to talk to people. Their problem was getting anyone to talk back. Constables could spend an entire shift being ignored. Nonetheless, their very presence, plus several coups when police caught raiders in the act, probably made the police seem more powerful than they actually were. Both the police and the council were paying close attention to the intimidators: the police by targeting organised criminals and the council by tackling households, known for threatening behaviour, which happened to be deeply in rent arrears. Using the arrears as an instrument, and their antisocial behaviour as the cause, the council used its powers to begin the eviction process against nine households.

During the summer there were signs that the fraternity were taking these developments very personally when 'tension indicators' – police officers' names, addresses and telephone numbers – began appearing on the walls of Meadowell. These surfaces – gable ends of houses and shops – were like the Peking Wall: they were where news and views, targets and threats entered the public domain. Graffiti was serious reading matter, it was a way of broadcasting injunctions, accusations, slogans and insults. Most important, it sustained a culture of fear by announcing the names of anyone suspected of being a 'grass'.

There were other tension indicators. Violent harassment was chronic and during the summer months became acute. The school holidays began with a wave of arson when nineteen houses were burned out in south Meadowell within a week and a half, according to North Tyneside's housing department. There were no arrests. Local housing officers toured the scorched streets to offer the remaining tenants alternative homes if they wanted out. 'By the beginning of August the estate was beginning to be ablaze. Properties we might have salvaged were completely wrecked,' said Rita Custance, the senior housing officer. 'It was a very frightening place for people to live.' The grip of intimidation was tightening. The summer was wild.

The incidence of car crime rocketed during the summer. In July the corpses of forty-seven stolen cars ended up at Meadowell. In August the total reached fifty-two. A battalion of boys were recruits to the circuit and at the beginning of September two of them died in a gruesome crash; their deaths started the countdown to the riot. On Friday, 6 September, twenty-one-year-old Colin Atkins and seventeen-year-old

Dale Robson were being followed by police when they raced eastwards along one of the coast roads in a red Renault turbo hatchback they had stolen in Newcastle. They were consumed in flames when the car crashed into a lamppost at around 130 m.p.h. and immediately blew up. Their identities could be traced only through the teeth, keys and jewellery found among their remains.

Dale Robson was due to appear in court three days after the crash on car-related offences. In an attempt to dignify his life, his grieving father, Mick Robson, made a public statement shortly after his death, reported in the *Newcastle Journal* on 9 September, in which he insisted that his son was not a joyrider, he was a professional car thief. Mr Robson said he had tried to warn Dale about the consequences. 'I tried to talk him out of it but if kids don't see sense, what can you do? He had no job and he told me he did it to make money. I know whatever he was involved in he was not a joyrider.' His efforts were regarded by respectable society as a mockery of making a living, and by Meadowell citizens as ruining their community's reputation. Nonetheless, he had made a poignant effort to give his son the status of a skill. This gave a dead boy, who had been an exile in his own society, much more than talent, though his father was paying tribute to that, too: it redeemed him as a social person by imagining a career and therefore a context, history, relevance and relationships.

The scandalous statement was probably one of the most illuminating things anyone said at the time about the meaning of a life on Meadowell. The distinction between the *profession* of thieving, and the *pleasure* of joyriding was an important struggle over meaning and the representation of desperate measures. It was a quest to clothe a life in moral virtue when it had ended in disgrace: profession implied a social purpose, a service that made Dale Robson a 'useful member of society'. Pleasure was pointless and Dale Robson's life was pointless, too. The passion of his life burned him up, it was suicidal.

The deaths stormed the imagination: the boys were so

young. A young person's death is lamented as a 'tragic waste',
as if youth is a life in waiting, ended before it can return the
collective investment and become more than a promise. But
these young men were already proof of a promise broken.
Their deaths were an explosive end to an unfinished journey.
Car crash victims are people making their way but who will
never arrive. They die in limbo, neither here nor there. But
where were these boys going? Were they going anywhere they
wanted to be? The imagery of motoring, travelling, speeding,
of mass, fast, perpetual motion, of going places, belonging to
a landscape and always leaving it, speeding without seeing,
fleeing, alludes both to the Club class air traveller and to the
mythic Levi jeans boy: a nomad, a restless, rich but classless
post-modern man. The irony of the deaths that caused the riot
was that they came out of an apparently peripheral place, a
closed culture which consumed these fantasies of modernity
and movement but was dominated by men who seemed atavistic, parochial, uncool and crazy.

There was a crisis of culpability in the debate about the
cause of death. Had the police in the Ford Sierra, who were
following the boys in the Renault turbo, driven them to their
death? The Sierra's top speed was 125 m.p.h., the Renault's 139
m.p.h. The Sierra could not catch the Renault – the car and its
drivers were too good. Police told the *Evening Chronicle* on
9 September: 'The officers were half a mile away when the
accident happened. They held back because of the excessive
speeds the other car was reaching – after all, our main priority is safety.' The inquest the following February heard from
witnesses, hidden behind screens to protect their anonymity,
whose evidence confirmed that the police car was well behind
the Renault. The coroner recorded verdicts of accidental death.
'Joyride fireball police blameless' was the *Newcastle Journal*'s
headline.[2] That was not how they were perceived on the estate,
of course. After all, the police had participated in a pursuit: the
police and the dead youths were *connected*. One police officer

---

[2] *Newcastle Journal*, 8 February 1992.

saw it this way: 'Everyone knew that there was a deadly game. The police knew their people were baited to pursue, they were drawn into the game in which the lads seemed to feel immortal.' Or suicidal.

There was a subdued pall over the estate the weekend after the crash. It was the quiet before the storm, and although the climate had been roughing up for weeks, the boys' inflammatory deaths seemed certain to ignite a new combustion.

Twice during the weekend, British Telecom manhole covers were pulled up on the estate, inflammable fluid was poured over the circuits and then set alight. Communications, including alarms, were silenced. The police were expecting a crime blitz.

Usually groups of half a dozen young people sat on the walls or lingered by the bus shelter near the Collingwood youth club on Waterville Road. On Saturday, bigger groups than usual gathered at the shelter. 'They were grieving, trying to swallow the news,' said one of the dead boys' friends. The erroneous conviction that the boys were driven off the road had been encouraged by people listening on their scanners to police bulletins during the chase. All these young men knew was that the police were in pursuit, and that was enough for them.

The destruction of telephone wires on Sunday put a swathe of North Shields out of communication, including the police subdivisional headquarters. Monday, 9 September, was expected to be a big day in the life of the estate. Nine evictions were planned by the housing department, all involving households known for harassment and massive rent arrears. In the event, only two of the evictions were carried out, and the tenants went peacefully.

However, all weekend the talk was that something was definitely going to happen, that the boys' deaths could not go unmarked. The attrition between the criminals and the authorities seemed set to enter another, audacious phase. All day Monday, telephone calls reporting rumours of a riot, many of them anonymous, were being specially routed through to Superintendent Broughton at North Shields police station, warning him to expect bother. He arranged for a team of Special Patrol Group officers to be brought back on duty that night.

Ashtak Ahmed, the owner of the Marina Fish Bar on the corner of Avon Avenue, began to have a feeling in the afternoon and early evening that things were not right. He was getting scared because the place had become still. 'Usually when something is happening, it goes quiet, you don't see the children out, you don't see the dogs out,' he told the Crown Court later. Calls got through to the police station that gangs were gathering at the Collingwood youth centre nearby. But when the police arrived there was no one around. When they returned a little later they were stoned, and withdrew.

That evening, Meadowell exploded. An old barn beside the youth club was set on fire at about 7 p.m. A tree was felled and hauled into a strategic position in the middle of Waterville Road, the main avenue between the north and south of the estate. It was after about 8.30 p.m. that people living around Waterville Road saw some serious organisation. Youths were clustering. 'At 8.40 I saw them cut down a tree and pull up fences,' said Robert Scott, a milkman whose evidence was heard in a Meadowell riot trial before the Crown Court in September 1992. The tree lay opposite the Collingwood youth centre, which was set on fire just after 9 p.m. It was the biggest building around, a fine place for a fire. The electricity substation near the Seine Boat pub in the middle of the estate was burned out after petrol was poured over its circuits. The flames could be seen from the pub, which called the emergency services. Televisions flickered and went blank. Lights went out. Northern Electric engineers tried to get onto the estate but were beaten back by lads throwing bricks. Wallsend fire station, which serviced Meadowell, received a call about the electricity substation at 9.18 p.m. and dispatched two fire engines. Once they reached Percy Main roundabout, the entrance to Waterville Road, they could see the massive fire at the youth club. Hundreds of youths lined either side of the road. The fire engines managed to get past the tree and close to the fire. 'I could hear bricks thudding against the sides. I instructed the driver to carry on,' said firefighter Michael Nielson. But soon, surrounded and fearing for their safety, they pulled out.

A youth worker had been called in to reset the burglar alarm and in all innocence drove to Waterville Road by about 9.30 p.m. 'I saw loads of people standing around. That was not unusual,' he said. 'There was lots of smoke, not unusual; people looking out of their front doors, not unusual either. I drove down and all hell let loose. There were flames on the road, the club was ablaze with flames coming out of the doors and windows, and the roof was going in.' From their build, he guessed that many of the masked men in the road were in their twenties. His car was being shelled by missiles, people were wielding clubs, branches and sticks, and he began to fear for his life. 'One of my thoughts was, How do I get out? What are my options? Dump the car? No, I'll be clubbed to death. Should I stay in the car and lock the doors? No, they could petrol bomb it. I just put my foot down. The tree was ahead, people were behind and suddenly a loud bang made the car swing around. I thought they were shooting at me. I skidded round.' In what was probably thirty seconds but felt like three hours, he fled and minutes later reached the home of a friend and got a message to the police. From the blow to his car's bodywork it was suspected initially that he might have been struck by a crossbow or a catapult firing a ball bearing – a mini cannon. A crossbow was later recovered during police searches.

There had been a few customers for fish and chips at the Marina on the corner of Avon Avenue that evening; several children had also come in asking for boxes of matches. Then a man wielding a metal bar appeared in front of Ashtak Ahmed and delivered a threatening message which intimated what happened to residents who disapproved of joyriders and professional criminals. 'He shouted at me, "He does not like car thieves!" As he walked away a few children followed and threw a brick which smashed my window. Then I realised there would be trouble for the shopkeepers,' he told the Crown Court later. Mr Ahmed closed his shop at 9.30 p.m. From his upstairs flat he could see a crowd outside stoning the shop belonging to his neighbour, Nashatar Singh. He called the police station. 'They said they were doing everything they could. There were no police in sight so I thought I might as well leave the place.'

Nashatar Singh was closing his food store and general dealer's at 81 Avon Avenue early when he saw a crowd gathering outside. The kids sitting on the wall opposite his shop were shouting; bricks started coming through the reinforced windows of his home upstairs; young men armed with bricks, sticks and iron bars were battering his shutters. He recognised some of them, they were regular customers from families well known to the police. His terrified children were weeping and his wife insisted that they must leave. Mr Ahmed rang and urged him to drive out with him. And so, gathered up by his friend Ahmed, the family threw themselves into the neighbour's car. Keeping the lights off, they fled. Their friend Ravir Rai Singh owned the newsagent's at 31 Avon Avenue and, like the other traders, lived with his family in the flat above. When his shop was invaded he, too, loaded his family into his car and fled.

Dinesh Sharma owned Gill's general hardware dealer at 36 Avon Avenue and had already had an intimation of what was to come. Just before midnight the previous night, a brick had been thrown through his window and a petrol bomb had hit the wall. After about 9 p.m. on Monday, bricks started streaming through his windows. His children gathered on the stairs, the safest place in the house, while he investigated what was going on outside. 'My escape routes were blocked. I didn't feel there was anywhere I could go.' He could see people coming out of Rai Singh's shop with crates and kegs of beer. And outside his own shop there were lads, some of whom he recognised, with crowbars and petrol bombs.

What the Asian traders were seeing from behind their broken windows was also being watched on the outside by other traders and residents. The pork butcher, Brian Mather, was standing outside his shop with his neighbours, Gladys Atkinson and her husband. Mrs Atkinson, the owner of the fruit and vegetable shop at number 39, had called her husband at his ex-servicemen's drinking club just before 9 p.m. and told him to get home because trouble was brewing. They watched the crowd filling the avenue when the Asian traders were being ransacked. They saw Rai Singh's white van being brought into the avenue by the lads and being used to ram his neighbours' shops.

Then a posse emerged from the crowd carrying bottles filled with petrol and walked towards the Asian shops. They were 'quite matter-of-fact', the butcher told the Crown Court later. 'They weren't trying to hide them.' As they passed him he turned to Gladys Atkinson. 'Did you see that?' he asked her. 'Aye, they're petrol bombs, them!' she told him. Several of the faces were familiar to her. The butcher watched them march past, moved across the road to get a better view and watched one of them light a petrol bomb and throw it.

'A crowd of women were watching and when they threw another, probably at Gill's, a couple of women ran out and shouted to them not to be so stupid, there were bairns in there. A woman ran across the road to stop them, shouting, "Stop it!" and went to the front door to get them out. A couple of women ran across the road screaming at them to stop it.' These women were the first people to challenge the rioters. They were also watched by the milkman, Robert Scott, who had seen the tree being felled, the bricks going through the windows of the fish and chip shop, and people pillaging the Asian shops along Avon Avenue. Now he saw Nora Casey dash across the road over to Gill's shop, where the Sharma family were trapped inside, and bang on the door to get them out. He heard someone shouting, 'There's bairns in there!' which briefly seemed to calm the crowd.

Earlier in the evening Nora Casey had registered a surprising stillness when she walked home from her daughter's house. Like Mr Ahmed, she noticed that while 'normally there are groups of youths congregating on corners', on that day 'there was a distinct lack of activity'. When the fire erupted at the Collingwood youth centre, she and her neighbour, Mary Barber, wandered down Avon Avenue to see what was going on, but were told by the young men to get away. On their way back they saw that the avenue was being stormed. 'I stood in disbelief at what was going on and I heard a voice shouting, "Let's do the shops next."' There were hundreds of people in Avon Avenue by then, some of them masked. 'Laden with cargo lifted from the shops, they were like little bees running around.'

'I was pleading, saying the Asians were a nice couple who should be left alone.' Then she heard someone shouting towards the besieged shop, 'They're all the same! You've got two minutes to get out!' She and Mary Barber shouted at the crowd to leave the shop alone. The lads backed off. Nora Casey seized the moment and thumped on the front door. Dinesh Sharma opened it and saw her. Behind her he saw 'lads standing outside with crowbars and petrol bombs. She was shouting to the residents inside, "Come out, come out, they'll petrol bomb your property." The moment I opened the door she grabbed hold of my daughter – she's nine years old – and I saw that one bottle was already burning.' Sharma looked at the man holding it. He knew him. 'I don't know why, but he turned away and threw it at the building opposite.' The women escorted the Sharmas over to the shelter of Nora Casey's kitchen.

Once she had settled the family, Nora Casey returned to her front garden and saw someone upstairs in the Sharmas' flat, 'with what looked like a lit newspaper. I had visions of the crowd turning on my house if they realised they were inside. I told him to keep away from the windows.' This woman had a certain authority, her family was close to one of the families with a criminal reputation on the estate.[3] Balaclava-type ski masks were everywhere: that was a sure sign, not necessarily

[3] Some of them later appeared as defendants in a Meadowell riot trial. Nora Casey gave evidence as a witness for the defence.

of anonymity, but of their wearers' wish to be invisible and a demand that they be not identified. Many people watching the spectacle would have noticed things that lingered low in their consciousness: a familiar pair of trainers attached to a body they would recognise anywhere. Meadowell was a community where people possessed so little that clothes and body language were like labels. Here, the claim that 'everybody knows everybody' was a reality.

Everyone also knew just what people were capable of, just how violent they could be. There were many women in that crowd who also knew that although they might not have the power to stop the violence, they had the power to prevent its worst excess. Nora Casey may have known that she might make the difference between murder and arson. She may also have known that the limits of her power meant that she was only being *allowed* to stop them doing the worst.

Mr Sharma sat in her kitchen with his head in his hands, crying. After the children had gone to bed he watched helplessly while Rai Singh's newsagent's was being rammed and raided, his neighbour's white van being driven into shop shutters and caseloads of goods – everything from nappies to beer – being carted out into the street; then he watched the crowd targeting another Asian's well-stocked liquor store.

Ann and Alan Ashworth had also watched the lads marching towards the shops. Mr Ashworth saw that, 'to my horror, a gang of four were making their way towards the shop opposite my home, wearing ski masks.' They started on the Sharmas' shop, looted it and moved on to another. 'I heard someone shouting, "Don't do that one, it's a white man's shop."' Then they moved to another Asian shop, Bains', and started forcing the shutters. 'My wife was shouting at them to back off and leave the family alone, and for some reason the group stopped and looked at each other as if they didn't know what to do. My wife started pleading with them.'

Ann Ashworth got the youngest Bains children out. Her husband went over, too, shouted through the letterbox and hammered on the door. When it opened he grabbed a little boy and, with two girls clinging on to him, raced back over the road and handed them over to his wife. Jacqueline Morris, who lived in a flat above the shops, had been out searching for her son among the crowd at the Collingwood centre. She shouted at the rioters on her way home and when she saw the white van ramming a shop front she hammered on its sides, shouting at the driver.

The white van was by now being backed into Bains'. The window shattered and inside Mr and Mrs Bains were throwing tins of food back at the boys throwing stones. 'I decided enough is enough,' said Alan Ashworth. 'I shouted, "Back off, I'm going to get them out." The crowd seemed to take notice and I got through.' He grabbed Mrs Bains and took her to his home, returned to find a dozen youths inside the shop and the van ablaze outside. 'I'm going to get this man out. He's not going to die!' roared Mr Ashworth, who grabbed Mr Bains and rushed him over the road to safety. Back in his own home he noticed there were flames coming from the Bains' flat. The family was devastated: their documents were stored up there, and money was wrapped up in the freezer. And so Mr Ashworth made yet more trips over the road and into the house, where he saw half a dozen youths filling their pockets. He retrieved the papers and the money. Altogether he made eight trips back and forth that night.

Currents of communication among the rioters seemed to have made the targets widely known. Adjacent to the Collingwood centre, there was an old building, known as the barn, and a modern health centre. The barn was torched and a fire had been started and then stopped in the health centre on the same site. A paint tin surrounded by scorch marks was found there the following morning. Little damage had been caused, and it seemed that although the youth club was deemed a legitimate target, the clinic was not. A fire was started at one of the schools, too. Fears that all the *public* buildings were at risk were unfounded – the word went out that the Cedarwood Centre, a church-sponsored community house on south Meadowell, was not part of the plan. The Community

Rights Centre on the corner of Avon Avenue survived intact,
too. Community activist Linda Craik had been trying to keep
an eye on it. Monday was bingo night for pensioners and while
they got down to business in the Community Rights Centre
building, known as 'the rights shop', Linda Craik popped out
for a bottle of milk and noticed lads lining the road down
towards the metro and Waterville Road. 'I just knew there
was something wrong somewhere. I went back in and got all
the pensioners out. I went home and phoned the police. But it
was preying on my mind – what were those people doing down
there? I phoned the police three times. I went down towards the
shops and I could see men in their sixties crying. Other people
were saying, "Where are the police?" I phoned them again and
they said they could not enter. People were shocked that they
were getting no response.' Some people just wrapped up their
babies and toddlers and fled to friends, who may have been
only a few streets away, but who felt safe.

All of this was happening in the hour or so after the
electricity substation went up in flames and the emergency
services were being kept off the estate. During that hour
Margaret Nolan, Meadowell's best-known community activist, had been at a meeting of credit unions in Newcastle and
overheard a reporter telephoning his office about rumours that
something was going on in Meadowell.

She rang home to check with her husband and teenage
children if all was well. It was not: they were frightened,
there were fires. She drove home and immediately set off
trawling the streets on foot to find her family and her friends,
Molly, Nancy and Linda, all community activists like herself.
Friends were fearful and flabbergasted. A little after 11 p.m.
she found her teenage son and daughter walking up from Avon
Avenue with Linda Craik and her son. As if from nowhere,
two police vans arrived. 'They were like the Keystone Cops.
They jumped out in riot gear and they went for our two lads
with their truncheons.' The mothers protested and according
to Margaret Nolan the police shouted back, 'Get in your fucking
doors and shut your windows . . . Get in, sluts!'

'That's what we were hearing from them. I said to one of them that that's not what they should be doing in a situation like that,' said Margaret Nolan. 'People weren't being cheeky, there was no panic, there wasn't even worry, just a nothingness. People were too frightened to panic or ask too many questions. We accept everything, we never ask questions. They marched our boys home. If we hadn't been there the lads would have been lifted. It was indiscriminate, they were looking for young men, because they would have been the likely culprits.'

By this time Northumbria's police helicopter had been mobilised and had been circling the estate for an hour. The police could not penetrate the heart of the estate but positioned themselves around the periphery. Superintendent Broughton did not have enough officers to send them in *en masse*, nor were his people properly protected. He was convinced, given the evidence of firebombing, that if officers had been thrown into the mêlée there would have been fatalities among the police. But desperate calls were flooding into the special North Shields operations room set up to manage the Meadowell crisis. They feared fatalities among the people. 'Listen, I don't know who you are,' said one resident to the police officer at the other end of the line. 'I'm a mother. Please, that family over there don't deserve this, their shop is opposite my house. I've been on the phone twice tonight ... All right, they're black, but they're a smashing family and they don't deserve this.' One of the Asian mothers shouted down the telephone, 'They will burn our babies.' Another called, crying, 'Please ... my kids ... please help me.' The switchboard staff could hear her children screaming in the background.

Just after 11 p.m. the police made another attempt to respond to calls for help from residents reporting fires in Avon Avenue, but police vehicles were beaten back by stone-throwers and petrol-bombers. A crowd of about four hundred people was still holding the Avon Avenue area, watched from above by the helicopter. And although it was a hot, dry night,

Waterville Road looked from above as if it was wet. The heli-copter patrol speculated that it might be petrol. Cars were spotted, going round and round the estate, repeatedly. Young men had been seen filling bottles with petrol at a nearby fill-ing station. A pattern was emerging: first it seemed that the purpose of the early fires had been to draw the police into the fastness of Waterville Road and thus into a trap. That failed. The police had not been drawn into the centre of the estate. If the police would not come to the fires, then it seemed that the fires would go to the police. North Shields police station, a few miles away from Meadowell, had been warned that it was going to be petrol bombed. The place was sandbagged and, sure enough, that night a convoy of suspected criminals approached until it was stalled by a barricade of police officers and dogs.

A trail of fires was now being lit on a route circling back towards Meadowell, which included a blaze at a big Coalite depot. When Wallsend fire brigade sent out a fire engine at about 11 p.m. it was pursued by cars full of youths, some masked.

It was almost midnight when the fire brigade and police tried again to respond to terrified calls for help in Avon Avenue. A fire engine reversed towards the parade of shops in response to calls carrying the conviction that people were stuck in their blazing homes. Meanwhile the reports coming down from the helicopter suggested that this was another trap, that there were young men waiting for them, offloading petrol bombs from car boots. Superintendent Broughton was the tactical commander who had to make a decision: to go in or not to go in. 'I remem-ber – and will do for all my days – hearing that we had persons trapped in an Avon Avenue burning building. We responded. We were forced to withdraw. There was another call about persons trapped in another building. I had to say, "We are not responding". It was the hardest decision of my life.' He dared not risk a confrontation without reinforcements. Running up to midnight, the police kept watch from the helicopter on the crowd contained around the avenue. 'We wanted to box them into a small area so that they could keep it and call it their own,' said Broughton. By then he was holding on in the knowledge that scores of officers were being drafted in, and was planning manoeuvres to recapture the estate. Squads were posted along strategic routes; a major Esso pumping station where tankers refuelled was under guard; garages were closed down; a hundred and ninety-seven personnel were gathered and positioned, ready to retake the area and drive the rioters towards the least populated southern edge of the estate. The final attack was organised as a military operation, coming from three directions: one unit moved from the east and the west towards the barricade in Waterville Road, another moved from the north down Ripley Avenue towards Avon Avenue. Once everything was in place the operation was over in almost no time.

It took seven minutes to scatter the rioters. At 1.30 a.m. the police moved into position. Two Special Patrol Group vans moved along Waterville Road, their lights flaring into the eyes of the crowd who would not have known whether there were two vans or twenty. At 1.37 a.m. the crowd disappeared.

That night had been a civil war. Hundreds of young men, apparently led by a fraternity that was making a big bid for power, had burned buildings, raided and razed shops, shared out the stolen goods – booze, bikes, nappies, jam, washing machines, biscuits, detergent, whatever anyone could lay their hands on. They were high, they partied on the looted lager and cooled out in their gardens until dawn.

At 5.30 a.m. Nora Casey's husband returned from nightshift to a place that looked like Beirut or Belfast, to a home packed with refugees. He drove the Sharmas out of Meadowell to a place of safety. Nora Casey never saw them again.

Margaret Nolan didn't go to bed. Like many others she could not sleep and was not allowed out to see what was happening: her only access to what was going on in her own neighbourhood was the broadcast media. 'I stayed on the settee and listened to the news. We found out what was going on from the telly and the radio. And I had to make sure that my lot stayed in the house.'

She got up at dawn and an hour or so later she and a corps of women, including Molly Woodhouse, Ann Divine and Linda Craik, made their way to the Community Rights Centre in Avon Avenue. That building was an ironic monument to survival – it was almost a year to the day that its occupants, community resource groups, had been squatters after the local authority grant had been withdrawn. Had they not kept the place occupied, its gas, water and electricity would have been cut off. Had they abandoned it then it would have gone the way of all voids – stripped of anything that could be stolen and sold; pipes, radiators, sinks. Everything was still working. They opened the doors, put the kettles on, and people started trailing in for help.

At the same time council officials, the cleansing department, the electricity engineers, advice staff, all arrived to clean the place up and take care of the refugees. It all worked well. 'The street had never been so clean,' somebody said. That day the public were not at war with the public servants.

But Meadowell had experienced a disaster. This was a community well used to catastrophe; it knew all about disassociation and displacement – that was how it survived emotionally all the time. But some people went into shock and several started turning up at the resource centre because they could not sleep: they were terrified that they would burn in their beds. After all they had had petrol bombs and broken windows. They feared that they would be next.

While kids who had stayed up all night in the thrall of incendiary pleasures staggered through the following week saying it had been 'fucking brilliant', anyone who had to put a dinner on the table or a nappy on a baby's bottom found nowhere within walking distance to replenish supplies – there were no more grocery shops or takeaways anywhere in the heart of Meadowell. You couldn't get a fresh loaf or a pint of milk. Meadowell was a place where people did not get their milk delivered: most people could rarely afford to come up with a weekly payment, and the bottles would be pinched anyway. 'This was a place where many people lived from day to day and they couldn't afford the fare to Shields to get their basics, like bread or nappies,' said Linda Craik. By the end of the week she was thinking maybe the women could set up a shop themselves, a co-op to cater for basics. But there was no bank on the estate and no one had any money.

However, they did have a community credit union. This was one of Meadowell's most useful self-help services, a people's bank comprising four hundred residents each saving about £1 a week. It was a bank for paupers, it had no capital other than that accumulated from these small savings, but it was the only source of credit – at rates that were repayable – available on Meadowell that week. The credit union came up with a loan of £200 for a food co-op. Linda Craik's daughter, Mandy, volunteered to be their delivery driver. Margaret Nolan lent her car to collect the stock from a cash-and-carry three or four times a week. A room in the rights centre was given over to the shop. A food co-op was created.

The riots had not exactly proved to be liberation by looting, they had left the place like a pre-*perestroika* downtown, where the supply bore no relation to the demand. A Meadowell stalwart recalled the craziness of it: 'People's houses were stacked high with daft things, like a hundred and fifty bottles of Fairy Liquid, or kids were walking around with pockets bulging with packets of cigarettes, but there was nowhere on the estate to buy coffee or sugar. There was a high for the first day or so and then people were finding out that they might have a load of shampoo, but there was nowhere they could get coffee.' There was nowhere to buy fresh vegetables either – the redoubtable Gladys Atkinson had been forced to call it quits, after twenty years as a trader on the estate, once it became known that she had given the police names of people she recognised in the petrol bombings.

The riots changed the police relationship to the place. They arrived in force and stayed for a couple of weeks, going from house to house. Everyone anywhere in the vicinity of the riots was visited. That, at least, offered a little protection – there was safety in numbers and nobody would know what was being said behind closed doors. If the lads with the scanners were tuned in to the police headquarters, they were not yet bugging people's houses. Nonetheless, the police interviewed six hundred people and came out of Meadowell with only a handful of statements.

When two CID officers went to see Linda Craik to ask whether she had been around Avon Avenue, 'I told them why I was there, watching our building because we'd fought so hard for it – though what I would have done if the lads had decided to burn it I don't know! The police asked for names. I said no, I'm not telling you because the riot was as much the police's fault as the lads' fault. If the police had responded right away then there wouldn't have been a riot, so much damage and so much terror. They said if I gave them names I would be guaranteed a house away from the estate right away, but I told them I didn't want to shift, I like the people here, I like where I am. One of the CID officers said he was very disappointed. I still say the police should have stepped in long before they did. The police were wrong letting it go.' Another Meadowell stalwart, who had felt terrified on 9 September, believed that 'in a situation like that people rely on the police to come in early. Everybody knows who is responsible, but they can't do anything about it. That's why they need the police.'

The evidence crisis was also a problem of strategic management. That strategic problem was aired during the first Meadowell trial at the Crown Court in July 1992. Superintendent John Broughton told the court that he was responsible for 'tactical, not strategic, command'. The strategic commander was Chief Superintendent Brian Duffy. He was not available on 9 September.

Neither was evidence-gathering equipment – cameras, photographers, video cameras aboard the helicopter which was requested only at 10 p.m. on the night of the riot. There was, therefore, no independent police corroboration.

The Superintendent agreed that there was no independent

source of evidence to support the community's witnesses. 'Not even a makeshift attempt to acquire independent evidence?' he was pressed. 'It would have required more than makeshift,' Broughton replied. He insisted that the police priority, when faced with serious disorder, is to put other issues aside and seek to restore peace. 'The priority is to restore order, not to make arrests.'

Challenged once again, when defence counsel argued that the reason for the absence of evidence-gathering resources to support serious criminal charges was 'not so much the ferocity of disorder but the command structure – it was just not available,' Broughton agreed, 'It was not available.'

The reasons were both political and professional. The absence of an alliance between the community advocates and police leaders had historically deprived the police of their most important source of intelligence – the community itself.

Nonetheless, the police had a resource problem that was both material and managerial. Superintendent Broughton was the *operational* commander of the Meadowell operation on 9 September. The staff shortage in Northumbria left Broughton spending much of the evening of 9 September gathering personpower to mount his manoeuvre to retake the estate. The force was in the midst of transition – the control of the constabulary was changing hands. The scale of the threat to both the community and the constabulary had not penetrated the *strategic* management.

But the threat had been gathering force before 9 September, long before the oaths to avenge the deaths of Atkins and Robson. The threat only revealed itself in the attack on Avon Avenue, and in the absence of resources to *control* the situation, to protect people and property. It was rumbling throughout the summer, when the estate began to feel the effects of the attrition between the fraternity and the police. Before that it was palpable in the failure of detection and the fraternity's confident command of their terrain. Most important, the ultimate victims of the attack had a long history of victimisation which had not been assimilated by the strategic managers.

The strategic commander responsible for the management of the territory that included Meadowell was Chief Superintendent Brian Duffy. He had been alerted several times to the dangers facing Asian traders. He had been briefed a number of times by local councillors and police specialist advisers in the Race Relations Unit. He had been warned in August 1990 and again in August 1991 by politicians and police professionals about the endangerment of the estate in general and the Asian traders in particular.

Police operations had not been guided by the intelligence offered by its own specialists and by the democratic agency to which the police were accountable, the police authority. The consequences were catastrophic. The traders did not just *work* in their shops, they also *lived* above the shop: if their property was torched their lives were imperilled. The failure to integrate the information about the conditions of the Asian traders' existence in a protection plan for the people of Meadowell meant that their shops in Avon Avenue were perceived only as commercial premises, rather than as homes in the heart of the community.

CHAPTER 4

Young Men Go West

Many of the Asian traders who fled from Meadowell, never to return, had relatives over in Newcastle's West End. During the riot on 9 September, some of them had tried to rush over and rescue them, but Avon Avenue was impenetrable. Only when escape routes were clear in the morning were they reunited, the refugees bringing with them only what they wore and what they had managed to retrieve from their burning homes. At least now they expected to find safety in numbers – the West End was where the majority of Newcastle's ethnic minorities had settled; it was the only place in the city that resembled a cosmopolitan, modern metropolis.

One of the besieged Meadowell traders found sanctuary with his brother, another shopkeeper, in the Scotswood neighbourhood on Tuesday. Their two families camped together in the Scotswood shop. The grocer's wife had begun her life in the West End, 'as one of hundreds of women who couldn't speak English. If someone swore at me – usually the young ones saying, "black bastard" – I could not say anything.' Times had changed and by 1991 she was an interpreter out and about in the city as well as working in the shop. 'Now I don't take racism from anybody!'

Groups of teenagers were touring her neighbourhood in cars on Tuesday; lads repeatedly paced up and down her street. People came into the shop constantly with the warning, 'They'll do your shop.' 'I would say, "Thank you," and carry on even though I was frightened,' she said. 'As soon as we heard the fire engines I told my husband to shut the shop.' The fire brigade went to thirty-one fires across Tyneside on Tuesday night. The refugees were terrified and, together with the children, were sent to stay with relatives in a middle-class neighbourhood several miles away. It looked as if the Meadowell script was about to be replayed in the West End.

But already that day folks were beginning to get organised. The police, ethnic minority leaders, activists, interpreters, West End councillors, youth workers and employees of the city's public works department moved swiftly to make the state and voluntary sectors proactive in trying to protect the city.

On Tuesday morning the director of Tyne and Wear Racial Equality Council, Hari Shukla, and Chief Inspector Steve Ransome, head of the Race Relations Unit at West End police station, drove east to Meadowell. 'It hit the heart straight away,' said Ransome, 'when we started talking to people, black and white, and heard some horrific stories of their helplessness and isolation and narrow escapes.' Those narrow escapes informed the policing and protection of Newcastle over the next few days.

An informal coalition came knocking on the police door. The Chief Constable agreed to meet black leaders and promised that potential targets would be protected. Hari Shukla and Zafar Khan, another prominent member of the Racial Equality Council, then scoured the streets of the West End, going from shop to shop, to the city's three temples and to Asian restaurants to spread the word: don't let yourselves be provoked, don't join in: if there's trouble, ring us. 'We spent almost the whole day moving from one shop to another, putting people in the picture. We didn't want to create fear, we just wanted to take precautions and tell people they could be supported straight away,' said Hari Shukla.

At the same time, over at the Civic Centre, an edifice to Sixties monumentalism that was, by the Nineties, acquiring the grandeur of middle age, a feeling of foreboding had hit the city's Race Relations Officer, Rajinder Singh, when he contemplated the fate of the Meadowell traders. This must not happen in the West End, he decided. A soft-spoken, resolute Sikh, he had cachet in Newcastle as a man who changed minds and made things happen. He had no doubt that 'the police containment policy in Meadowell meant that the Asians were trapped. The police should have known that they would be at risk. We didn't want a repeat of Meadowell, families stranded without help.'

He had helped transform institutional consciousness of racism in a city which traditionally, and wrongly, believed that it had no problem because it had so few black citizens. It was commonplace to assign the problem of racism in the city not to whites but to the presence of blacks. Newcastle was home to Chinese, Vietnamese, Indians, Pakistanis and Bangladeshis who formed about three per cent of the population, though in some wards that presence was more than twelve per cent. In any case, numbers were neither here nor there. Singh's experience was that Newcastle was often more *overt* about its racism than elsewhere. 'People are bold enough to swear at you in the street, which they wouldn't do in some other places. Our mere presence represents a threat here.' This view was supported by a Civic Centre survey in 1990 which found that fifty-seven per cent of black people had suffered personal abuse. Attacks on property had affected forty-five per cent (compared with twenty-five per cent in Sheffield and fourteen per cent in Waltham Forest in north-east London).

Singh asked for a direct telephone link and an office at the Civic Centre which would be the community's conduit to emergency services, and recruited a team of black and white volunteers to staff it day and night. Word went out immediately to the ethnic minorities that there was a hotline at the Civic Centre.

Off the Elswick Road, in one of the terraces that typify the Tyneside landscape, West Enders, police, dogs and children, were, on Wednesday night, all watching an everyday burglary that entered history. What in any other week would have been a simple scam became a spectacle. A woman arrived home from work around 6 p.m. after stopping at the shops for her supper. She put the plastic bag on the step and the key in the door. That was as far as she got. She lived alone; she heard banging inside her house. Burglars, she thought. This woman had been burgled half a dozen times. Leaving the shopping on the step, she ran to her neighbour's house and called the police. Her neighbour had been in all day – waiting for the joiners to fix her door which had been kicked in over the weekend by burglars.

When the police arrived a little later, two boys, the burglars, sped out of the back door, over the wall into the neighbour's yard, through her back door and found themselves face to face with her. They recognised each other. Only the day before, the boys had knocked on her door asking for a fictitious friend – they had apparently been stalking the street to see which houses were empty. She ran at them, shouting and swearing. The boys raced out and up the drainpipe to her roof. There they stayed for the next couple of hours.

The women called the police headquarters again. 'You'd better do something because there will be a riot,' they warned presciently. As if they had overheard this conversation, the boys responded from the roof, 'If you think Meadowell was bad, just watch, we're gonna burn the place down. Meadowell was nowt compared to this.'

A large crowd of onlookers was collecting in the street. Local gangsters in souped-up motors circled around. The boys had an audience, including police officers who were videoing their show while they stripped tiles off the roof and chucked them into the street. 'We're very critical of the police communication skills,' said the neighbours. 'They just let it happen. The boys seemed stuck, they didn't seem to know how to extract themselves.' The lads' solicitors arrived on the scene but their presence made no immediate difference either and they, too, became frustrated. 'Obviously, the police were trying to contain the crowd,' said one of the solicitors, 'but they were simply standing there, they weren't trying to move people on.'

Up above, the boys were collecting the tiles and stacking them into piles. Inside the house, the children in their bedrooms listened to them rustling on the roof. Downstairs, the two neighbours stared out of the window, watching the roof boys' reflections dancing across the windows of the house opposite. 'We could see the lads piling up the slates, like ammunition.' They began to feel that the very roof over their heads was being stripped away while a crowd of spectators – including the police – watched no more than twenty yards away. 'They were just methodically taking the roof to bits,' said the neighbour. 'I was beginning to feel like a hostage,' said the householder. 'I've had half a dozen burglaries. I felt myself feeling so vulnerable that anything or anyone who will protect you is your friend. I was becoming a law and order freak.'

When the roof boys were finally persuaded to come down, on condition that their solicitors would accompany them to the police station, the crowd moved off towards the derelict Dodds Arms pub in Elswick, animated by rumours that something was going on down there. Several took sticks from rubbish near the terrace as they set off. On the way to West End police station, the roof boys and their solicitors heard the news on the police car radio. There was a fire at the Dodds Arms. By the time they got to the station a riot had already started.

A crowd of about two hundred was moving around Elswick. Some were stoning the firefighters aiming for the Dodds Arms, which had been set on fire at 8.20 p.m. Riot police had to be brought in to surround the building just after 9 p.m. Masked men in stolen cars were screeching into handbrake-turns outside the pub, youths were throwing petrol bombs and others were slashing fire hoses.

That evening the Racial Equality Council was hosting a farewell dinner for Chief Constable Sir Stanley Bailey when a message came through for the chief that there was big trouble in the West End. He was taken to operational headquarters and the ethnic minority community leaders gathered where they could be reached with the latest information.

There were two hundred calls to the fire brigade that night. No ethnic minority targets were damaged. The leaders contacted their communities with the news and after 1 a.m. rang restaurant workers and urged them to contact the police when they were ready to leave and be escorted home.

The area had been known for racial attacks on black households and harassment of anyone who challenged crime. On Wednesday night a rough-and-ready telephone 'tree', which had been developed to support residents under attack, was activated. Local Labour councillor Nigel Todd went over to Elswick as soon as he heard about the fire and called in on a woman who, he suspected, might be in trouble. She had supported an Asian family when they were being victimised and now she was desperately trying, in vain, to get a taxi to take her children out of the area. She was immediately taken out. Councillor Todd, a modest, tenacious member of the tiny Left caucus on Newcastle council, stayed around with his constituents that night.

No places of worship, restaurants or homes went up in flames. That was a triumph. Between 5.30 p.m., when the first débâcle was reported off the Elswick Road, and 4 a.m. on Thursday morning when everything went quiet, fire had damaged eight empty buildings, two pubs, one of them derelict, and seven vehicles. None of them was one of the potential targets identified by the black communities. Indeed, these were protected throughout the rest of the week. The only incident at a symbolic site was when a petrol bomb hit the door of the mosque and drained away. Had it ignited, a thousand plastic chairs stacked behind the door would have gone up. That petrol bomb was thrown in the short period – a matter of minutes – between the departure of one Police Support Unit and its replacement by another.

The morning after, an early audit of the riot territory was carried out by one of its councillors, Mo O'Toole, with Rajinder Singh and the city's policy planning manager, George Robertson.

O'Toole was chair of Newcastle council's racial equality committee, a member of the REC and one of the council's few feminists. She knew the West End well – she had grown up there. Not yet thirty, she was a local government specialist. After seeing the streets, they set up a second hotline from the Chief executive's office to coordinate council resources and responses.

Their journey into the streets registered an eerie stillness: the only difference been Before and After was at the Dodds Arms – it wasn't there. The pub had been notorious, associated with trouble, prostitution and skinheads. When it had closed a year or so before the riots, it remained a boarded-up blot on the landscape. The disappearance of this derelict landmark opened the view to the Tyne and thus it had few mourners. O'Toole and Robertson noticed that the streets were 'so quiet and cleaned. It was the quiet *after* the storm.'

CityWorks, Newcastle's public works department, which had a reputation for being fast and efficient in the care of this hard-pressed city's public space, had cleared up the mess. The talk in the depots that week was that 'Mr Ramsay must have been on.' Alec Ramsay was one of the maintenance managers and in the week of the riots he was indeed on call continuously from 8 a.m. on Monday until 8 a.m. the following Monday. 'He's a person who just won't see a man beaten,' said CityWorks boss Tony Atkinson. 'If we have a skill, it is to shift problems, and we have people who thrive on it.' CityWorks had mobile patrols out during every night of the week, and during the riots they turned their night eyes to signs of danger or destruction. One patrol noticed that a store of bricks – enough to build a house – had been delivered to a Scotswood street. 'We didn't think *bricks*, we thought *ammunition*,' said Atkinson. After securing permission from the Civic Centre CityWorks shifted the bricks to a place of safety.

Apart from the police and the local politicians touring the area, activists from the Black Youth Movement and workers from the Big Lamp Youth project, situated strategically on the corner of Elswick Road, took to the streets on the Wednesday night, to check on frightened families and to keep an eye on young people. An extensive network of interpreters, many of them women, had been developed since the mid-Eighties by the energetic Area 4 office of the Social Services Department, based in Scotswood, to support clients in their dealings with the world. They and the Area 4 office were to contact all potentially vulnerable clients several times that week.

Half a dozen places in Newcastle had been identified by the police as possible volcanoes, areas that shared a similar axis of poverty and danger. The West End of Newcastle suffered the worst health and mortality rates of anywhere in the city. The city and the region were the sickest and the poorest in the country.

Male unemployment in the West End had risen fourfold between 1986 and 1991. The area had more men on the dole than anywhere else in the city. In the Elswick neighbourhood alone there were 290 *young* men without jobs. Of these, 55 were on government training schemes. That left 235 young men with no money and nothing to do. Scotswood was even worse: there were 432 young men on the dole, of whom 180 were on temporary training schemes, leaving 252 young men with absolutely nothing to do.

On Thursday morning, 12 September, there were serious suspicions that some of them were about to do *something* in Scotswood. For a start, it was signposted. Scotswood, like Elswick, is emblematic of old Tyneside, a ragged place teetering on the high river bank. One of its focal points is the Bobby Shafto pub in the middle of a junction where the Armstrong Road meets streets running down to the Tyne and into the Scotswood estate. The pub looked like a prison, a lavatory, a fortress, an eyeless place keeping its secrets from the scrutiny of passers-by. The junction was a local shopping centre with a kebab shop, a bookie and a post office – the poor people's bank, where most of Scotswood's citizens collected their state benefits.

The Bobby Shafto was a rendezvous for the Scotswood underworld. Apart from cars, the lads often stole the neighbourhood's televisions, rings, videos, radiators, jackets, anything that moved. The Bobby Shafto was where they would show off and stake out their territory. On Thursday morning the lamppost outside the pub displayed a public announcement: there would be a riot that night. Some of the lads were seen putting up the poster and the talk raced around their networks. They were hyper, they were thrilled, they were in control and they were telling everybody. Their traffic back and forth between Elswick and Scotswood operated like a telegraph system. They were getting ready, they were organising, hungry for action.

All morning, people passing noticed the sign, and by midday its news had been transmitted to the police by several Scotswood citizens. That meant *everybody* knew. An even more specific and sinister threat was posted in the West End around the same time. This announced personal targets – women known as community activists in the neighbourhood – and escalated a tradition of retribution developing in the West End in the Eighties: the lads who preyed upon the neighbourhood also punished those who challenged them. Scotswood was the last episode in the summer's serial of riots, when so great was the lads' confidence in the control of their community's territory that they made public announcements of their actions and their victims. For some reason this information did not define the law enforcement agencies' policing practices that day. Maybe it was because the targets were women and because the community was one whose collective security had only ever been defended by women. For sure, the women had no institutional equivalent to the Racial Equality Council, no easy access to civic or constabulary leaders, no formal conduit to process their experience.

During the afternoon local people began to notice that a white van, which had been spotted in Elswick and Scotswood the night before, ferrying youths back and forth, was circling around delivering its cargo of teenagers to the Bobby Shafto. The van was also spotted in Elswick, where it shipped a group of youths into a house in one of the long terraces, followed by a man wearing shades, a suit, a tie and greased hair, and carrying a brief case. It looked odd enough to be noticed. By early evening the van was spotted by vigilant neighbours, returning to Scotswood every fifteen minutes or so with a new delivery.

This was not the only odd thing happening. Groups of lads wandered up and down the road opposite the Area 4 Social Services office during the afternoon. A gunshot hit the window of the office, too. No one knew what to make of the shooting, it just seemed another sign of the place going crazy. Nonetheless, the Area 4 SSD office and its network of Asian interpreters contacted all their vulnerable ethnic minority clients to monitor their safety.

A police car was in and out of Scotswood all day, but there was no permanent presence, nor were symbolic locations offered police patrols. Riot squads were at the ready, however. Just after 7 p.m. a police officer spoke to the white van's driver when it parked near the Bobby Shafto, and noticed a group of young lads inside. By the early evening a crowd had gathered outside the pub. Among them was a man who pulled a mask over his face. Other people were 'known' to the neighbourhood, the police and the magistrates; some were habitués of the pub who were known as the Bobby Boys. The rest of the crowd were the people who just lived there, who were coming and going to the shops near the pub while their neighbours watched the spectacle from their gardens nearby.

A little later, boys screeched up and down the Armstrong Road in a stolen car, doing handbrake-turns. They got out and there was a loud boom as it burst into flames in the middle of the road. At 8.30 p.m. a police car appeared in Armstrong Road and confronted the sight of the burning carcass of a vehicle surrounded by a crowd. The police officer decided that 'it was dangerous to approach the scene and informed other officers via my personal radio to stay at a safe distance.'

Less than half an hour later, a white Vauxhall Nova SR burst into the arena to do the handbrake dance before it was put to death by a petrol bomb. The two dead cars blocked access by emergency services.

Several young men then attacked the shutters of the post office with a sledgehammer and, although they didn't pierce the shutters, the window smashed. They did manage to break down the door to the flat above, however, and the crowd watched them run up the stairs with petrol bombs, grabbed from a crate behind the kebab shop, and appear in the front window to face the crowd, like champions. Suddenly the curtains began to burn. On their way out, they petrol-bombed the stairs and rushed back into the crowd to watch the effects of their work.

All this was witnessed by children living around the Armstrong Road and who were friendly with the man whose flat had just been torched. Like them, he kept rabbits; they were pals. 'We saw the naughty boys break into that man's house,' said a couple of primary-school children. 'They went up the stairs and they hoyed petrol bombs. It was disgraceful because the man lived there, but we weren't too worried because he wasn't there, he was staying at his friend's. The naughty boys who did it are the ones who usually hang around.'

The man had evacuated his flat above the post office because he had heard the night before that there was going to be trouble – and a home beside the Bobby Shafto was no place to be during a riot. Just after 9 p.m. he was tracked down and told that his flat was on fire. When he got there he found that all he had left was his life and the clothes he stood in .

The first fire engine had been called to Scotswood during the afternoon. More than four hours later, the police and fire service finally arrived in force to a territory that had already been captured by a wild bunch. Carloads of men sat around the Armstrong Road eavesdropping on the police manoeuvres with their radio scanners and watching vanloads of riot police moving into place for a pitched battle. There was a running battle between a group of lads, armed with an arsenal of bottles, and riot police stationed near the shops. The police jumped out of their vans armed with truncheons and shields and made for the coteries of young men, the people who, despite the mayhem, were still queuing for chips, and residents in their front gardens. One woman standing at her front door was horrified when she, too, was the object of a police charge. 'Riot police came at me with truncheons. I shouted back at them, "I live here."' Women in her street had campaigned for two years to make the police pay attention to the incessant harassment, burglary and car crime which overwhelmed their everyday life. They had failed. *Being there* was bad enough any day of the week for these residents, but this day it meant being to blame as well. A few streets away residents were reported to be filling their baths with water in case fires spread to their streets. One mother, whose children had been sent home early from a targeted school, only to see flames eating the air in their own street, was silenced by her child's question, 'Mammy, mammy, are they going to burn us?'

On Friday morning schools were full; subdued children turned up in greater numbers than usual, as if there they were sure of security. Only one school had by then suffered serious damage, when a car rammed into a wall and was then torched. Children were not deterred by the drama in the streets from attending school. 'School was fuller than usual,' said the headteacher in one of the West End's multiracial schools. 'School is reliable in a shifting world. Like it or lump it, the school is still secure. We are very used to our Asian students being frightened, because they are targets so often – they are spat at all the time, that is the reality they put up with – but at that time everybody was frightened. That increased our desire to make sure that we would stay open, even if we were in tents in the field.'

The post office, like the school, was a significant social space. It was not just a stamp and stationery shop, a place to spend money, it was also a place to receive it. In a neighbourhood where eighty per cent of the population lived on benefit, it was its most significant source of finance. The post office was an intimate place that carried the reassurance of regularity and convivial queuing. It was people's conduit to the big wide world, where they posted their 'Letters to Brezhnev', where they got the postal order for the grandbairn's birthday or the football pools. Across the counter from the customers was a public servant who knew how much they lived on, but whose relationship to their poverty contained no element of power. In their transactions they were equals. The post office was a symbolic location, like a temple or a bank.

Scotswood post office had not warranted a police guard during the riots, however. An elderly woman stood outside its remains on Friday morning and said, to anyone who might listen, 'Where am I going to get my pension? I can't understand why they've done it. This post office has been here for sixty years. I've been coming here since I was a little girl.' Other women turning up with their benefit books were vexed by the perversity of the boys' behaviour. 'Most people are unemployed round here, this is where they get their money from. Why burn this down, of all places?' they said.

On Friday the city centre was added to the half dozen sites which, it was feared, might combust. The divisional commander, Superintendent Bob Wright, had already warned the Chief Constable, Sir Stanley Bailey, that the police were in a hopeless position without extra support. Officers were drafted in from North Yorkshire and Durham and the city was well covered by the weekend. There were no riots.

On Friday morning senior police officers, politicians and public servants gathered at the Civic Centre to brief each other after the city's cathartic week. There had been an unprecedented level of multi-agency cooperation, and the police switchboards and Civic Centre hotlines had produced reservoirs of information. The council leader, Jeremy Beecham, a solicitor whose reputation for political managerialism during his seventeen-year stewardship replaced an earlier era of corruption, presided over the meeting. A sense of failure shadowed palpable successes.

No black shops, restaurants or places of worship had been

destroyed. No one had been killed. Just as the riots were about to spread westwards, the police had been briefed about the implications of Meadowell. There the strategic management had not appeared to interpret threats to the police and to black traders as implying a threat to the community in general. A manoeuvre that was almost militaristic in its design had contained the conflict but it had left a commercial community terrorised and a neighbourhood abandoned to its most dangerous members. There, a white neighbourhood had been unprotected because its black presence had been de-personalised as 'commercial premises'.

The lesson was that when the police were proactive and preventive they were effective: 'One of the best things we did was focus our attention on vulnerable places,' said Superintendent Eric Lewis. That did not describe the fate of the woman whose house in Benwell was besieged for two hours while the police waited for two boys to come down from her roof; nonetheless, the force could be confident, nay proud, that where it had targeted locations in Elswick it had protected them. Likewise, people were protected by a well-established series of relatively autonomous networks, ranging from the black communities' streetwise activists to their powerful patriarchs, the Civic Centre's black professionals and the West End's interpreters. Through the race equality committee of the city council they had worked with progressive white politicians, powerful civil servants and the police. Young blacks and their elders, professional women and police officers, who were defined by their diversity, had therefore shared the same civic discourse. During that week they became a potent resource for the city. As in a kaleidoscope, a dynamic rearrangement had happened when their stable world was shaken, when Ely, then Blackbird Leys and then Meadowell had announced a warning: danger. That had placed these people on the *qui vive* and they became the agents of a larger coalition wrapped around endangered people and places. They were the reason that no temple or trader was torched in Elswick.

Elswick, therefore, marked a major break in the history of

riots and race in Britain. In the early Eighties *race* and *riot* had been synonymous because policing practices identified black people as the problem, as people who did not deserve a service and who were not entitled to protection. It was part of collective wisdom in Britain that young black men were police targets and riots were their mode of resistance. It was because the world witnessed their victimisation that their response was forgiven.

By the end of the decade, police procedures had been modified and incorporated the opportunity for the victim's experience of victimisation to be *recorded*. That did not necessarily change operations, but it did change the record, the official story. Ely became a riot because a black shopkeeper's history of victimisation was invisible to the very organisation which had registered it. The irony of Ely was that the police denial of racism was negated by the police themselves, by their own archive. That archive had not been allowed to impinge on the force's operational consciousness. The tactics adopted seemed to suggest a confusion about who was the victim and who was the culprit.

In Meadowell the riot did not begin as a racially motivated incident. But what started as a crusade against the police became an assault on the Asian traders: when the police refused to make themselves available for an attack, then low-flying endemic racism made the Asians – who lived there – available to drive a mission that was drifting. The threat came from poor white working-class men – therefore, Meadowell could have been anywhere.

Elswick began where Ely and Meadowell ended. But the experience of Elswick in mobilising a civic coalition to keep its citizens safe did not define the protection of Scotswood, its post office, its streets and its sense of security. Recent history suggested that black people would be targets in Elswick and that women would be the targets in Scotswood.

On Thursday the police force had 'rearranged' itself. It maintained a proactive presence in locations where danger, according to Superintendent Lewis, 'was most predictable or particularly sensitive. Where it was less predictable the police took a reactive stance.' He explained the police constraints. 'Our options were to show a strong presence, which some people can see as provocative, or be ready to respond. Resources were limited and we were geared to responding.' But the ability to respond depended in turn on the swift management of knowledge. A vast amount of information came from the public. The police problem was whether to turn information and rumour into intelligence, whether they could pattern and profile the data and match it with what they already knew about the locality. They could not. The information could not be sifted and shifted fast enough and translated into something the Divisional Commanders could use.

Scotswood had given clear signs that it was going to go wild on Thursday night, and it did. The force was befuddled, its head was turned this way and that by indiscriminate detail, while joyriders and petrol bombers were taking control of the streets. 'If we had handled the information more effectively it could have manifested itself as the flashpoint it turned out to be,' said one senior officer. 'The problem in Meadowell had been that they were not getting information rather than not knowing what to do with it. The problem in Scotswood was that we knew what to do with the information, but it got lost in the volume.'

No alliance was created with the women who were Scotswood's active citizens and yet also its most exposed targets, to pre-empt the riot and prepare proactive patrols. 'We knew that women were being fingered,' said Mo O'Toole. 'The women had a lot of hassle from the local lads because they were reporting burglaries. It was the women involved in the Scotswood Strategy who were trying to sort something out in the community.'

Furthermore the women had no backers, no representatives, among the great and the good. 'They had no champions,' said O'Toole. Councillors were aware of a high level of general harassment. But harassment that had no name also had no institutional impact. Where there was no place to record the women's reality, there was no responsibility for future redress. Women's endangerment *as women* was no more perceived as a political problem than men's dangerousness *as men*. 'There's an enormous amount of everyday harassment going on, but it is not on the political agenda, it is not recorded or reported and nobody takes it seriously when we complain about harassment in the community,' said one municipal manager. 'When women make complaints they're told by the police that "lads will be lads" and "you can't expect us to control them."'

Unlike in Elswick, where attacks on its black citizens had become a matter of public record, attacks on women in Scotswood were only everyday life. Unlike in Elswick, where black citizens had access to an established forum, with statutory rights to act against discrimination and harassment in the community, as well as at work, women – both black and white – had no agency, supported by the state, to share their grievances about the hazards of everyday existence. Unlike in Elswick, where black community leaders networked with civic and constabulary leaders, the women of Scotswood (as in Meadowell) who were the *advocates* and *organisers* of communities' collective interest, had little access to authority.

That had left the police to their own resources and reactions, and left the population to their panic. Superintendent John Broughton presciently believed that the authorities, including the police, needed to support women's challenge to men's dangerousness. But that philosophy did not define the defence of besieged neighbourhoods.

When senior professionals and politicians met in the Civic Centre on Friday, the Divisional Commander, Chief Superintendent Don Wright, a respected officer, shared his sorrow. He was choked, devastated, as he described the week they had all lived through, with candour and courage. It was a terrible feeling that they had failed to keep neighbourhoods within their city safe.

PART II

THE BOYS IN BLUE

*Public disorder and policing
in the Eighties*

What were all these explosions in British cities during the late summer of 1991? Were they just 'events' or 'disturbances' or real 'riots'? Did the nomenclature matter? Certainly embarrassment ebbed and flowed around the terminology. These were riots that no one wanted to claim or own, that no one could be proud of, that could not explain themselves. These riots lacked the one thing that legitimises lawlessness: a just cause. They could not easily be translated into the syntax of political struggle, even though they were immediately mobilised to service a law and order rhetoric on the Right and an unemployment rhetoric on the Left. Ironically, both had a point, but no inquiry at the time reached beyond the slogans and sought to explain what economies, powers and cultures sustained the forces that produced these pyrotechnics. The reason lay in the riots themselves – they did not do what riots are supposed to do, they did not expose the exigencies of everyday life, they did not carry within them *a critique of oppression in the present or a fantasy about the future.*

The argument of this book is that the riots of 1991 did not represent the people's collective will, they represented its defeat. They happened in communities that were like battered women left alone to manage their marauding men. The police had offered only absence, then inertia and paralysis and finally havoc before they took control.

Historically, riots express a crisis – the impossiblity of politics and of protest. They are the moment when challenge becomes chaos, when disorder becomes danger. Any discussion of the riots in 1991 needs to start with the decade that created

them, a decade that displaced an earlier era of political dissent.
In mainland Britain the era of the New Right is also the era
of the riots. The explosions in London, Bristol, Birmingham
and Liverpool happened in a decade which lost confidence in
the politics of resistance and witnessed the rise of the riot. It
became the term that connected poverty and crime, policing
and public order.

In 1979 the Conservatives came to power after two decades of unprecedented popular protest, bearing the promise
of order to a nation that thought it knew all about disorder.
Thatcherism brought an ultimatum to end the era of protest
in which political life had been punctuated by direct action,
by marches, sit-downs, sit-ins, work-ins, strikes and student
occupations. Resistance would no longer be represented in
Thatcherism's rhetoric as being concerned with disagreeable
but nonetheless just causes; resistance would come to be
criminalised.

However disparate the forms of political action during pre-
Thatcherite Britain, what was perhaps underestimated at the
time – by both the Right and the Left during the Sixties and
Seventies – was that protest in the form of a strike or sit-in
may have implied a purely temporary rupture in stable institutional relations and procedures. The action brought together
values and interests that were both *inside* and *outside* institutional life, which presupposed the potential of change, and
which implied a rough-and-ready dialogue across autonomous
political cultures. Protest carried a case or a cause into the
public domain; it became a quest for public endorsement or
pressure. Protest assumed opposition, argument and activity
which, however rude or raunchy or risqué – drugs and sex
and bad manners were not unknown in student occupations;
drink and bad language were not unknown on picket lines –
was predicated on a negotiation, a conversation with the world.

The practice of protest had its own cultures and forms:
meetings were held, committees were formed, events were
imagined and organised, demands were discovered. Above all,
the activity was perceived as a particular kind of privilege, not

of having or consuming, but of belonging, of being *in* society, of being a social subject, an active citizen. Indeed, so resonant was the equation between *challenge* and *citizenship* in the Sixties and Seventies that Thatcherism campaigned against the very language by which people represented their own events, and thus the image of the 'active citizen' was reinterpreted and then reinvented as the 'active consumer' by the New Right.

Resistance was represented as crime. It had always been thus in Northern Ireland, where the Establishment's refusal to negotiate an egalitarian social settlement with the forty per cent Catholic population had led it to criminalise acts of resistance. Bloody Sunday in Derry in 1972 was the epitaph to any truce between the minority and the British State when thirteen unarmed civilians were shot dead by the British Army during an anti-internment march. But now it applied also to the traditionalist *modus operandi* of the 1984–5 miners' strike and the improvisations of the Greenham peace camp.

After a decade of Thatcherism a large cohort of young men and women found themselves not only on the edge of politics, but exiled from the social world. They were neither legitimate citizens nor consumers. Mass unemployment among teenagers, the generation which constitutes the largest 'criminal' category, priced them out of social institutions altogether. There is a national shortfall between the number of unemployed school leavers and the number of places on government training schemes – in Newcastle alone, a year after the riots, 870 school leavers were completely unemployed and, therefore, without any income, according to the careers service. Their student contemporaries may be poor, too, but they have an income and a passport to a world of libraries, canteens, clubs, unions, concerts, seminars and conversations. Unemployed school leavers who are not enrolled in training schemes have no income and no access to the public domain.

School was both their first and last point of contact with a society beyond their family and their neighbourhood, their first and last contact with a social culture of cooperation and compromise. By the eleventh year of school it was not unusual for schools to record a twenty-five per cent rate of absenteeism among fifteen-year-olds. In the year of the riot the absenteeism rate in year eleven was twenty-three per cent in one of Newcastle's West End schools. An average of twenty children were excluded for at least one day for violence. Almost all were *white boys*. Adrift from all institutions, how could they experience themselves in a system, how could they discover the power they might have in a process, the influence they might have through negotiation? For a lad whose culture celebrated a man's authority and power, and lethal weapons as the solution to social problems, the discovery of his own illiteracy or incompetence could, of course, carry the dread that 'being inside society' meant 'being defeated'. That was the scenario some of these lads repeated in the riots, where *power* only meant *brute force*. 'They have no idea how society works,' says one of their lawyers.

CHAPTER 5

The Riotous Decade

The 1991 riots became memorable not for their message or their martyrs, but for their management. They tested the success of new regimes of public order and community policing which had been promoted after riots a decade earlier when the policing of black people became a public order crisis. The earlier riots had prompted a full-scale public inquiry by Lord Scarman in 1981. The prelude to the 1981 riots saw 'flooding', saturation policing which overwhelmed and criminalised communities; but the 1991 riots were preceded by the absence of the police from the neighbourhoods that erupted. These events could have been seen as a test of what was supposed to have been put in place across the nation in response to the Scarman report: community policing. In fact, these neighbourhoods were abandoned by crime managers; they had been given little or no police *service*. Crises in public order erupted in the absence of effective investigation and intervention. Though the riots were more or less modest events compared with the great protests of the Sixties and Seventies, they were catastrophes for their communities. The police chiefs, all of them schooled in the new ethics of public order management, heaved a sigh of relief that at least no one had been killed. But in all of the riot territories a local problem of *crime* prevention had produced panic or paralysis among the law enforcement agencies. The Tyneside riots happened in the week that Northumbria police reported their highest-ever crime figures.

The Tyneside situation had to be seen against a larger and more mundane picture of policing and crime prevention in many other cities. Detection in the decade of the riots had been subject to unprecedented criticism in the wake of notorious cases of corruption and was accused of a more banal professional crisis in the context of record crime figures. Sir Stanley Bailey's successor as Chief Constable, John Stevens, tried to confront the problem by abolishing the habit of hoisting detection rates through admissions secured from convicted prisoners. It was a common practice in police forces that created only the *appearance* of crime resolution.

Professional crime was the fourth largest industry in Britain and the fastest-growing business, employing on both sides of the law as many people as energy and water and almost as many as banking.[1] This had followed a boom of unprecedented conspicuous consumption, what some socialist economists came to call the 'casino economy'. There had been a renaissance of the Conservative 'You've never had it so good' propaganda of the Fifties when the notion of *affluence* was 'essentially an ideology of the dominant culture *about* and *for* the working class, directed *at* them.'[2] Stuart Hall *et al.* argue that what mattered was not the passive remaking of the working class in the image of affluence, 'but the *dislocations* it produced – and the responses it provoked.' One of the phenomena that grew within the polarised economy of Thatcherism was recorded crime: sanctions-busting, car crime, computer crime, financial fraud on a grand scale, sexual crime, crimes against children and finally 'survival crime'. But the visible criminals were the poor, the people bearing the brunt of the economic recession and believed to be those who 'under current conditions of deprivation are prone to innovative criminal responses.'[3]

Policing could not cope; the costs of clearing up crime in London and the South East were nine times the national average. Police managers all over the country were

---

[1] Duncan Campbell, 'Crime Becomes Boom Industry' in the *Guardian*, 17 September, 1992.
[2] Stuart Hall and Tony Jefferson, eds, *Resistance Through Rituals: Youth subcultures in post-war Britain*, Hutchinson, London, 1976.
[3] Stephen Box, *Power, Crime and Mystification*, Routledge, London, 1983.

experiencing the effect of the Government economic attack on their employer – local government. The police appeared to be the most inefficient of all state agencies, protected by the patronage of the Conservative Party and by structural immunity from public scrutiny. 'If the police were a private-sector operation they would be hauled over the coals,' said the criminologist Professor Jock Young in 1991.[4]

Amidst this crime crisis, 'rioters are much easier to put down than burglars,' wrote the journalist Andrew Brown in the *Spectator*, on 19 July 1986, when the Metropolitan Police Commissioner, Sir Kenneth Newman, announced new proposals to deal with future riots. In the first half of the decade, a Conservative Government pledged to the restoration of order had presided over the worst serial of public 'disorder' since the Second World War. Crime rates soared and detection declined during the very period which had promised to be most commodious for the police.

In the Seventies and Eighties the association between crime, class, race and place infused the rhetoric of law and order. Most potent was the particular inflection of race. They were racialised.[5] Race and riot became synonymous in public rhetoric. The difficulties of cosmopolitan neighbourhoods came to be blamed not on their economic crisis but on a spectre: the young black 'mugger'. His imaginary entry into the public domain carried the assumption that he smashed and grabbed his way around the streets. This provided symbolic capital, it sustained a strategy of street policing which became self-fulfilling: young black men became police targets.[6] The notorious 'suspected person' law allowed the police to stop and search anyone in the street. 'Sus' became the dominant

[4] *Sunday Times*, 24 May 1991.
[5] Stuart Hall, Chas Crichter, Tony Jefferson, John Clarke, Brian Roberts, *Policing the Crisis: Mugging, the State and Law and Order*, Macmillan, London, 1978.
[6] *Ibid.*

dialogue between black people and the police.

A white woman living and working in south London before the 'sus' law was abolished in the Eighties recalled with shame seeing 'these young white policemen who had been given permission to run their hands all over these young black men's bodies in the street. I remember thinking it was like the slave owners. No one could stop them: it was sanctioned in a liberal society, apparently in the name of crime prevention, for white men in the street to intimately touch black men's bodies. Of course, a white person touching a black person's body has a historical significance for all of us.'

The demonisation of young black men in the image of the 'mugger' was dramatised not only in the everyday policing of public order but in the riots of the Eighties. The 1981 Scarman inquiry into the Brixton riot was to give a modest but official endorsement to black people's experience of humiliation by police in the inner cities. In its recommendations, it proposed a new relationship between police and public, to be formalised and institutionalised in the practice of consultation and accountability.

However, the Chief Constables in the most devastated riot territories, London and Liverpool, mounted a rearguard resistance. In London the Metropolitan Police Commissioner, Kenneth Newman, launched a proactive propaganda war. Newman's authoritarian interventions in public debate were satirised on the massively popular television show, *Spitting Image*. After fresh outbreaks of riot in 1985 the political debate about policing was compelled to reorient itself, not least because the police had been exposed as being trapped by tradition and inefficiency. The Metropolitan police, under new leadership, initiated debates of a very different timbre about modernisation, which prioritised public service and which started not from triumphalism but from an admission of failure. It had failed in the protection of public order and property, and it had failed to control itself.

In Liverpool, Chief Constable Kenneth Oxford, who had already been involved in a rowdy dispute with the elected police authority and its Conservative chairperson during the Seventies, became emboldened in his defence of police autonomy and in his scorn for notions like community policing. This became a public tournament in the Eighties between the Chief Constable and the police authority, by then in Labour control. The contest came to an end a decade after the 1981 riots when the testimonies of two women brought into the public domain the prejudice and belligerence of a butch, boozy culture in the constabulary. It all came out during the marathon hearing of an industrial tribunal which heard the charge of sex discrimination against the Merseyside Chief Constable, James Sharples, the Chief Constable of Northamptonshire, the Home Secretary and Her Majesty's Inspector of Constabulary. The women were Britain's best-known leader of a police authority, Lady Margaret Simey, and Britain's top woman cop, Alison Halford. Simey and the Merseyside Police Authority, of which she was chair, were responsible for the appointment of Halford to a position that no woman had ever occupied before, Assistant Chief Constable. Simey's hope was that a woman might make a difference to the way the constabulary served the community. But things turned out differently, as we shall see in the Liverpool story.

Bristol was where the contemporary riot season began in Britain, not Brixton or Toxteth. Bristol is an exemplar of the English city, a handsome old colonial port whose grandeur was bankrolled by the slave trade, home to manufacturing, to a middle class and to a well-established black community. A third of Bristol's twelve thousand black people lived in the poor inner-city neighbourhood of St Paul's.

On Wednesday, 2 April 1980, the sun was shining. It was the first hot day of the spring, and Grosvenor Road was full of people coming out of hibernation. The Black and White Café was a corner of Jamaica nesting in St Paul's and that day three police officers from the drug squad paid a sudden visit. They had made no contact with the force Community Relations

Officer. They drank cups of coffee and left. Less than an hour later they returned with a warrant to look for drugs. A search came up with bottles of Red Stripe beer, but no drugs.

There was an argument when a young black man in the café complained that the police had torn his trousers, and another later, when a crowd protested as the police loaded the beer bottles into a van during the afternoon. Within an hour, fighting had broken out, a police car was burnt out and about a hundred and fifty young men, both black and white, were throwing stones at a police presence of between sixty and eighty officers, including some dog handlers. Two black women approached a policeman and offered to try to calm the crowd, but the officer was attacked and the women pulled him away to safety.[7]

Early in the evening the police made a desperate effort to retrieve their burnt-out car but were forced to retreat and returned only at 11.30 p.m. when reinforcements had been gathered from several other constabularies. 'It seemed agonisingly slow. But it was necessary,' concluded the Home Office. This was after fires had been started, a dozen shops had been looted, Lloyds Bank and the post office had been gutted. Shops where Asians and West Indians worked were exempted from the looting.[8] According to a report by the Commission for Racial Equality, 'Throughout the period of rioting there was no violence between black and white members of St Paul's community, it was purely directed against police and property.' There were a hundred and thirty-two arrests in the riot and its aftermath, mostly for minor offences, but twelve people were tried almost a year later in March 1981 for riotous assembly. Only six were convicted.

In the immediate aftermath of the riot, the Avon and Somerset Chief Constable, Brian Weigh, conceded that the

[7] Home Secretary's Memorandum, 28 April 1980, on *Serious Disturbances in St Paul's, Bristol, on 2 April 1980*, House of Commons Library.
[8] Paul Stephenson, *Report of Bristol Disturbances April 2, 1980*, Commission for Racial Equality, 29 April 1980.

operation had been, in effect, a mess. As a law enforcement exercise it had not solved a problem, it had created a crisis. Worse, it had all happened at a time and on a day when the streets were full of children. 'The day and time chosen were not the best,' said his report. The Chief Constable's proposals for reform anchored the policing of St Paul's in the community beat, on the one hand, and in top management, on the other. Decisions on such raids would, in future, 'not be made at a lower level than Assistant Chief Constable'. He planned to extend community units to each division and to ensure that officers would be given training in the background and cultures of their areas.[9]

How odd, therefore, that Avon and Somerset Constabulary should launch an extravagant, though well-planned, drugs raid at about the same time in the same neighbourhood six years later. Operation Delivery began by closing off the area during the afternoon, positioning furniture trucks nearby and spilling officers into the streets. Again, about a hundred and thirty people were arrested, mostly on minor public order charges. Only one person received a custodial sentence for drug dealing.

'Operation Delivery caused chaos while creating the appearance of control,' commented one community activist. 'If things are presented like military operations they look like control, but this was about setting an example – the people they got were small fry – it was not intended for the benefit of the community. All these kinds of operations do is victimise the community – what they should have done was target the criminals, not criminalise the community.' Operation Delivery was politically expensive – the price was the end of dialogue. Community representatives withdrew from the St Paul's Liaison Committee, which had been set up to prevent precisely such a situation and to improve relations between the people and the police.

During the afternoon of 11 September 1986, about three hundred riot police occupied the area after Operation

[9] Chief Constable's Memorandum, 28 April 1980.

Delivery had organised raids on half a dozen premises in
St Paul's where alleged illegal drinking and gambling were
taking place. Riot police sealed off streets after the raids provoked violent confrontations. Once again the police had made
their move when the movement of children and parents around
the neighbourhood was at its maximum. One of the mothers
making her way home recalled, 'I was over six months
pregnant. I had my two small kids with me. They were so
frightened and the police would not get out of the way so we
could pass.' She was a member of a mother's group which
collated their feelings about the effect of Operation Delivery
on their homes. 'Children were scared and upset by it. Mothers
were distraught. Some were trapped in their houses or streets
by riot police. Some were prevented from going home or
going out,' said the group. People had been made to feel that
'their area was worthless'. Others were subjected to the
racism that was supposed to have been rooted out by the
police training proposed in 1980. A police officer noticed a
bowl of fruit on one woman's dining table during a raid and
said, 'Only monkeys eat bananas.'[10]

Brixton was home to one of Britain's best-known Afro-Caribbean communities which had reinvigorated this seedy, stressed
neighbourhood south of the Thames. The area had been in economic decline since the First World War. In the late Seventies
ethnic minorities comprised twenty-five per cent of its population, but a quarter of its black workers were unemployed and
young black men on the streets were prime police targets. In
1979 a hard stop-and-search strategy was pursued with confidence and commitment but without a community mandate,
and without consulting the Brixton Community Liaison Committee, where the police met with local leaders. That led to a

[10] Quoted in *St Paul's, The People and the Police raid: A Grassroots
Account*, by Members of the Bristol One-Parent Project, in Local Government
Policy Making, vol. 15, no. 2, September 1988.

crisis and to the collapse of formal communication between political representatives and the police. The force commander defended the refusal to share information with local MPs, beat officers and senior officers of the local authority. Someone might have leaked it, he said.

Home beat officers were again kept in ignorance of a massive street search in 1981, notoriously named Operation Swamp. About a hundred officers, purportedly armed with search warrants, were launched into mass raids. They yielded only seven arrests.

During Operation Swamp, in April, Brixton became the first place in mainland Britain where petrol bombs were used by members of the public against the police. The nation turned on its televisions and watched war in the streets of London. In his influential report, Lord Scarman later described it as 'an instant audiovisual disorder watched by the British people.'[11] One of the witnesses felt that the place looked like 'the aftermath of an air raid'. The confrontation was caused by fleeting moments, brittle, brief encounters between police officers and black men.

A young man was running. He was bleeding. He was stopped by a policeman who assumed that he was up to no good. When finally the young officer realised that the young man needed help it was too late to staunch the bystanders' angry reaction to his pursuit. What people thought they had seen was *hostility* towards the bleeding runaway, not *help*. What people thought they had seen was, of course, only what they were always seeing: a young black man being hunted by young white men in uniforms. That was the first incident. The second involved two young, white, plain-clothes officers who interrogated a taxi driver after seeing him stuff something into his sock. They assumed it was drugs. They were wrong: it was his bank. He showed them his sock: it was where he stored his takings. Undeterred, they asked to search his taxi for drugs, all

[11] Lord Scarman, *The Brixton Disorders, 10–12 April 1981*, HMSO, Cmnd 8427, 1981.

the while watched by a group of increasingly angry youths. The taxi driver let them look; they found nothing. Betraying what Scarman later described as a lack of 'discretion or judgement', they arrested one of the young men who was watching and complaining.

Lord Scarman described the raw material of what then happened on Saturday, 11 April, as 'the spirit of angry young men', including the policemen who had 'failed to recognise the real signals and strike the balance between enforcing the law and keeping the peace.' It was the police intervention that produced the problem which became a riot: two hundred and seventy-nine police officers and forty-five members of the public were injured when phalanxes of officers and young men who had assembled bricks, bottles and petrol bombs confronted each other in a series of charges. During one of these the crowd captured some of the police shields, and a senior police officer grabbed hold of a firefighter's hose and turned it on the crowd while he ordered his fellow officers to do the same.

The individual actions which ignited the riot were part of a larger and longer war of attrition. They were 'nothing unusual', commented Lord Scarman. Police managers, despite pressure from community leaders, refused to call off Operation Swamp although there were clear indicators of a volcanic feeling on the streets.

Lord Scarman's report laid down the basic principles of police practice: prevention of crime, protection of life and property, preservation of public tranquillity. He recommended that operational management should always be available for discussion. He concluded that saturation policing did not tackle street crime, it only displaced it. Furthermore, if law enforcement within a community caused acute friction, then another way had to be found that would carry the commitment of the law-abiding community. Pre-empting police criticism that consultation interfered with police independence, Scarman concluded that this was a 'non sequitor': consultation should *inform* the police, and in any case *any* operation likely to inconvenience the public – a bomb scare, for example

– demanded their cooperation. 'Any aspect of police policy should be regarded as a matter appropriate for discussion . . . including operational questions.'

Scarman argued that although the police could only be responsible for policing, and not for social conditions, he felt that unless they were sensitive to 'the difficulties, social and economic, which beset the ethnically diverse communities', and unless they handled these difficulties with 'imagination as well as firmness', they would fail, 'and disorder will become a disease endemic in our society.' Although the report rejected the possibility of institutional racism it concluded that some officers were racially prejudiced and abusive, inflexible and unimaginative. It suggested politely that some police constables in the Met were racist and that they had to be taught to serve in a cosmopolitan country.

In one of the report's important insights about black households – ignored by subsequent theorists of the 'underclass' – Scarman refused to endorse white myths about the 'decline' and 'fragmentation' of Afro-Caribbean families. The Scarman report identified the *strengths* of extended black families sustained by women. He noticed men's marginality as, at best, supportive, and that at worst a man was 'an absentee of little or no significance'. The crisis of the black family was the impact of *British society* on the women, the dislocation of their networks and the lack of support offered to black women by British urban structures.

What many senior police officers thought they were reading when they scanned Scarman was the repudiation of action. What Lord Scarman actually asked for was not *no action*, but *firm* and *imaginative* action. When he insisted that the composition of the police reflect the community they served, did the people of Brixton wonder what might have happened in 1981 had the force been commanded by a middle-aged black woman?

*

The political aftermath of 1981 brought a great debate about the politics of policing. The Metropolitan Police Commissioner, Sir Kenneth Newman, made few, if any, concessions to Scarman's discrete cautions. Newman refined his own rather anti-cosmopolitan notion of community policing in his theory of 'symbolic locations'. The theory conflated ethnicity and urban crisis in the capital by blurring the boundaries between black, poor and criminal in precisely the terms predicted in the exhaustive critique of racism, policing and moral panics by Stuart Hall *et al.* in *Policing the Crisis*, a germinal socialist study of crime and ideology written in the late Seventies.[12] Newman's theory revealed the very estrangement from ethnic minority experience that had already so worried Lord Scarman. Two years after the Brixton riot he targeted four 'symbolic locations' and by 1985 expanded this to nearly a dozen. These were the places where 'unemployed youths – often black youths – congregate . . . They equate closely with the criminal rookeries of Dickensian London.'[13] Newman was the former Chief Constable of the Royal Ulster Constabulary and seemed to have imported his experience of Ireland to London. He appreciated Scarman's commitment to a strategy which balanced law enforcement with the preservation of tranquillity – Scarman had placed a priority on the latter – but suggested that 'it is a strategy which raises difficult moral, legal and political problems for the police.' In a talk to the European Atlantic Group in November 1983 he argued that there were 'problems arising from ethnic minorities in the UK, the USA and in Continental Europe.' He was not referring to racism, he was referring to 'what many commentators refer to as the "underclass" – a class that is beneath the working class.' In 'multi-ethnic areas', he went on, youths congregated in 'locations associated with the sale and purchase of drugs, the exchange of stolen goods and illegal drinking establishments.

[12] Stuart Hall et al., *Policing the Crisis.*
[13] Quoted in *The Broadwater Farm Inquiry*, an account of the inquiry chaired by Lord Gifford, Karia, London, 1986.

The youths take a proprietorial posture in this location: they regard it as their territory. In general they will regard the police as intruders and as a symbol of white society that is responsible for all their grievances.' If a police officer made an arrest, 'there will be a confrontation which could escalate to a full-blooded riot. A similar situation exists in many ethnically mixed housing estates.' While supporting Scarman's plea for sensitivity, he argued that 'an over-regard for individual liberties' could put order and security at risk.

Newman focused on 'two particular problems' in the West that would tilt the balance between order and freedom: 'multi-ethnic communities' and 'indigenous terrorist movements'. Just as the Prevention of Terrorism Act restricted Irish individual liberty, so Newman envisaged that 'areas with large black populations might require similar sacrifices.'[14]

Commissioners appeared rather like great white settlers doomed to preside over territories teeming with what must have seemed to be restless natives. These seemed to be perceived as problems rather than as communities deserving full protection by the police. Broadwater Farm is one such place, a council estate, built in the 'brutalist' mode in Tottenham, one of the cosmopolitan working-class districts in north London. In 1985 it became a household name when a community police officer was killed during a riot between black youths and police. It was a place where Newman's notion of symbolic territory became a self-fulfilling prophecy. His disposition had given an endorsement to local police managers who found Scarman's recommendations too difficult.

The Gifford inquiry into the riot heard that the police division did not engage in consultation with community leaders and boycotted a local authority police committee, and that home beat officers were told not to meet community groups, though the estate had an unusually high level of residents' organisation. The reluctance to cooperate on any terms other

---

[14] David Rose, *A Climate of Fear: The Murder of PC Blakelock and the Case of the Tottenham Three*, Bloomsbury, London, 1991.

than their own, produced an impregnable and closed police culture. The police regularly and publically criminalised the whole community in Broadwater Farm by describing it as a 'haven for wrongdoers'. The approach to the place confirmed the findings of a study of Met officers, *Police and People in London*, by the Policy Studies Institute, commissioned by the Metropolitan police themselves. Researchers found that 'many individual officers and also whole groups were preoccupied with ethnic differences.' It was black drivers whom white officers obsessively stopped around Broadwater Farm – a phenomenon that was tested by a white councillor who deliberately set himself up to be arrested, and failed. Tottenham police priorities, meanwhile, differed from the community's own clearly published priorities for policing – sexual offences, burglaries, theft, harassment.[15]

Ultimately, it was not the police but the residents themselves, together with housing managers, who secured the most dramatic reduction in offending on the estate in the first half of the decade. Lord Gifford's inquiry into the Broadwater Farm riot noted that crime was *halved* by a combination of council security systems and the formation of the Broadwater Farm Youth Association to engage the young people with time on their hands. In the month or so before the riot, the estate's inability to engage the police, however, was again evident when the place suddenly became a station for drug traffickers displaced from a neighbouring borough. According to the Gifford report, divisional police managers appeared not to respond, to the frustration and fury of residents and home beat officers. Whether it was out of paralysis or pique, they did not intervene to protect the neighbourhood from known perpetrators of serious criminal offences. To the residents this meant the Scarman report had made no difference, to the rank and file police officers it meant Scarman had scared their managers into inaction. It was the latter that became the conventional wisdom among police officers across Britain.

[15] *The Broadwater Farm Inquiry*, 1986.

Towards the end of September, rumours of riot were pouring in to Tottenham police. However, on 1 October, police mobilised a day of action to stop and search all vehicles going in and out of the estate, apparently looking for stolen goods. Described as a provocative 'disaster' by Haringey's chief executive, Roy Limb, the enterprise was abandoned.

On Saturday, 5 October, Floyd Jarrett was stopped in his flashy BMW. His tax disc was several months out of date but he was arrested at lunchtime on suspicion of stealing the car. Actually, he owned the BMW. Jarrett was a founder member of Broadwater Farm Youth Association – the object of many police officers' hatred – and was held in custody for four hours. At teatime officers raided his mother's home. There remains a dispute over whether they sought a search warrant before or after the raid. In any event, when they barged into the flat they knocked over his mother, Cynthia Jarrett, a forty-eight-year-old woman who had led an active life despite suffering from heart disease. The police, of course, could not have known this. However, it was not denied that she had been knocked down. Cynthia Jarrett was a well-regarded and respectable resident. To the people of Broadwater Farm it seemed that her respectability was invisible to those who only saw her colour – black. She was dying of heart failure while the police searched her house. Her daughter said they had pushed her over when they swept into the flat and the doctor who gave evidence about her death to the inquest said that a push followed by a fall would have been 'an important precipitating factor'. During the raid her daughter tried, in vain, to raise the emergency services. She told the police to leave. By then Cynthia Jarrett was dead.

Almost immediately the police surrounded the estate, and so began the swift descent into disaster that night when, in a massive confrontation between the police and the youths, a white police constable, Colin Blakelock, was murdered, hacked to death. Three young black men were ultimately convicted of his murder. Their conviction was later deemed to have been unsafe. One of them, Winston Silcott, appeared as the ultimate 'black devil' in the media representations of him after his arrest. He was typical of a generation sucked into the criminal justice system not by committing crime but by being black – he was first searched and charged for having faulty brakes on his bicycle.[16]

PC Blakelock's gruesome death shrouded the importance of everything else, particularly the police conflict with the community. Now two people were dead: PC Blakelock and Cynthia Jarrett. The suave suspicions that infused the rhetoric emanating from headquarters ricocheted around this catastrophe.

The saturation 'swamp' operations did no more for clearing up crime than they did for community relations. Finally, it was the police themselves who initiated a critique of the Met's dismal record in detection. It was Newman's successor, Sir Peter Imbert, who tried to change the corporate culture of the Met. By the end of the decade a searching review came up with a radical report, the *Investigation of Crime in Territorial Operations*, by the Met's Priority Project, in 1989. This report made more than a hundred recommendations for the reform of criminal investigation. It concluded that the organisation was ill-managed and unprofessional, it had failed to make objectives clear to officers, and gave little satisfaction to the main 'users' of criminal investigations – victims.

This was followed by the Met's 1990 *Operational Policing Review*, an important document in what was becoming a desperate quest among police managers to bring their profession into line with the public will. It exposed a fundamental breach between police perceptions and community wishes: the public wanted a service and the police wanted enforcement. About twenty per cent of police time was concerned with enforcement, however: thus front-line officers were in fact focused on what was only a minority aspect of their work.

On 2 June 1991 the annual conference of one hundred

[16] David Rose, *A Climate of Fear*, 1991.

and twenty senior managers in the Metropolitan Police, called by the Commissioner, completed the Met's auto-critique by reforming the way that police budgets and strategies were formulated and by uniting both in a five-year plan. Commenting on the 1990 *Operational Policing Review*, Sir Peter Imbert said, 'It revealed a basic incompatibility between what our officers saw as our role in the community and what the community itself identified as the role of the police.' His own report to the conference was candid: 'As an organisation we have an almost unparalleled ability to adopt the vocabulary of change without changing the substance.' The citizens of Ely, Blackbird Leys, Meadowell, Elswick and Scotswood would know what he meant – they, too, had heard the vocabulary of modern, community policing before they ended up with a riot. Imbert's report stressed that officers on the streets were being encouraged to think only in terms of *measurable* enforcement. This was evident, said Imbert's report, in a commitment to the appearance of detection, and the 'low priority given to crime prevention'.

Imbert's warning about the attraction of measurable enforcement, worryingly, had apparently not tempered the Home Secretary's introduction of 'performance indicators' in his dramatic reorganisation of policing in the spring of 1993. What he offered to the police was the discipline of measurement rather than the discipline of service.

In 1993 the Prime Minister John Major intervened in the great debate about communities, children and crime, with an extraordinary call for a crusade. 'I would like the public to have a crusade against crime,' he declared in an interview in the *Mail on Sunday* on 21 February, when Britain was mesmerised by the murder of two-year-old Jamie Bulger by perpetrators believed to be children. 'Society needs to condemn a little more and understand a little less,' said the premier.

Crusading, of course, was exactly what the women of Scotswood and Meadowell had been doing. Neither the premier, nor his butch Home Secretary, alluded to the sense of abandonment that had often accompanied these community campaigns, nor to Central Government's reluctance to retrieve the relationship between an aggrieved public and a weary police force – since detection depends on the public, whose information is the vital ingredient in solving crime, their estrangement starves the police of their major resource, the community they serve.

The new Home Secretary, Kenneth Clarke, had already shaken the welfare state with his reorganisation of education and health, and in 1993 he announced his reorganisation of the strong state, the police, along similar lines. This swiftly followed his launch of the third attempt by the Conservative Government to *shock* men and boys into good behaviour, in the wake of Jamie Bulger's death. The announcement of the introduction of more secure units for young offenders was driven by public panic rather than by the Home Office's own research into trends in crime since the Second World War, which showed the correlation between crime and the effects of the economy on poverty and patterns of consumption.

The mothers in beseiged communities across the country had appealed to the institutions to support them in their efforts to protect their neighbourhoods. The crusade against crime in Scotswood was an exemplar – there the women had made an assessment of how realistic were their own responsibilities for the lads. What they discovered was that they carried responsibility without congruent influence. Like any good managers, they looked beyond themselves, to the institutions with power and responsibility, to share the attempt to influence the boys – they still felt alone.

One of the great issues of our time, the discovery of just how dangerous a time childhood could be for children living in it, whether in the care of the family, the Church, the community or the State, produced a political crisis about children and adults. No politician during that era of discovery sponsored a community campaign against the sins of the fathers. Indeed when children *en masse* complained about abuse, primarily by their fathers, the discovery of their pain was followed by the commitment to listen to children, balanced by the consolidation of the State's 'partnership with parents' enshrined in the 1989 Children Act. When children's distress or their defeat expressed itself in dangerous deeds, when children went to war, when children could not be constructed in the collective imagination as *innocent*, then they were not victims but only culprits. The Prime Minister's crusade dramatised, therefore, not a new moment in the war against crime, but a new turn in the balance of power between parents and children on the one hand, and a bid to blame its historic ally, the police force, for a problem of the Government's own making.

The efforts of radical, reforming chief constables to publicise their auto-critique were barely supported by the Home Secretary's initiative. The poor management discovered in the 1989 Priority Project survey had been confirmed in Imbert's report to his conference: only fifteen per cent of officers questioned in an anonymous staff survey thought top management was any good, while forty-four per cent rated them as poor. The Commissioner was as critical of public order management as he was of criminal investigation. By the beginning of the Nineties, therefore, it was clear that senior officers' scrutiny of the police's ability to provide the service for which they were paid damningly endorsed the public criticism of the police throughout the Eighties. It was also echoed in chief officers' grumbles about the efficacy of community policing. Of course, that was partly rooted in resistance to any challenge to their autonomy and their authority, discussed in Robert Reiner's revealing study *Chief Constables*,[17] and the perception of its limits as a tool to challenge crime in the community at the same time as providing a service to the community.

The political problem of reform was cemented by the difficulty of the police, as a determinedly masculinised profession, to admit its fear of failure and its self-doubt. Its impregnable, insular, closed culture was challenged, rather than enlightened, by cooperation. The experience of the neighbourhoods

[17] Robert Reiner, *Chief Constables*, Oxford University Press, 1991.

overwhelmed by crime in the Nineties was that despite the rhetoric of community policing, communities as a whole were contaminated by the tag of criminality, and constabularies had difficulty differentiating between the distinct responses of community action and crime. It was as if they had difficulty *empathising* with and *learning* from their primary victims and witnesses, women.

The difficulty of that public dialogue was mirrored in the interior life of constabularies. In March 1993 the Home Office published a searching report by Her Majesty's Inspectorate of Constabulary into equal opportunities and harassment. It showed that women suffered 'persistent low-level harassment unchecked by supervisors', that physical harassment had been ignored by managers, that women who complained were not protected by their seniors, and that racist abuse was 'accepted' by supervisors who were often 'unprepared to challenge, or worse, were prepared to join in.' How could a corporate culture that expressed contempt for women and black people also provide them with protection against those who harassed them in the outside world?

Police culture, crime management and public safety were the crux of the crises which came together, conjuncturally, in the 1991 riots. Chief officers complained that they had received little help from the Home Office in their efforts to secure clarification about how to handle this matrix, and at the beginning of the Nineties, a dangerous decade, they felt uncertain about their responsibilities when the lore of minimum force met fierce disorder.

Several cities experienced riots in 1985. It was in Birmingham in September that they were deadly. The West Midlands had experienced several 'disorders' during the riot season in 1981, but they had been relatively minor. However, streets in Handsworth, in the heart of the city, were besieged on Wednesday, 11 September, and two Asian traders who ran a post office in Lozells Road died when their business was burned down.

The limits of Lord Scarman's recommendations on account-ability were apparent when the Home Secretary, Douglas Hurd, supported the refusal of the Chief Constable, Geoffrey Dear, to give evidence to Birmingham City Council's inquiry into the riot, conducted by Julius Silverman, QC.[18] However, the Chief Constable produced his own hugely detailed report, giving an hour-by-hour account of the events.[19]

As in Brixton, Toxteth and Tottenham, Birmingham's young black men suffered unemployment as high as fifty per cent in some areas. The West Midlands was devastated by the economic ravages of the late Seventies and by the restructuring of the motor industry and its staple sources of employment. Metal industries had employed half of Handsworth's workers. Indeed, the expanding metal manufacturing industries had attracted Caribbean migrants in the Fifties. But thousands of jobs, mostly in large manufacturing companies, had dis-appeared. By the middle of the decade the multinational corporations had evacuated, and the pattern of manufacturing was transformed – most jobs were in clothing factories, and were almost exclusively filled by the Asian community. Drawing on the findings of the 1981 census, the Chief Constable commented that seventy per cent of the people of Handsworth were 'extremely deprived'.

Handsworth had a tradition of locality-based community policing after 1977, though this often suffered from the pres-sure of conflicting community interests. These were becoming very visible in 1985 and the Silverman report concluded that there were 'tension indicators' that should also have been recognised in the weeks before the riot. The Chief Constable's report rated them as only 'short-lived episodes of disorder and criminality which are not uncommon in the area.'

Some of these incidents happened during the Handsworth

[18] Julius Silverman, QC, *Report of the Independent Inquiry into the Handsworth Disturbances, September 1985*, Birmingham City Council, February 1986.
[19] *Report of the Chief Constable, West Midlands Police: Handsworth/ Lozells, September 1985*, West Midlands Police Headquarters.

carnival over the weekend of 7–8 September. Several shops were attacked. Asian traders called the police, but were told that the police did not have the time or resources to help them. Silverman, and the traders themselves, felt that this response was racist. The Chief Constable's report acknowledged that there had been no arrests, but added that 'smash and grab' incidents had been increasing during the summer and were 'not unusual'.

A longer war of attrition had been fought between the police and drug dealers selling mainly cannabis. There were spectacular raids in 1983 and 1984, and in 1985 there were three big raids in the spring and summer. Only the third of the raids, a couple of weeks before the September carnival, netted a hard drugs haul of any great value. There was undoubtedly support in the neighbourhood for the raids; there was also a reaction against them.

A couple of days after the last raid, a routine campaign against illegal parking, the source of much complaint in Lozells Road, not far from Handsworth Park, because parked cars choked the road, triggered a confrontation with a black driver. A crowd gathered, police reinforcements arrived, there was a fight, and then, to prevent more damage, the police withdrew. According to the Chief Constable's report three telephone calls were made to the police, reporting fictitious incidents, apparently in the hope of drawing them into the area. The police resisted the temptation. By early evening petrol bombs were being prepared and shops were being set on fire.

Although the Scarman report had recommended that police forces be issued with protective clothing in the event of riots, none had been distributed to Birmingham police. They dared not, therefore, withstand the hazard of petrol bombs and stones being thrown at them as they tried to move into Lozells Road. The police acknowledged that this seriously slowed their mobilisation while shops were being burned and burgled. Barricades were also being built across Lozells Road to stop the emergency services getting through. 'Missile throwing and the movement of rioters appeared to be orchestrated by the loud blowing of whistles,' wrote the Chief Constable in his report.

Both Silverman and the Chief Constable record that between 8.44 p.m. and 9.36 p.m. the brothers in the post office telephoned the police, desperate for help. 'Please help, they are smashing their way in, they want to kill us,' was their last recorded appeal. The shops were burning; the flames did not die down until well after midnight. The following morning the bodies of the postmaster, Kassamali Moledina, and his brother, Amirali Moledina, were found.

For the next couple of days there were more outbreaks of looting, described by the police as 'criminal opportunism'.

The debate about the 1985 riots followed a familiar pattern: there had been an *enforcement* strategy in a cosmopolitan neighbourhood, directed at black drug dealers; and an inadequate *service* to protect residents from everyday harassment and theft. In his report, the Chief Constable acknowledged that the Lozells Road area had been targeted for drugs trafficking, indeed the police believed that 'drug abuse in this area appears endemic.' The entire area was thus described by the predilections of one part of it. The police were committed to a strategy to stamp it out. The Chief Constable's report concluded that the 'disorders were at the outset orchestrated by local drug dealers who had become fearful for the demise of their livelihoods.' It does not comment on whether the constabulary had calculated how to control or cope with the consequences of its strategy. By contrast, the Silverman report criticised the police for failing to recognise the tension indicators, the incidents in which people either felt harassed by the police or neglected by them. Furthermore, said Silverman, the police simply did not seem to believe that the riots would happen. He urged West Midlands police to look again at the Scarman report.

Economic crisis and crime, detection and obsession, politics and professionalism – these were the themes behind the Eighties riots and their aftermath. The events exposed not only the lack of police accountability to the people they served but also police authorities' passivity in monitoring and managing police priorities.

Merseyside was the paradigm. At the beginning of the Eighties Toxteth's riots generated a new era in the politics of policing: under the leadership of Lady Margaret Simey, the police authority's challenge to the Chief Constable pushed democratic accountability to its limits. A decade after the riots, the mothers of Toxteth 'took the law into their own hands' and finally exposed the failure of reform: something which could have been so simple had become so difficult – cooperation between the police, the council and the community to cope with traffic, car crime and deadly dangerous driving in a neighbourhood street. All of this had been the source of much complaint. The mothers barricaded Granby Street after two children were killed by 'death riders'.

The larger story revealed that by the end of the decade public order training, which counselled caution and clarity rather than aggression, had penetrated police culture. But it had remained immune from the impact of the Scarman report: operational issues were not open to public scrutiny, collaboration with other agencies was underdeveloped, enforcing the law was still preferred to confronting the problem of crime – reaction to incidents commanded status and resources, compared with the low profile of proactive prevention. These themes were central to the conditions that created the riots. By the Nineties they were the subject of intense professional and political inquiry.

It was also beginning to seem that the recent history of challenge by police authorities was a blip in a longer story of supine support for Chief Constables. A study by the Association of Metropolitan Authorities showed that police authorities were not exercising their legal powers either to insist upon accountability or to bring some stringency to the development of police priorities and practices. They rarely attempted to advise the Chief Constable or to influence force objectives. They seemed satisfied with what the Chief Constables told them, because they rarely asked to be told more.[20]

However, though the police authorities were remarkable for their passivity, there was a strong critique from elsewhere, from the Metropolitan Police Commissioner, who in 1991 challenged the priority given to law enforcement rather than crime prevention. A Home Office report of 1991, *Safer Communities*, criticises the narrow interpretation of crime prevention as a police responsibility, and urges the adoption of 'community safety' as a term that implies the participation of all sections of the community.[21] But recent research has shown that the police sponsor fewer prevention initiatives than other agencies. 'Data provided by Her Majesty's Inspector of Constabulary suggests that prevention initiatives undertaken by police are heavily outnumbered by those taken by other agencies,' argues the criminologist Barry Loveday.[22] More than five times more initiatives were sponsored by other agencies, particularly by local authorities, than by the police. And according to the 1991 National Audit Office Report the number of police officers designated as prevention officers were fewer than half of one per cent of police staff. Was this cost-effective, the Audit Office wondered?

Heavy-duty policing, in the absence of crime prevention, may do little to attack the conditions that create crime in hard-pressed neighbourhoods. The police tradition as an 'incident-led' service leads to a narrow focus and affirms macho habits. According to Barry Loveday, 'although the tradition emphasises the use of authority and powers of arrest as "real police work", it does very little in terms of dealing with the underlying causes which may generate the original incidents. This is unfortunate, if only because the analysis of crime demonstrates

[20] *Final Report of Working Party on the Police Authority Role: Strategic Issues*, Association of Metropolitan Authorities, 1991.
[21] *Safer Communities: The Local Delivery of Crime Prevention Through the Partnership Approach*, Home Office, August 1991.
[22] Barry Loveday, 'Police and Government in the 1990s' in *Social Policy and Administration*, vol. 25, no. 4, December 1991.

that few incidents with which police deal can be construed as isolated events.' Loveday argues that effective crime control strategies need cooperation between the police, the council and the community to move away from incident-response towards a problem-solving approach, one that concerns itself with the conditions which create crime in communities.

CHAPTER 6

Women of Merseyside

Merseyside is the place that unites the main riot seasons of 1981 and 1991. It is the exemplar of the crisis in public order policing, in the provision of a police service, and in constabulary culture. Women came to be the spectre haunting these crises and the complacency of the constabulary's corporate culture. Riots hit Liverpool 8 in July 1981, three months after Brixton burst into flames. Ten years later, when the riots elsewhere had calmed, mothers in the heart of Liverpool 8's Granby Ward built a barricade where a car had crashed into three children. Two of them, a boy and a girl, died. The car, driven by joyriders, came to a halt up a lamppost. The mothers were protesting against the joyriders who had captured Granby Street as their own arena, and also against the police who had failed to intervene on the side of the community against car crime. Granby Street was a symbolic space within a 'symbolic location'. Blocked off at one end by traffic managers after the 1981 riots, it had become a circuit for joyriders. The 'Women of the Barricades', as they came to be known, were a model of active citizenship in Britain's hard-pressed places, they were pacific vigilantes whose direct action challenged both the passivity of Neighbourhood Watch and the butch fantasy of High Noon traditionally associated with the image of the vigilante. Mothers organised the resistance to what Superintendent Broughton had designated the 'deadly game' in Tyneside, in Liverpool 8 and in Ely in 1992. Their barricades were an epitaph to community policing.

Between 1981 and 1991 the city had witnessed the most potent challenge to any constabulary by any elected police authority. It was led by a magisterial former suffragist,

Margaret Simey, who had been Granby's Labour councillor for more than twenty years. She brought a certain grandeur to municipal manners, though she never herself recognised her reputation as an amazon. 'It was my middle-class façade that frightened the police. They really were at a loss as to how to deal with me,' she said later. Merseyside Police Authority challenged the reality of community policing, which never matched the rhetoric, and pushed out the frontiers of democratic policing. The police authority took its powers to the limits and offered unprecedented criticism of authoritarian management by Merseyside's Chief Constable, Sir Kenneth Oxford, and of inefficient policing within the constabulary. By the end of the decade a new generation had resurrected an old alliance: Simey's successors at the police authority were collaborating with Oxford's successor as Chief Constable, James Sharples, to defeat yet another challenge from a woman. The leaders of the police committee supported him in a discrimination case brought against the Chief Constable, the Home Secretary and Her Majesty's Inspector of Constabulary by Britain's most senior policewoman, Assistant Chief Constable Alison Halford. Halford's appointment had been an effect of Margaret Simey's attempt to reform the notoriously macho character of the force. After Simey's retirement, the old-fashioned Labour lads, led by Simey's former deputy, George Bundred, supported the Chief Constable's campaign against the Assistant Chief Constable. What had been a problem of powers became a problem of politics.

In 1981 Liverpool was not part of Lord Scarman's brief. Merseyside Police Authority conducted its own inquiry. It confronted the disaster that hit the heart of the city by bringing the politics of public order and the conduct of everyday detection together in a campaign for constabulary accountability to the community.

The riot in Toxteth, formerly a genteel neighbourhood built on the site of a forest, began on 4 July when a young black man on his motorbike was stopped by the police who challenged his ownership. The motorcyclist, Leroy Cooper, was surrounded and supported by friends and he escaped. But this latest episode in Liverpool 8 was the last straw. At midnight the following night, a black community worker arrived at the door of Margaret Simey, a white woman who represented one of the great cosmopolitan neighbourhoods in the old port city. She not only represented the ward on the County Council but was also the chair of the police authority. The community worker was shivering and shocked and he had come to tell her the worst – there was war in the streets.

That weekend, local landmarks like the Rialto Cinema, the Racquets Club and Lodge Lane, went up in flames. Black and white locals were rioting and there was looting – largely by white adults, according to the police.[1] Although rioting continued sporadically for weeks, the major confrontations happened during the first weekend, when damage was estimated at £12 million.

What Toxteth already knew was then revealed to the nation: 'A chasm of devastating dimensions had opened up between the police and the policed, a gulf so wide that the sole means of communication across it was by the beating of plastic shields and the throwing of milk bottle bombs,' said Simey. One of those who watched the riot consume her community was Maureen Lamb. Her son went to school with Leroy Cooper, the motorcyclist whose encounter with the police had sparked the riot. 'It was frightening. I hope I never see another riot. The youths were mad, nobody could have stopped them,' she said. 'They'd had enough because of the racial harassment. It hasn't changed. The police here only see black and white, they don't see you as a person, they only see colour.'

Lord Scarman visited the city, although it was not part of his brief, and noted in his report on the Brixton riot that 'relations between the police and the black community in

---

[1] Margaret Simey, *Democracy Rediscovered: A Study in Police Accountability*, Pluto, London, 1988.

Toxteth, as was made plain to me when I visited Liverpool, are in a state of crisis.' The aggressive tactics of the police had been sanctioned by the Chief Constable. He had provoked Simey's predecessor in the police authority, the Conservative Sir Kenneth Thompson, to make an extraordinary complaint about the 'distant authoritarianism of certain ego-inflated police officers'. The Chief Constable's attrition with the community that July was symbolised in the deployment of CS-gas canisters against the crowds in Toxteth.

Margaret Simey's record of those days is an intimate cameo of the death of democracy itself – when she tried to go out into the streets to see for herself, 'a car whizzed up, two men from CID bundled me into it and smartly deposited me on my own doorstep.' Here was the ward councillor, the leader of the police authority, being banned from her own streets, powerless, 'because I was an old woman.' She came to believe that 'it is in regard to policing that the breakdown of democratic practice has been taken to its most frightening extreme.' She had watched her neighbourhood exploding from her bedroom, where she sat on her bed looking out, 'watching the flames and smoke shoot up beyond the roofs of the houses in the next street.' Suddenly 'the flames had died down and the shouting had died away.'

The National Council for Civil Liberties noted at the time that 'the use of CS gas was abandoned in Northern Ireland in the early 1970s because it was considered too dangerous. It is particularly unacceptable that CS gas has been introduced without any public discussion or approval by Parliament, local councils or police authorities.' Margaret Simey was later to become a stringent critic of the model of 'policing by consent' and 'community policing' proposed in the Scarman report because her own experience showed that the powers of police authorities would never be allowed to have any impact upon the operational mastery of chief constables.

The traditional passivity of police authorities had 'left the police to their own devices' and thus they had 'taken over decisions which should properly have belonged to the politicians,' she said. 'Almost unobserved, they have acquired an astonishingly comprehensive control over every aspect of the service – even the extent to which they shall be accountable for what they do.'

After the riots, Chief Constable Sir Kenneth Oxford rarely disguised his disdain for the Scarman report. Merseyside Police Authority's angst about its own political paralysis and the constabulary's reluctance to communicate with its constituents over anything designated 'operational' – which meant the actual practice of policing – were the very problems that were aired in the Scarman report. Police forces reluctantly conceded the right of democratic institutions to impinge on operational matters in the decade following the report. Their resistance had a profound impact on the content of public debate about policing, since the public had so little access to knowledge about police practice. Not surprisingly, there was no inquiry into police tactics in the 1991 riots by any of the police authorities.

However, in the early Eighties Merseyside Police Authority audaciously tackled operational issues, management and complaints and created a web of specialist subcommittees to cope with its newly-stringent concern. It produced illuminating inquiries into police operations and accountability which were pertinent in the Nineties, not because the riot territories of 1991 were policed by cavalier chief constables – on the contrary, all of them were managed by modernising chief officers who had been chastened by 1981 – but because Merseyside's economic conditions and high crime rates mirrored their own difficulties and clarified the elusive connections between public order and criminal investigation.

Merseyside, like London and Bristol, was beset by the criminalisation of black men in the Eighties. Stop-and-search tactics which echoed the old 'sus' law and 'swamp' operations seemed to many people to be a staple in the police strategy for criminal investigation. The result was that a quarter of young men in

Granby Ward in the heart of Toxteth had been searched. The rate was seventy per cent higher among black than among white residents. The historian of Liverpool policing, Professor Michael Brogden, has shown the long trajectory of that *modus operandi*. The police, operating rather like 'uniformed garbage men', had a mandate to keep the streets clean, and thus the 'traditional objects of public order police work were the poor, who were the objects of 'incursive patrolling of the lower-class city.' However, 'arrests, other than for minor misdemeanours, were rare.'[2]

As a mode of criminal investigation, the 'sus' strategy was absurd. Only 4.3 per cent of stops resulted in arrest.[3] As an intervention it was disastrous, because it carried the message: you're all criminals. When stop-and-search was studied by the academic criminologist Richard Kinsey, he suspected that its efficiency as an investigative tool was far outweighed by the harm done by raising resentment against the police.[4]

Recorded crime increased by sixty per cent in Merseyside in the decade after 1974. Detection increased equivalently, but only as a result of admissions from offenders in custody. Either these offenders had dramatically increased their productivity, or crime figures were being massaged – there was no increase in the number of offenders being caught, cautioned or prosecuted. Police problems were compounded by a decline in detection before 1985 when there was another serious riot in Liverpool. Burglary and car theft (which, next to sexual crime and violence, were the offences which ordinary citizens perceived as having the most impact on their lives) saw the main fall in detection rates between 1983 and 1985, down twenty-three per cent. Again, this had no impact on the number of offenders locked up, confirming the earlier

---

[2] Michael Brogden, *On the Mersey Beat*, Open University Press, London, 1991.
[3] *Policing: An Agenda for Merseyside*, Report of the County Solicitor, Merseyside County Council, 1986.
[4] R. Kinsey, *Merseyside Crime and Police Surveys: Final Report*, Merseyside County Council, 1985.

criticism that the police depended on admissions by people in custody. At the same time detection actually declined – a time when Merseyside had the highest burglary rate in the country and when diplomatic relations with the community were at a fractious low.

After the 1981 riots the police were criticised for exceeding the Government's 'minimum force' criteria. But approval of *operational* methods was deemed by the Chief Constable to be beyond the remit of the elected police authority. The Scarman recommendation that all operational matters should be up for discussion was not favoured in the constabulary's culture. Indeed the concept of community policing, which became part of the vernacular of law and order in the Eighties, seemed foreign to the Chief Constable. 'I have yet to find a definition of "community policing",' he told a seminar on the Scarman report. 'It is all very well to call for community policing as the panacea for all problems with which we are faced when it is obviously not the case.' Having dismissed the concept as a mystery, he then predicted its failure, but not before he claimed that he'd been operating it for years: 'We've had police liaison officers for fifteen years,' he said.[5]

When Alison Halford was appointed Assistant Chief Constable in 1983 she knew nothing of the politics of the police authority and, coming from the Met which was accountable to no elected authority in the capital city, was not familiar with the attrition between the authority and the Chief Constable. But, like all senior officers in the city, she soon became familiar with the Chief Constable's well-known contempt for his challenger, Margaret Simey. And, like all senior officers, she soon discovered that the citizenry had much preferred the officers drafted in from other counties during the riots. That was enough to

---

[5] Kenneth Oxford, 'Policing by Consent', in *Scarman and After – Essays Reflecting on Lord Scarman's Report, the Riots and Their Aftermath*, edited by John Benyon, Pergamon Press, Oxford, 1984.

know that there was a problem in the city.[6]

Rank-and-filers in the police hated Simey. 'She was seen as challenging everything that Oxford did,' said one manager. 'They thought they'd been out doing their jobs during the riots, when their lives were wrecked, and she was giving them no support. I totally agreed with them. I saw people in uniform dripping with blood and petrol and I had to listen to rubbish coming from that woman. I was appalled. Now I can see,' the manager said, alluding to the well-known criticisms of the Chief Constable's budget plans by both Conservative- and Labour-led police authorities, 'that she was just trying to stop an arrogant chief constable spending the public's money in a way that some people feared was profligate.'

Halford had been appointed not only because she was a woman but because the authority was attracted to her expertise in management, staff selection and training. Five years later, she was also given the complaints portfolio. That placed her at the heart of modernisation in Merseyside – though the industrial tribunal which heard her discrimination case was to learn just how far her ability to influence constabulary culture was minimised.

During her first year Halford introduced communications training for criminal investigators, the importance of which she had learned during her time in the Met. Traditional police culture had relied on gut instinct and 'masculine intuition' in criminal investigation and public order management. It had rarely offered its officers training in communicating with the public. 'Police officers had not been shown how to conduct a conversation in the street, how to handle confrontational situations or how to conduct interviews,' said Halford. 'At the time police officers were often very heavy-handed, didn't read the signs properly, and were often aggressive and abusive to the public.'

It went without saying that policemen had learned little

[6] The following material comes both from Halford's evidence at her Industrial Tribunal and from an interview with the author.

from policewomen, who could not rely on brute strength to manage a crisis, and who had not even been issued with batons until relatively recently. During the Eighties the resources described by Halford as 'guile, tact and diplomacy' came to be affirmed publicly by several senior policewomen in the great debates about public order management in the police press.

While responsible for staff development at the Met's training college in Hendon, Halford had worked with Dr Eric Shepherd, a clinical psychologist who specialised in interrogation and communication skills. They were the first to introduce British police officers to the human awareness training which was already part of modern corporate culture. Halford brought this experience to Merseyside where she introduced Dr Shepherd to the force as a consultant. It was a critical moment. Police communications in general and confessions in particular were subject to unprecedented public criticism, and after 1984 were to be controlled by the Police and Criminal Evidence Act. Officers would no longer be allowed to bark around an interview room and badger a suspect. At the same time police officers' communications with victims were being challenged by the new consciousness of sexual offences against women and children, and domestic violence. The police needed help.

Halford's chief, Kenneth Oxford, approved the new training but refused to pay for it. Indeed when Halford asked him for his signature he rebelled. 'Take advices, madam, you need a holiday,' he told her. Apparently she should have known that he didn't like putting things on paper. By contrast, it was Halford's habit to record everything. It was a habit that gave her an archive when she made her formal complaint of sex discrimination against the police.

Despite Oxford's brusque evasion, Halford found the money and the people to prepare and then present Shepherd's communications courses. After about a year Oxford, so impressed by Shepherd's courses, appropriated the initiative. Shepherd was to remain a consultant with Merseyside until 1991.

'The CID loved the interview development course, which

was unheard of, because it taught them skills they'd never had,' said Halford. 'They always wanted more courses. They felt I had *given* them something useful.'

In the year of her appointment the highest endorsement was given to the police authority's efforts to engage the Chief Constable in a cooperative plan for policing their city. It came in the form of Home Office circular 114/83. This document had emerged from a working party embracing civil servants from the Home Office, local authority leaders and chief police officers, and it obliged elected authorities and chief officers to develop a joint approach to policing policy. Margaret Simey invited Dr Shepherd to enlighten the authority about training. The Chief Constable rejected her request in a note dated 17 October 1984.

Working with the Home Office circular, a series of seminars was organised in Merseyside for the authority and the constabulary to discuss 'Planned Policing' – a prospectus of agreed aims and objectives to be implemented across the force by chief superintendents after discussions with their colleagues and the community.

The initiative, which was designed to reform police management, had the mandate of the Home Office and the approval of Her Majesty's Inspectorate of Constabulary. And although the police authority was perceived as politically challenging, it was also seen to be doing what police authorities should do: bring democratic scrutiny to a public service. Furthermore, the HMI had concluded that the authority was giving 'positive support' to the constabulary, and that it was properly exercising its responsibilities under the Police Act.[7]

The police authority was enthusiastic because the initiative offered elected councillors the opportunity to influence priorities. According to senior police managers, officers were enthusiastic about Planned Policing because it gave them a framework and offered them 'the opportunity to participate

---

[7] Barry Loveday, *The Role and Effectiveness of the Merseyside Police Committee*, Merseyside County Council, 1985.

in the management of the force.' Alison Halford reckoned that chief superintendents were excited by it because it 'gave them responsibility for looking at problems in their own areas of command and for making changes. They were to consult every member of their staff and consult with the community, with the Community Forums which had been introduced in 1984.'

However, the Chief Constable refused to produce a joint statement of priorities with the police committee after the seminars organised to elicit a shared view. Instead, he wrote a provocative report of his own in which he stated that the local authority displayed 'simplistic arrogance which clearly reflects political expediency rather than a wish to improve.'[8] This moment was a watershed in the drive for community policing and the principle of accountability. A process had been put in place to make those terms part of professional practice. But it was a process that the Chief Constable found difficult. The call to cooperation counselled both by Scarman and by the Home Office circular, and now sought by the elected councillors, seemed to represent not a resource but a threat. He argued that it 'would attempt to interfere with the statutory responsibilities of chief constables.'[9] Nor were senior staff confident that he would let them have their head.

The police authority appealed to the Home Office for help after the Chief Constable had refused to issue a joint statement. It declined to intervene. The argument exhausted itself and after the Chief Constable and the police authority had consulted each other's documents they issued their own statements.[10]

Planned Policing died. 'He killed it off by his vehement attacks on chief inspectors and superintendents,' said Halford. 'He was happy with the rhetoric of Planned Policing as long

---

[8] *Ibid.*
[9] *Ibid.*
[10] *Ibid.*

as chief superintendents did not take responsibility or do anything without his personal knowledge or approval. There was a whole head of steam: they had poured a lot of resources into the process but it fizzled out. The Chief Constable's power was absolute and the structure gave him permission to use it.'

Another senior manager in Merseyside reckoned that 'the clock stopped on Planned Policing in 1984. Merseyside could have been the pioneers then, but that wasn't allowed to happen.' Many years later the format was pulled out again and polished up in a fresh effort to modernise management practices and communication with the police committee. 'We wasted all those years,' said the manager. By the time the effort was renewed in the early Nineties Halford had been exiled.

Planned Policing was one of many initiatives designed to reform relations between the community and the constabulary. It was defeated. 'It would be fair to say that since 1981 all the forms of exercising local accountability of the police have been explored and utilised by the Police Committee,' concluded the Loveday report on its effectiveness, which was published by the County Council in 1985. The committee having exercised its public powers to the full, the Merseyside experience confirmed that those powers could not overcome the resistance of an absolutist Chief Constable. 'It must be asked, however, if in exercising those powers the Police Committee has yet been able to establish a more accountable Police Force for Merseyside ... Where the Police Authority has attempted to exercise influence over policing policy it has rarely gone unchallenged by the Chief Constable who has viewed it as an infringement of his operational autonomy.[11]

The constabulary's formal contact with the community came to be seen as 'a format more suited to a public relations exercise than a serious attempt to tackle police–community relations.'[12] In 1986 the metropolitan authorities were

---

[11] *Ibid.*
[12] Merseyside County Council, *Policing: An Agenda for Merseyside,* 1986.

abolished by a government that found their independence inimical, and police authorities were replaced by joint boards.

Just as the elected representatives had been publicly humiliated, so the Chief Constable's professional colleagues were subjected to his imperial behaviour. None more than Halford. She was seen as an innovative and rigorous manager. When her life and times at Merseyside were revealed at the industrial tribunal into her sex discrimination case in 1992, the public domain was admitted to the interior life of a culture struggling both with the effect of masculinisation and the effort of modernisation.

Halford's fate shadowed key themes in the reform of the police: professionalising the *discipline* of *detection* by honing the skill rather than relying on authority and intuition; empowering officers by giving them skills; organising the complaints and discipline systems so that they conformed to a rigorous and respectful hearing of issues raised by the public – a hotly-contested theme in public debates during the Seventies and Eighties; alerting the police hierarchy to the changing priorities of a public that was more aware than ever before of both its troubles and its rights. Women all over the country were challenging the police over the investigation of sexual crime and domestic violence, both of which attracted a disdain in 'canteen culture' which camouflaged the weight of the challenge. The fate of these reforms, which were being slugged out in constabularies all over the country, revealed much more to the tribunal than the character of the protagonists – they exposed the difficulty of making the *force* into *a service*.

Although the tribunal was concerned with Halford's case that she had suffered discrimination when other, less qualified and less experienced men were preferred in promotion to the next rank on nine occasions, it was also invited into the inner life of the of the hierarchy when the tribunal heard Halford's answer to forty-seven episodes cited as evidence by the Chief Constable. However, *after* the tribunal heard Halford's sex discrimination case and her vigorous response to the Chief Constable's case, but *before* the police side put their own case, the proceedings were halted, apparently under pressure from the Home Secretary. In any case, Halford was believed to be exhausted by her gruelling performance at the tribunal. It seemed that the police hierarchy was in disgrace – the revelations reflected so badly on the police that the Home Office was disinclined to let the marathon go on running.

'The Alison Halford affair could not have exploded at a worse time for a police service already on its knees from a succession of miscarriages of justice, shattered public confidence and rising crime rates,' commented the *Independent* newspaper's report on the settlement on 22 July 1992. 'Accusations of drunkenness, misogyny . . . appeared to confirm the worst public suspicions that sections of the service are brutish and sexist.'

Apparently, under pressure from the Government, the Chief Constable and the Merseyside Police Authority reached a settlement with Halford and the Equal Opportunities Commission. Part of the deal included EOC monitoring of equal opportunities in the Merseyside police.

Much of Halford's work was concerned with staff management. Her training reforms were followed by the review of occupational health within the force, a review of force firearms training, the stringent enforcement of complaints protocols, and a review of the response to child abuse and domestic violence. The following are examples of her fate. Her occupational health brief was handed over to a less experienced colleague. She proposed streamlining of firearms training, which reduced the number of officers entitled to be armed – and needing to be regularly trained – from four hundred, or ten per cent of the force, to a specialist squad. She heard no more of her proposals until her industrial tribunal, when the firearms file was produced and she discovered that her plan had been adopted – in the name of another chief officer. Early in the Eighties she initiated research into the prevalence of domestic violence against women and suggested setting up a specialist unit. The answer was no. In the mid-Eighties, she proposed a rape crisis suite. The answer was no. In the Eighties there were nineteen official inquiries by the Government into the preventable deaths of children at the hands of their carers. But by the middle of the decade child deaths through cruelty were producing stiff political pressure on both the police and Social Services to provide new services for children being abused in the community. Halford consulted other professionals in Merseyside and then set up a multi-agency seminar on child abuse and domestic violence. These initiatives were being echoed by a few other progressive constabularies around the country.

'Children were being abused. Detectives handled that badly. Detectives didn't like dealing with domestic violence because it was so unpredictable and so dangerous. So the seminar had merit all round,' said Halford. Participants received invitations to attend the seminar on 14 February 1986. It was cancelled by the Chief Constable.

These incidents were few among many in which her professional impact was denied or stolen. It was a way of telling her that a woman would neither be allowed to show prowess, nor be seen to have influenced the force. Her attempts to bring discipline and modernity to a chaotic and capricious corporate culture provoked a crisis similar to the challenge from the police authority.

Even after Oxford's successor, James Sharples, took over in 1988, butch values prevailed. Sharples' reputation as a modern management man did not extend to his response to the most senior policewoman in the country, nor – the tribunal discovered – to police discipline or to the community. He had respected Halford's professionalism and sought her counsel, but he did not promote her. She was not given the prestigious criminal investigations portfolio, but was assigned instead the minefield of complaints and discipline. Merseyside had suffered a barrage of criticism since the Seventies and complaints and discipline lay on the boundary between the public domain and the police. Halford resolved to treat the public's complaints with respect.

The public domain preoccupied the Chief Constable. He never forgave Alison Halford for contributing to the *Police Review*'s debate on the fate of women officers, in a critique of constabulary culture published in October 1987, even though she had written it *before* he took over as Chief Constable. He cited it in his response to Halford's discrimination case. He expressed alarm at the prospect that she might write a book on her experiences – not an unexpected project for the country's top woman cop. Sharples' objection to Halford's contribution to the *Police Review*, the tribunal was told, was that it had 'not been submitted for approval', that it 'damaged working relations', and that it was 'inaccurate'. Halford had written the article in response to what she had regarded as a cosy and complacent review of a woman's life in the hierarchy. She argued that a woman was given little of the 'support, guidance or empathy' that would be afforded to a male Assistant Chief Constable. A few years later the Metropolitan police were to concede as much and more when the new Commissioner, Paul Condon, initiated a great debate into equal opportunities in 1993. However, Sharples not only repudiated Halford's experience, but her audacity in sharing it with her professional peers.

An incident which shocked reporters at her industrial tribunal, even though it was unreported in the national press, revealed an intemperate and authoritarian response by the new Chief Constable, and showed that the frontier between the public and the police could still be a war zone.

The incident was unravelled at the tribunal. The Chief Constable's complaint was that Halford had unjustifiably criticised him for his handling of a case in August 1989, and that she had failed to inform him of her correspondence with the Police Complaints Authority.

This case concerned a man who lodged a complaint that a police officer had beaten him up with his truncheon while arresting him for a motoring offence, and that a fellow officer had failed to stop him. He provided medical evidence of injuries to his eye, legs and back. The case was serious enough to have attracted the scrutiny of the Police Complaints Authority, which supervised the proceedings. The investigating officer, Detective Superintendent Robert Cody, and the PCA concluded that the complaint merited the consideration of disciplinary charges against the officers. Thus the Chief Constable presided over a disciplinary hearing. However, he aborted the proceedings before hearing how the man had received his injuries. The tribunal heard that the Chief Constable had 'no faith whatsoever in the complainant', that he was a 'liar' and his case was 'a load of rubbish'.

The view of the investivating officer, Detective Superintendent Cody – who was later in charge of Operation Cheetah into local authority corruption – and of the Police Complaints Authority, was that whether or not the complainant was a liar, a beating could not be excused, and in any event deserved investigation.

Detective Superintendent Cody alerted Halford that the Chief Constable should at least have heard how the complainant came to suffer his injuries. When it heard that Sharples had blocked the investigation, the PCA wanted to know why a case which it believed 'had considerable merit' had been abandoned. The PCA pressed Halford, who was the officer in charge of the complaints and discipline portfolio, for an explanation. She advised the Chief Constable of the PCA's concern. When she was asked again for an explanation, Halford alerted the Chief Constable to the PCA's correspondence.

That generated a dyspeptic response from the Chief Constable which was presented to the tribunal. Sharples dispatched an angry riposte to the PCA, refusing to give any answers, with copies to Halford and all her senior colleagues. This, of course, publicised her humiliation: 'I have to say from the outset that I have not the slightest intention of giving any information,' wrote Sharples to the PCA on 29 November 1989. 'Direct your inquiries to me personally, but I can assure you that you will certainly not receive any answers.' He added that he could understand why 'other chief constables have become somewhat prickly.' He also sent out an instruction, which was read to the tribunal, saying, 'I am instructing chief officers that under no circumstances will any officer of mine comment on any decision of mine.' These audacious rebukes had been cited as challenges to an uppity woman. In fact, they boomeranged back to accuse not the woman but the boss.

Journalists covering the case were riveted. We carefully checked our notes in the press room. Had we heard it right? Was he that bad? Was the constabulary so capricious in its treatment not only of complaints but of the PCA, the public and its own senior staff?

'What the police are terrified of is exposure to the outside, because they know they're a shambles,' commented a Merseyside criminologist.

The evidence of a butch, boozy force culture which emerged during the tribunal shocked even seasoned drinkers in the journalists' community. Drinking had been cited by the Chief Constable in his case against Halford. She had attended a race meeting at the Chief Constable's invitation in December 1988, when she was 'under the influence'. Halford replied that it had been her day off. She then parried with a picture of a hard-drinking environment. There were 'drinkie-poohs in the office at the drop of a hat on the CID floor.' Towards the end of an HMI inspection week in 1986 an 'enormous booze-up' resulted in two of her colleagues becoming 'legless' and two spending the night at force HQ. On another occasion duty officers out on patrol rescued a drunk colleague seen wandering around the city centre, being eyed up by youths.

'I know of no other force where drinking among such senior ranks seems to have been so prevalent,' commented the long-standing editor of the *Police Review*, Brian Hilliard.[13] 'It is like *Just William*,' commented a senior policewoman in another force, after following the tribunal saga in the press. 'But it could be anywhere – that's what is so dreadful.'

[13] The *Independent*, 22 July 1992.

The Merseyside force did not seem to see any reason for self-criticism in their reputation for hard drinking. But that reputation was mobilised against Halford when she took her discrimination case to the Equal Opportunities Commission after being refused promotion nine times while less qualified men were preferred. The force and the police authority resurrected an allegation that she had been involved in drinking and partying at the home of a local businessman while she was the senior officer available. This had been disposed of in an internal disciplinary hearing. It was exhumed when she went to the EOC with her discrimination case. 'I believe the whole affair has been dirty,' commented Hilliard, 'but the dirtiest thing the police authority did was to reopen the disciplinary case.'[14]

When Halford lodged her equality action her sexuality was recruited as an *accusation* against her. The Chief Constable in November 1990 had recorded a rumour about her sexual orientation – prompted, apparently, by her taking a woman with her to football matches. Men's pleasure in the company of men had never, as far as we know, generated rumours of homosexuality. The rumour surfaced again after she had taken her case to the EOC. The chair of the police authority, George Bundred, a powerful mover in municipal circles, was heard complaining that Halford was a lesbian. According to an affidavit for Halford signed by Merseyside Liberal Democrat Councillor Simon Shaw, Bundred had said that she was 'a lesbian and it was bad for discipline'. The gossip had been overheard and then disclosed by one of Bundred's colleagues on the Association of Metropolitan Authorities police committee, Neil Taggart. He was appalled by the notion that an officer's sexuality had any bearing on her professional performance.[15] The gossip exposed the precarious success of the Labour Party's efforts at modernisation during the Eighties, a decade which had witnessed formidable inner-party struggles over the

14 The *Independent*, 22 July 1992.
15 *The Times Saturday Review*, 22 February 1992.

enfranchisement of women, gays and black party members
– everyone who failed to fit in a party made in the image
of middle-aged, white, working-class men.

Halford's reluctance to throw herself into all of the force's
bouts of corporate drinking was also used against her. 'Being
the one woman in male company at fairly boozy do's is not
the best way to spend an evening,' she told the tribunal.

Police managers' failure to learn about her or from her was
reinterpreted by the HMI when it considered her application
for promotion. 'She is an enigma,' commented an HMI report
quoted at the tribunal, which noted her 'reluctance to mix
socially with the force' as well as the fact that she had
'crossed swords with her peers'. The HMI report admitted
that this was 'not entirely her fault' but made no effort to
elicit an explanation from Halford herself.

Despite the HMI's plentiful visits to Merseyside, Halford
was not consulted about her progress nor was she never offered
any feedback about her performance. Indeed it was not until
her equality action, when she got sight of the HMI's reference,
that she discovered her reputation as an enigma.

Neither the Home Secretary, nor the HMI, nor her colleagues in the Association of Chief Police Officers came
forward to protect her. It appeared that none of them thought
her deserving of the professional solidarity they themselves
enjoyed as *men* – the companionship of her peers, senior
women. On the one occasion when she found herself in a
department working closely with another woman of senior
status, their friendship was frowned upon and discouraged.
There was no other woman in the force whose rank brought
her close enough to be a companion.

None of the men with whom she worked, or who passed
judgement on her professionalism, was ever confronted by a
woman in their professional midst who was his equal. Nor
were these men ever in the position in which she found
herself, of being surrounded only by otherness, being denied
supervision or support by anyone who knew how that felt, or
who knew what *difference* might bring to the organisation's

professional repertoire. None of them knew what it felt like
to work entirely without empathy. But they all monitored her
in her quarantine and allowed her chiefs to effect her decline
and destruction. None of them decreed: this must stop, we
are interested in the survival of our top woman cop! They all
responded with surprise to her resistance, and they treated her
as a problem rather than as a resource.

At the time of Alison Halford's sex discrimination complaint against the Chief Constable, the Home Secretary and
the HMI – which she lodged in 1990 and which was heard
in public in 1992 – the residents living around around Granby
Street in Toxteth were tormented by white youths joyriding
up and down Granby Street and dumping stolen cars in their
neighbourhood. The two scenarios appeared to be uncon-
nected. Yet these struggles both revealed the readiness of the
police to learn from women inside and outside their own ranks.

Granby Street had been blocked off at one end after the
1981 riots. The once bustling thoroughfare was, by the end
of the decade, a deserted relic supporting only a post office,
a barber and a couple of general stores. The residents never
discovered why the street had been blocked off. 'We don't
know why; just one morning there it was. The police don't
communicate with us when they do things. They don't think
about what is in the best interests of the people, they think
of the convenience of the police,' complained Maureen Lamb,
a tenants' leader. 'If another riot was to happen they'd have
us boxed in.' Her kitchen overlooked the opposite boundary
of the neighbourhood which was bordered by a grassy bank
between housing and a main road. Only the grass on the side
of the bank that faced the road was cut by the council. That,
too, communicated a clear message to the residents about who
the council thought was important.

The effect of the barrier at the end of Granby Street was
to turn it into a circuit for joyriders. They often used the
playground of Granby Street primary school, too.

Maureen Lamb was just returning home from a meeting of Merseyside community organisations with her long-time friends Flossie Cofi and Josie Burger on 31 October, Hallowe'en night. They got off the bus a little after 9 p.m. and were approached by young men from the neighbourhood. Maureen Lamb recalls, 'Two big lads came to us and said, "There's been an accident outside your house, Flossie. Can you come?" They said a girl was dead and two other children were hurt.' No one knew the identity of the girl but the other children, boys, were well-known locally. The women saw the killer car wrapped around a lamppost. Two lads had been driving the car and had been recognised. They had fled, one of them leaving one of his shoes behind.

The three women got the children in the street to go round the neighbourhood to find out who the little girl was. The following morning flowers began appearing where she had died. She was twelve-year-old Adele Thompson. Two weeks later one of the injured boys, Daniel Davies, died. He was nine years old. They had been among the children collecting 'a penny for the guy' on the street when the high-powered stolen Mazda hit them. It was being driven in a 'ludicrously dangerous' way, said the prosecution at the driver's trial in 1992, when he was imprisoned for seven and a half years.

Mothers, both black and white, delivered their children to school as usual the day after the crash and on their way home Flossie Cofi and Josie Burger began to build a barricade across Granby Street from the wood being collected nearby for Bonfire Night. They wanted to stop all cars using the street. 'The big grown-up lads went to get the youths who'd been driving the car and took them down to the police station,' explained Maureen Lamb.

They called a meeting that night in St Bernard's Church – Granby community politics is energetically sustained by St Bernard's and by the local Methodist Centre. It was packed by hundreds of residents. 'It was mostly women. It's only women who do things. Very few men ever come to meetings, anything that gets done round here is done by women,' said Maureen

Lamb. For five months the Women of the Barricade, as they came to be called, maintained their vigil in Granby Street.

Out of the barricade emerged a new tenants' movement which was then favoured by regular negotiations with the local authority and the police over the rehabilitation of their devastated neighbourhood. The Women of the Barricade conducted a house-to-house survey of the whole neighbourhood to find out what people wanted. They wanted the road reopened and the removal of the traffic blockade erected after the riots. A year later the blockade was still in place.

A year after the children died the women's complaints to the police – about young men bringing stolen cars to their streets to strip them, about youths who harassed neighbours, particularly young mothers, and shouted 'grass' and spat at anyone known to be active in the community or to have called the police – appeared to have yielded little response. 'The police say there's nothing they can do about it,' said Maureen Lamb. A decade of community forums since the 1981 riot had failed to commit the police to the residents of Granby Street. But the allegations of racism that had infused the 1981 riots still surfaced. 'If you are black round here they search you,' said Maureen Lamb. Her own son is a skilled cabinet-maker and a well-known amateur footballer. On his way home one night after the children's deaths his car was followed by the police. They made him pull over and asked if he was lost. 'I beg your pardon?' he said. 'Don't fucking patronise me,' said the officer. 'What made you think I was lost? I live here,' said the cabinet-maker. They detained him for an hour or so and when he warned that he would make a formal complaint he was told, 'Don't waste your fucking time, we look after our own.'

The residents did not feel looked after, however. Dangerous drivers had killed five people, both black and white, in as many years: Adele Thompson, Daniel Davies, a four-year-old child, a man, and an elderly woman. She was Daisy Showers, a well-known resident whose son was in prison when she was killed. Through Simey's successor on the police authority, George Bundred, he appealed to be released to attend his mother's funeral. Halford was the duty officer. She consulted her colleagues and sought Sharples' opinion. He didn't like the idea, he told her it might cause mayhem.

In memory of Adele Thompson and Daniel Davies a massive street party was held in August 1992 and two streets were named after them, to celebrate their lives. 'You have to wonder what it would take for the police to take any notice of us,' says Maureen Lamb.

PART III

COMPONENT PARTS

Community, crime and culture

Like the so-called symbolic locations of the Eighties, the estates that were overwhelmed by riots in 1991 were regarded as places contaminated by crime. They were thus deprived of the service and support they would have expected had their class character been privileged. Primarily white, their inhabitants indeed perceived as poor white trash, they did not attract the same attention as neighbourhoods with a strong black presence.

The history of the black body as a figure of white fantasy and contempt is embedded in British culture, nowhere more or less than in the police canteen, among the last bastions of white, working-class male supremacy. In the prelude to the riots of the Eighties, police potency was constantly put on parade in street encounters with black men. The power of the badge, the uniform and the institution was mobilised to service not law and order but officers' masculinity and authority. The stop-and-search 'sus' law yielded little for the management of crime or the calming of communities but gave young white men many opportunities to overpower black men.

What had been a provocative and intrusive police presence in the Eighties was in the Nineties an experience of episodic, passive or capricious policing. When the police were jerked into action then the problem that had been caused by the lack of a police *service* became a problem of public *order* and police *force*.

The distinction between service and force holds the key to the decline of Britain. A passion for force, authority and competition became the currency of an entire era of domestic politics. They appeared to comprise what, in the Thatcherite mind, made the world go round. Coded accordingly, the nation was comprised only of individuals who were goodies or baddies. Competition was good. Crime was bad. Margaret Thatcher, when offering one of her most memorable mantras – 'there is no such thing as society' – improvised an ideology emptied of *social relations*, of classes, communities, cultures, generations and genders, races and regions, emptied, of course, of history and power. And yet, all these elements were vital and visible in the riots of 1991.

The New Right invoked government as a moral manager of visceral drives and original sin. Competition was, therefore, represented as the eternal energy that made the world go round, as liberation, while crime provided a perpetual alibi for authority and paranoia.

These values were echoed by young men patrolling the streets all over Britain. They well understood the potency of competition and any challenge to their authority was perceived as a crime against their reputation which could provoke the ultimate force.

The following chapters explore the ways that key terms like 'competition' and 'crime', 'service' and 'solidarity' shadowed the riots in 1991.

CHAPTER 7

Unfair Competition

Competition and crime defined the triumphs and tribulations of that key character in the Conservative chorus,
the shopkeeper. Small business was supposed to be the life
and soul of the party, the state and the economy in the political revolution initiated by Thatcherism. The shopkeeper was
like the housewife, endlessly invoked, though rarely admired;
given grandeur only in retrospect, for services rendered but not
particularly enjoyed. It was the *image* of the shopkeeper that
was important in Conservative ideology: as the representative
of capital in the community, as the shield of individualism
against collectivism, as being in the community but also
above it. Grantham's Alderman Roberts was, of course, the
archetype.

Though powered by *competition*, the shopkeeper was also
plagued by *crime*. Together they were a dynamic trinity in
the service of the 'authoritarian populism' that characterised
the Thatcher revolution. Theft was an occupational hazard for
the shopkeeper. The social contract between the trader and
the community carried both mutuality and an intimate and
unmediated suspicion. Unlike the relation between customers
and the corporate trader, proximity made this tension *personal*.

This relationship was, therefore, a caution to any sentimental notion of community as a homogenous, unified group with
a universal interest. In Conservative ideology the community
was only a context, a market. It was a space, not a society.
The citizen, by extension, was a consumer – a customer or a
thief. The trader was a merchant and a vigilante.

All these terms, *competition*, *crime* and *business*, hovered
subliminally over the Eighties and Nineties, organising our

moral circuits, our certainties about right and wrong. But
there was a rogue in the firmament, and it was *race*. It
disturbed the rank and meaning of competition, crime and
punishment. What was stable and self-evident in one currency
was destabilised in another. What if the shopkeeper was black?
How did Abdul Waheed's race affect the way competition and
crime worked for and against him? How did they define
his context? Why were the traders who were burned out
of Meadowell all Asians? Why didn't political commentators
hesitate in front of the questions? What we will see is a rush
to judgement.

A contrast between Agius and Waheed that was noted
among other Asian traders, but which did not filter into the
public debate, was carried in their complaint that they had to
work hard for their capital, and then exploit themselves and
their families. And yet still they were *envied*. They were harassed, and even then they were envied – what for? they asked
themselves. Race became a filter through which all of Abdul
Waheed's travails were reinterpreted. It was as if he was not
allowed to be the successful businessman that he was, nor
was he allowed to be a victim. His shop was successful. His
neighbour and rival, Agius the newsagent, was failing. But that
was never invoked in any discussion of their dispute. Indeed
Waheed's success as a businessman was represented by some
people locally as *unfair competition*. His ability to invest in
chilling and freezing equipment, to store more stock, to secure
his shop, all of this was the standard stuff of domestic disputes
between small shopkeepers and yet, in this case, seemed so
much the object of envy that it had to be explained away:
Waheed's capital investment was not allowed to be about
expansion based on trade, it was about exploitation.

The perception of the newsagent's problem was similarly
skewed: it was not seen as a business that was failing; it
was Waheed's fault – the newsagent was represented as the
victim of Waheed's success. Clearly a black man could not be
allowed to be better than a white man. But the relationship
between the two shops was constrained by a more or less

conventional covenant that was designed exactly to eliminate rivalry by engineering a clear division of labour. The covenant, introduced by the previous owner of both shops, limited what each could sell. Both Agius the newsagent and Waheed the grocer were buying that covenant when they bought their shops. That separation of functions should have enabled the shops to be mutually supportive neighbours rather than rivals.

The newsagent refused to abide by the covenant. When he began selling goods banned by his legal contract he presumably thought he could get away with it. Indeed he converted a legal challenge into a right, and then into a community campaign. When Waheed challenged the newsagent's breach of the covenant he was not perceived as legitimate and law-abiding but as a mean man. When the conflict went to court at the end of August the newsagent was required to abide by the covenant and to pay his neighbour £3,000 in compensation. The grocer was vindicated; he had been wronged. But the mythology prevailed: the newsagent was the victim and the grocer was the villain. A covenant designed to *control* competition was then represented as defending *unfair* competition.

'That's the racism that lies in all of this,' said REC director Rita Austin, 'to expect to do all this with immunity, to expect to get away with it because you are doing it to an Asian.' Of course, bouts of commercial attrition afflict small businesses, particularly during an economic recession. The night life of corner shops and restaurants is notoriously volatile and has always provided an alibi for those who need to insist that the hassle is not racism, that it is what happens with late-night shopping! People get pissed! Too much lager and vindaloo! 'As if being drunk was any excuse for breaking up a restaurant on a Friday night,' commented Rita Austin.

Ely's shopkeepers were trading in a hard-pressed neighbourhood where the frontier between commerce and crime is fragile and frequently crossed. In all economic ghettoes, where credit is debt, where a cash-flow crisis cannot be resolved by a credit card, a corner shop is a dangerous place. In the Eighties, the rise of impoverished neighbourhoods all over the United

States and Britain brought with it a new orthodoxy. On both sides of the Atlantic, Asian and Korean traders' self-defence in these economic war zones has been deemed aggressive, hard and over-the-top. And so it was with Abdul Waheed. Before the riot, it had become the consensus that Waheed had wished trouble upon himself by his 'hard' treatment of suspected shoplifters. When he locked a suspected shop-lifter in by flicking a security switch, and when he called the police, the man threw himself out of the window and escaped. In the story's circulation around the estate, the star, the window-breaker, was reincarnated as a boy rather than a man. That made him a more suitable victim. And Waheed's tactics against theft were reframed as aggression.

During the weekend campaign outside his shop, the demand that he had to go because he was unpopular hardly held up. 'If he was that unpopular,' commented one police officer, 'why didn't people vote with their feet? People weren't *forced* to go to his shop.' Rita Austin reckoned that once again there was an implicit assumption that Waheed should let anyone get away with anything, including stealing. 'This is racism. The belief is that shoplifters can get away with it with impunity.' Police officers who had tracked the shopkeeper's life and times in Ely agreed. 'Why was he regarded as unpopular? Because he wouldn't have it. That's it, in a sentence,' said one officer. 'Shopkeepers in Ely had a rough time, but Asian shopkeepers had a rougher time than their white counterparts. Fact.'

So, race was the factor around which moral certainties imploded, when a suspected thief became a goodie and Waheed became a baddie. The window-leaper was transformed into a martyr, whose heroic flight attached the virtue of desperation to his metamorphosis into a victim. There was no point at which Waheed's *class* as shopkeeper secured for him the moral high ground. His *race* was always mobilised to put him in moral jeopardy. The case against him always depended on a denial of his *class* relationship with competition and crime.

'Sometimes it is difficult to say what is the motivation, or whether the aggravation is racist, because it won't be written all over it,' said a Cardiff police officer. 'The police will want to say that white shopkeepers suffer problems, too. But it's a fact that the vast majority of late-night shops are run by Asians. It's also a fact that they put up with a hell of a lot. There's a shop surrounded by barbed wire, video cameras over the chiller; you think to yourself: it's a corner shop, for Christ's sake! Anyway, are you telling me that if Waheed had been white the incidents would have been so extreme? I'd have to say no. It gave people a way of letting racism escape.'

By fortifying his shop, Waheed forfeited support precisely because he affirmed his confidence in his class and a clarity about his customers – he was behaving like a shopkeeper. He was not even a trader who Asianised his environment, his was a Heinz-and-Hovis shop. But he knew a racially motivated attack when it hit him in the face, or in the pocket. His refusal to be victimised, which was registered in police records if nowhere else, was apparently too challenging. Even Agius, a white man, had a story to tell. In another conversation with the REC, after the riot, he distanced himself from racism as an issue by revealing that he too suffered racist taunts – he was Maltese – but that he shrugged them off. Rita Austin assured him that no one should have to put up with it. The community's consciousness of itself, of what it was capable of doing, of what people had to put up with, was untouched by the experience of racism. Waheed's story was censored, the space into which he could speak was rationed, and no one in the community felt any responsibility to *represent* him. His voice was hardly heard in the calumny which brought riot police to the streets of Cardiff for the first time since the Second World War.

That he was a Pakistani did not necessarily make it a race riot, but the *relevance* of race was evident: everyone went on and on about it. In the repetition, Abdul Waheed's ethnic origin was inescapable; it was endlessly invoked during the riot and yet instantly repudiated afterwards.

Ely's political leaders had not hesitated in the face of this contradiction. None of them felt the need to stop and think, to consult him and create a space in which he could speak.

The only two agencies that had been informed by Waheed's experience were *outside* Ely: the REC, not surprisingly, and the police.

Such was the strength of the drift towards denial, however, that the police were caught by it, too. According to a police statement in the *South Wales Echo* on 2 September, the rioters were of 'different races and the trouble was not racial . . . There are no racist undertones.' But the force itself had recorded the events that detonated the violence against Waheed's shop on 28 August as being racially motivated. They subsequently recorded another nine racially motivated incidents in the month after the riot as being directly attributable to the 'Ely effect'.

Police managers had been urged by their advisers to play down the racist element, though not to deny it. Apart from the fact that the focus of the riots had shifted away from Mr Waheed to the police themselves, the police sought to influence Pakistanis who might feel bound to respond to his troubles. The police had heard reports of Pakistanis making their way to South Wales, and in any case that weekend there was the hockey international in Cardiff. The black community in the city had already done its bit. The REC was enrolled to calm them. However much Rita Austin might have wanted to stand by her own people, and however much she wanted them to stand up for themselves, her *function* was mobilised to pacify them.

The police statement played down the racism in the riots in the hope of pre-empting a response from visitors. Neither the police nor the REC wanted young black vigilantes descending to defend Waheed. The propaganda was directed at black people, not at white people. This suggested the paralysis the institutions felt in the face of a white crowd. There was only one protagonist in the public debate that day who was insisting on the relevance of racism, who was drawing attention not only to Waheed's travails as a black trader, but to the behaviour of a community's *white* crowd. But the distinction between minimising and denying had escaped police managers.

Although the BBC Television news in Wales at 6 p.m. included white politicians, a pre-recorded interview with Austin was not shown. It was, apparently, lost. The BBC resorted instead to broadcasting an audio tape of her words. Strangely, she was described as an 'Asian community leader', something that she was not. None of the white, male politicians were described as a 'white community leader' ...

Assistant Chief Constable Bob Evans was alerted to the error by his advisers – the police *must not* make a denial. Evans went on television and acknowledged that there had been a racist element. Throughout the disturbances, Rita Austin was the only person to engage in an *argument* about what that might mean and why it might be important. There had not been a 'race riot' in Ely in the sense of a set-piece confrontation between black and white youth, she said. But she found it 'disgraceful' that the underlying racism in the whole saga had been denied, particularly by the Reverend Bob Morgan. As the local councillor, chair of the County Council and for ten years chair of the County Council's race advisory committee, he would have known the guidelines laid down by the Association of Chief Police Officers and the Home Office about the recording of 'racial attacks'.

Politicians did not seem to think Waheed himself or his experience was worth representing. Rhodri Morgan announced on television that he didn't know exactly what was meant by a racial attack. To help him, the REC faxed a reading list – including two Home Affairs Select Committee reports available in the House of Commons library.

The Labour politicians had apparently not apprehended what the most conservative agency, the police, already had in its filing cabinets: the evidence of racially motivated incidents, including the riot. The irony was that political pressure had been more effective within the police than within either the community itself or the political parties: the reform of the system of recording, and therefore *naming* racial motivation. That had placed the power of *interpretation* with the victim as well as with the police. The effect had been dramatic – reporting of racially motivated incidents increased by two hundred per cent in Cardiff in 1991. Records held by the police, therefore, dramatised the prevalence of racism more than those of any other white institution in the city. The irony was amplified when, several months later, the Labour leaders were still minimising racial motivation while the Crown Prosecution Service mobilised it as an 'aggravating circumstance' when Ely's riot trials came to court in 1992.

Home Office guidelines oblige the CPS to cite racism as an 'aggravating circumstance', but the CPS may only do so if it has been filed by the police in their record of an event. The prosecution's recruitment of racism to fortify its case against rioters in the Crown Court vindicated the rigorous record-keeping by the police's Ethnic Affairs Unit at Butetown.

But the potency of the record was always only a potential – the archive of racial attacks in Ely did not necessarily influence police practice as keepers of the peace and protectors of people and property. The responsibility to *record* did not carry an equivalent responsibility to *prevent* racial attack.

There were no arrests on the day that detonated the Ely riot, the Thursday when Waheed tried a citizen's arrest of a shoplifter. There had been no strategy to challenge the racist tenor of the crowd over the weekend. Finally there was a chorus of denial by both police and politicians. And yet there it was in the record.

'The police denied evidence of racism and then miraculously offered it for the CPS and the trial,' commented Rita Austin. 'White agencies will ignore or invoke racism as it suits their purpose and not when it reflects black experience.'

The economic – if not the existential – consequences for Asian traders were serious. Their insurance premia rocketed in the wake of racial attacks. Amidst Waheed's personal tribulations, his insurance company insisted that he barricade his business even more before they would agree to renewing his cover.

When Waheed reported this to Austin she contacted his

insurance broker and much to her surprise found herself having 'the best conversation I had with anyone during the riots. I had fully expected to have a very robust talk, but I found myself having a conversation with a most helpful young man who was appalled at what had happened to Mr Waheed and promised to get on to his insurance company immediately to get his cover reinstated. I had tears in my eyes when I put the phone down.'

None of this touched the political domain, where the Reverend Bob Morgan ruggedly denied not just the racism but whether it mattered. He returned to the row with a provocative *riposte* a week after the riot: 'Only ignorant outsiders see race as a community issue in Ely.' Did he know what he was saying? Did he know that Ely was one of the significant sites of racially motivated incidents in the city? And did he know how the deployment of 'outsider' as a pejorative term would sound in a city that had been home to some of the early black communities in Britain? The poignancy was not lost on the person at whom his remark was targeted: Rita Austin, whose family had belonged to the West Bengal intelligentsia, whose mother was an academic and whose father, one of India's progressive lawyers, finally became the Attorney General. Austin had been schooled in the ways of the British and had lived her adult life in England and Wales. 'I don't object to being called an outsider, I'm comfortable with that, it is essentially what I am. But ignorant I am not.'

Ely's political representatives could have used the public domain to create a political space in which the community could contemplate what had happened to itself. Instead, they defended themselves and the community from a penumbra of 'outsiders'. Waheed did not appear to be numbered among the politicians' constituents because his story was never to be told by his elected representatives. It fell to another Asian, Rita Austin – who had been an insider when she was a member of the Country Council with Reverend Bob – to interpolate Waheed's experience into the public debate. When she did so she was met with another repudiation. Against the outsiders

were the motley of insiders, who ranged from rioters to politicians, and who were united only by their denial of the black
experience.

Labourism once again minimised the importance of political
debate as an environment for collective self-discovery. And
it also dissembled the experiences of 'the other'. Labourism,
typically, operated in Ely as a landlord and a lobbyist to secure
a leisure centre here and a library there. Politics buried the
evidence of racism beneath a more comfortable discourse –
that of poverty, unemployment, jobs and housing – which
confirmed Labourism in its role as a begetter and the
community as a beneficiary, rather than as a political subject
in itself.

Ely's ethnic minorities, four per cent of its population,
matched the national average. Ely could, therefore, be seen as a
paradigm. All that irrationality and denial was a benchmark by
which to measure the limits of British cosmopolitanism. South
Wales ports had been blessed with a visible and stalwart black
community from the Middle East and the Caribbean ever since
the middle of the nineteenth century. They had been subjected
to political and moral panics, crusades against black and white
men and women consorting with each other, and campaigns
against their right to work. Corralled around the docks in
Butetown and Barry, the black communities expanded during
the coal bonanza that made Cardiff briefly but massively rich.
They grew again during the Second World War.

However, what the Welsh historian Neil Evans has described
as 'probably the most violent race riot to occur in Britain' hit
the Cardiff black community in 1919, leaving three people
dead. During the Twenties and Thirties, the black neighbourhoods built their own networks and organisations while white
workers campaigned to ban black people from the seafaring
and firefighting unions, supported by the local Labour Party.
The local authorities were reluctant to offer relief to destitute
seafarers. A government Aliens Order required black citizens
to register with the police – from being British subjects they
were suddenly required to report regularly to the police. 'Being

black and British had become almost impossible.'[1] A couple of generations later the city's police told a government select committee: 'there is no record of any serious disturbance involving the indigenous and immigrant population.'[2] Evans has argued that although Cardiff probably had the biggest black presence in Britain before the Second World War, 'there is little for the city to be proud of in the way that minorities have been treated, and often the unions and Labour Party branches have played an all too active role in discrimination.' A determination to deny racism is part of Cardiff's cultural history.

In the wake of this history it was not surprising that the debate about the Ely riot was preoccupied by whether it was about race at all, when it needed to ask a different question: what was the riot about if it was not about race? It is a peculiar fact of British politics and criminal justice that when it comes to racism and sexism it is reluctant to rely on the evidence of the victim, preferring instead the protestations of the perpetrator. In no other categories of offending would the denials of the accused be so readily believed.

Meadowell provided another model of denial. Once again, people protested that the attack on the traders could not have been racist because Ladbroke's, the bookies, was among the wrecked shops. But Ladbroke's didn't live there! Ladbroke's was a business, not a person. The Asian traders lived above their shops, they were citizens of Meadowell. Like any small shopkeeper at the nub of a neighbourhood they might have been expected to know its secrets, its habits, its proclivities. And they did on the Monday teatime, hours before the riot: a petrol-bombed shopkeeper contacted Northumbria police ethnic affairs unit and shared his worries about the attack he had

---

[1] Neil Evans, 'Regulating the Reserve Army: Arabs, Blacks and the Local State in Cardiff, 1919–45' in Kenneth Lunn, ed., *Race and Labour in Twentieth-Century Britain*, London, 1985.
[2] Neil Evans, 'The South Wales Race Riots of 1919' in *Llafur*, the Journal for the Study of Welsh Labour History, vol. 3, no. 1, Spring 1980.

endured the night before and about attacks to come. He knew something else was about to happen. That information was passed on but did not penetrate the police planning of the operation to protect the people of Meadowell. When, several hours later in the middle of the evening, the fires were lit and the petrol bombs were thrown, police protection was not in place. It took several more hours before enough officers had been mobilised to move in on Meadowell.

A black trader's *personal* experience did not, therefore, inspire a plan that might have safeguarded not only the black traders but the neighbourhood as a whole. Either there could have been evacuation of the traders or the mobilisation of police personnel could have begun there and then. Evacuation did not arise, apparently because the area had been designated in the police mind as purely commercial. That allowed the Meadowell operation to become a military manoeuvre across terrain as if it were peopled only by warriors.

Neither was a black trader's professional experience allowed to inform what was known about a white estate. That rejection was compounded by the Balkanisation of police structures, which led to the containment of something known about the traders – that they lived above their shops. The Meadowell riot was a bid to take territory from the police. But once its initial motivation had metamorphosed, the riot found other targets, and as one senior officer put it, ruefully, 'in the heart of the riot, racism surfaced.' One of Meadowell's Labour councillors, Rita Stringfellow, agreed: 'The racist element was played down, probably because it did not spark off the riots. But the riots enabled the prejudice to come out.'

The discussion of racism was subjected to a self-imposed embargo by the media in the North East. That silenced what should have been a drama of self-discovery for a region where racism is displayed with a certain pride. It meant that Tyneside could not learn how black people had felt fear, and how they had developed strategies for survival.

The 1991 riot certainly detonated the conventional wisdom that the region had up to then been spared riots because it was

– or rather saw itself as – white. 'Local politicians and police officers explained the lack of rioting in the North East during the 1980s purely in terms of race,' argues a criminologist from Durham University, Dick Hobbs.[3] 'Conversations with senior police officers during the winter of 1990–91 consistently explained [away] the region's lack of a major public order problem with the lack of a coherent, visible black population. "Blacks equal trouble" was a sentiment cited to me on several occasions,' he added.

Clearly, these officers had been talking to the wrong people. A retired teacher in Elswick explains, 'I'm an educated person, I think positively, but when people shout at me – Paki, black bastard, nigger, blackie, darkie, we hear it virtually every day – my heart feels like a smashed windscreen.'

A retired Sikh elder in the West End was so fearful when the riots moved from Meadowell to Newcastle that he did not leave his home for two days. 'It was a very scary time. I slept for only a couple of hours, and I didn't go out of the house for a couple of days. Then I had to go out for food. The councillor, Nigel Todd, came to see me. He was an encouragement, and my relatives telephoned all the time. My brother came over to take me away but I said I wouldn't leave my house, I'd rather die than come back on my own and find it burned down – I've lived here for nearly forty years.

'We can never leave the house empty. My wife and I never go out together because if we do the place is ransacked.' Every door in the house has been fitted with locks. 'We've had all our doors broken. When they wreck the place we have to pay £200 for a new front door – you come back to the house and find it lying in the lobby.' His street used to have half a dozen Asian households. Most have moved out. 'It's because some harassment happens every day. It all got much worse a year or so before the riots.'

A translator, fluent in several languages, has lived in the

[3] Dick Hobbs, 'A White Riot or The Sound of Breaking Class: Meadowell, 1991' in *Youth and Policy*, no. 37, Tyne and Wear, 1992.

West End for twenty-five years but says she would leave, if only she could sell her house in one of Scotswood's terraced streets. 'This is a prison. We feel we are being watched all the time. They wait for us to go out. The other day the young people in the street were smashing the street lights. I phoned the police and the next day when I went out they were shouting, "That's the fucking lady who called the police." So, what's the point? The neighbours are scared to phone the police because then people would know, and they'd be in trouble. All of our people are sick of life because of these troubles.'

Asian, Chinese and Vietnamese teenagers brought up in Scotswood and Elswick plan their routes as they make their way around their neighbourhoods. There are certain places and bus routes some of them boycott. They are tactical about their movement and their networks – what they do not enjoy in the place they live is freedom of movement. 'The thing I hate most is when people spit at you,' says a sad fourteen-year-old Muslim girl who lives in Elswick. A white girl recalled the time her mother had helped a black woman on the bus: 'She sat the woman's baby on her knee and then this man started shouting at her and calling her all the names under the sun.' A sixteen-year-old British Asian girl who goes to school in one of the West End's middle-class areas explains, 'You hang around with the Sharons and Trevors, the tough ones at school, because you have to stay alive and in one piece and they are your protection.' She adds, 'If they get angry they'll be racist, too, but you have to be strategic, you either have nothing to do with them or hang out with them.' She told her parents she wanted to go to martial arts classes. 'I want to learn karate,' she said. 'I want to save my life.'

Some eight-year-old friends at West End primary schools complain, 'The bullies pinch your hairbands and fight you and call you racist things like darkie and blackie. If you tell the teacher, they say, "Look at the grassers."' They are taken to their youth club in an elegant, black mini bus belonging to the Asian community which used to bear the title Black Youth Association. The word 'Black' has been removed. 'We took it off because we got so much hassle,' says the driver, a woman who came to the city from Pakistan fifteen years ago. 'When white kids see the van we get trouble. They bang the door, they kick the door, they throw stones, they break its windows, they shout at us if we are delivering children to their homes. Newcastle is horrible now. Children in the street shout and swear at me; they shout, "Bloody blackie! What are you doing here, you blackie bastard?" I never shout back, I try to understand how they feel, but inside I am really hurting.'

A black teenager in Meadowell says, 'They call me blackie and nigger. And they call my cousin goofy and fuzzy-hair. My mam has already been to my school about it because kids blackmail me and say things like, "If you grass on us we'll fill you in." There's been conversations about racism in assembly and the heads tells us, "I will not have racialist remarks," but it doesn't make any difference. They beat up my sister – they broke her jaw. I used to like school but I don't any more. I want to move.' Her friend, a white girl aged thirteen going on a hundred, adds, 'We've broken friends with half the people.' With a tired, bitter voice she says, 'I can't stand it, I just can't stand it.'

CHAPTER 8

Space and Power

The recruitment of active citizens for law and order, by the engagement of communities in crime prevention, became the Government's primary law and order innovation in the Eighties. Neighbourhoods were not to take the law into their own hands, but they were to be the eyes and ears whose vigilance would be rewarded by a rapid response from the police, and whose cooperation would help catch criminals. That was the theory behind Neighbourhood Watch. The scheme was to borrow several politically neutral or mobile themes for the dominant discourse of law and order. It enclosed concepts of community, neighbourhood, self-help and fear within its own circuit. Crime was outside, outcast, other.

Neighbourhood Watch was launched in 1982. In terms of growth, it was phenomenally successful and reached eighty thousand schemes, covering four million homes, in 1990, although by then chief constables were resisting their expansion – apparently at a rate of six hundred a week – because of their claim on police resources.[1]

The watch schemes were one of the few contexts in which the Government conceded the concept of community. Like community care, a way of emptying hospitals, its ideological force was its anti-Statism. Its economic merit was that it cut costs, or rather that it redistributed costs from Government-funded institutions to individuals citizens who were increasing driver to fortify their own homes. The potency of Neighbourhood Watch was that it reverberated with nostalgic echoes of the

[1] Les Johnston, *The Rebirth of Private Policing*, Routledge, London, 1992.

night watch, it was an ideological wedding between community and protection, between security and surveillance. In practice it was neither about community nor about crime because it could not cope with the consequences for citizens and communities alike of crime in their midst.

The Conservatives had traditionally traded in fear. Law and order had been Conservatism's political forte. Just as in hospital operations and love, everyone felt they were experts in law and order. Women's fear of men, coded in the 'men are beasts' *patois* that circulated around the Tories' private networks, had always found a voice in Tory rhetoric. Indeed, the hangers and floggers, the hell's grannies who embarrassed the Tory enlightenment during the period between the Second World War and the rise of the New Right, were the historic spine of popular Conservatism. Their visceral cries for revenge against 'hooligans', 'vandals' and 'child molesters' were sustained by *personal* fears, grounded in mass experience. Fraud never attracted the opprobrium of the law and order lobby unless it was spectacular in scale. White-collar crime attracted empathy rather than outrage. But calls for law and order were always fuelled by panic about the integrity and safety of the person, a panic that its exponents perversely projected *out there* and yet sensed also in their midst.

Neighbourhood Watch could not navigate its way around the phantoms and realities of local crime. It was predicated on the assumption that crime against property was incidental and opportunist and came from outside. It was, therefore, a pessimistic project which could not promise any greater police presence in besieged neighbourhoods. The paranoia behind Neighbourhood Watch and community policing was fixated on 'stranger danger'. It echoed the postwar panic that *public* places were the dangerous places, full of strangers and surprises. 'Stranger danger' minimised the sense of safety that could be promised by public space, by visibility, tolerance, cooperation and collectivity.

Stranger danger undoubtedly attracted real fears, but assigned them to *places*. The *perpetrators* could, of course, have been anywhere, everywhere. But popular dreads were assigned to open and shared space rather than the mythic sanctuary of the home. It was assumed that danger lived in public places, not in the private domain. The weirdo waving his willy in the park, who was the classic object of parental fear and loathing, was more likely to be an ordinary dad abusing his wife or children at home. Home may be a frightening prison for a battered woman. The neighbourhood may feel like a prison to residents, a local landscape is as likely to be endangered by members of its own community as by any intruders. The lads who take over the streets and refuse to share them are sponsoring a lacuna which is filled with such a sense of threat that it is evacuated by their neighbours. Typically, Ely, Blackbird Leys, Meadowell, Elswick and Scotswood had already been the site of a struggle over young men's criminality and control over their shared streets. Since Neighbourhood Watch was predicated on the protection of communities from intruders, not insiders, as a mode of crime prevention it had shown no stamina for the conflicts of interest which may shatter neighbourhoods' abilities to look after themselves. Nor could Neighbourhood Watch and community policing cope with the difficulties of places overwhelmed by economic desperation, and therefore by petty crime.

In the year before the 1991 riots, despite the impressive four million households covered by schemes, there was the sharpest increase in recorded crime since records began in 1857. The notion heralded by the Home Office minister, John Patten, that the schemes were reuniting communities and cutting crime at the same time was shattered – Neighbourhood Watch was, it seemed, neither here nor there. The postwar annual rate of increase in crime in general of about five per cent had grown, by the end of the Eighties, into a sixteen-per-cent increase in theft, an eighteen-per-cent increase in burglary and a twelve-per-cent increase in criminal damage.

Crime might be personal or it might be business. It could be casual, opportunist or organised. In the year before the riots in Tyneside there were forty ram-raids, a North Eastern speciality: warehouses, sports shops, electrical goods shops – located at industrial estates or in shopping centres – had their shutters and windows rammed. Ram-raids were an audacious modernisation of the old principle of smash-and-grab. One of the most spectacular ram-raids happened only months before the Tyneside riots, on 21 May 1991, when thieves drove their car through a domed mall at the Gateshead Metro Centre, having burst through the entrance and into the mall, and rammed the vehicle into the shutters of an electrical goods store. A group of men poured out, dashed into the store, aimed swiftly for the electrical goods they wanted, noticed the security camera on their way out and smashed that, too.

In the Nineties the Government was deeply embarrassed by the inexorable rise in crime to record levels. This was despite the massive expansion of public vigilance through the medium of Neighbourhood Watch, and despite investment in the police – the one public service agency to enjoy an enthusiastic mandate from the Government. Having exempted only the police from its stranglehold over most other public agencies, it was virtually alone at the beginning of the decade in failing to face what everyone else already knew, including the police themselves: that they were not able to do their job properly. The major victims were people living economically *in extremis*, in places like Meadowell and Scotswood. But the citizens' efforts to engage the police in their problem were disappointed. Their failure expressed a political blockage at every level, from the personal to the political: there was no mechanism, whether by personal complaint or by political pressure through the police authority, that could guarantee a response. There was no device which could influence whether there would be an investigation, or the mode of intervention.

Neither Neighbourhood Watch nor community policing was designed to cope with domestic violence or strategic theft. It was known that ram-raiders were 'known' in their areas, but in the absence of a police service that was, in the words of the Scarman report, 'firm and flexible', these communities had enjoyed little or no service from the police. They felt engulfed by a criminalised coterie. Diligent detection depended on the cooperation of communities who had felt abandoned by the police, and who reciprocated by giving little or no information about the criminals of whom they were afraid. This is not to describe those entire communities as criminalised – police and state agencies had done precisely that and then walked away from them, leaving the neighbourhoods to survive as best they might against forces that the police themselves would not or could not confront. It is to say, however, that neither the constabulary nor community policing, nor crime prevention initiatives like Neighbourhood Watch, lent their support to citizens who were trying to survive crime and its oppressive cultures of domination. The riots were only a matter of scale: they were how scores were settled.

Meadowell did not need Neighbourhood Watch. People knew what was going on, they were familiar with the power of the criminal fraternity. The lads ensured that the graffiti announced who was innocent and who was guilty. Some man up for murder in the week of the riot was, of course, deemed to be innocent; some man up on sex offences was a pervert; some girl was a slag; some person was a grass.

The lads in neighbourhoods in every hard-pressed estate in Britain adhered to a cult of honour and loyalty which exempted them from everything that demanded responsibility. At the same time it conscripted a communal complicity – everyone kept *their* secrets for them. It was the ancient solidarity of silence. The injunction against being a grass was sustained by a long history of class solidarity that was contingent on an economic ethic: the working class could accommodate respectable villainy, it could forgive fugitives from the class enemy, those whose crimes came from poverty and whose pillage afflicted only the privileged.

The cult of honour also positioned the villain as a victim. The poor boys had a point, of course: they were victims. But the helpless heroes were also villains whose freedom of movement was never to be impaired, whose tyranny in the streets brooked no challenge. Their solidarity was exclusive.

A measure of their power in these neighbourhoods was the extent to which almost everyone felt silenced. Active citizens, mainly women, who had witnessed the riots refused to give evidence against the rioters because they *knew* they could not name names and remain in their community. For these citizens their community was synonymous with their social being, they could not think of leaving it. The police would only offer them safe passage out, apparently they could not offer protection within. Their safety depended on the solidarity of the other women and the strong-arm of a man in the family. If they had neither, they were doomed. Neighbourhood Watch and a community bobby combined could not take care of them.

It was significant that in the Meadowell trials which took place a year after the riots only those people who had fled the estate identified culprits in court. Potential witnesses who had given statements about the riots to the police usually refused to give evidence to the court. 'They tried to pressure us into giving evidence, but I said no, because I would be putting my bairns in danger. No way could we be witnesses in open court,' said one resident.

The police were aware that people lived in fear and they were painfully aware of their inability to help them. 'It is a matter of concern, whether we can reduce the fear of intimidation,' acknowledged Superintendent Eric Lewis in Tyneside. Again, the primary instruments of connecting localities to the police, Neighbourhood Watch and community policing, could not withstand the pressure people had to endure.

Before and after the riots, residents who might bear witness became *suspects* in their own space; their property was attacked, their persons were abused in the streets. Potential witnesses in the riot trials needed no reminding of the rioters' power to damage and brutalise, because they had seen it all before. The lads' power, together with their paranoia, had well-known effects. Paranoia might be excited by nothing more than the facts of city life – having neighbours, being seen, being known. Everything that was supposed to be sublime about an urban community became unsafe. Being seen might mean being watched. Having a telephone might mean owning the means to grass. On one of the estates a young woman, among the few in her street to have a telephone, was fingered as a target after the riots, apparently because she had the means and because she was vulnerable. Her windows were broken and her children were threatened. On another estate dead animals – a cat, a bird – were dumped in one family's porch and a fire was lit at another family's front door. A woman well known in another neighbourhood was walking to the shop when a car aimed straight at her and knocked her down. 'Fucking grasser!' shouted the voices in the car. These women were targeted because they had at some time challenged the lads.

The police could not offer protection to the people *they* needed. Nor could they offer support to people whose status as victims often slipped into the status of symbolic culprits on the poor estates – single mothers. They became the point at which Conservative moralism met monetarism: they were the *undeserving* poor of their time, a part of the community whose stamina was unseen, whose vulnerability was rebuffed and whose needs were used as an accusation against them. The single mother, in her demonisation as 'problem family', united the theorists of the 'underclass' as the rough rabble outside society, on both the Right and the Left.

In a neighbourhood where distinctions between ally and enemy had disintegrated, a person did not need to 'grass' to catch trouble: a person needed only to be alone. 'We are seeing attacks on single parents just because they're vulnerable,' said Joe Caffrey, a former shipyard worker turned community worker in Scotswood. 'It's just because they are available for attack. They don't have men to protect them from men. They don't have other networks, other men in their family, to be deterrents. It's not that these women are inadequate, which is what the underclass theory argues, it's just that they're vulnerable.' A lawyer who often represents poor women reckoned that 'unless you're tough and hold your own, unless you have big male relatives, you get shat on.'

A divorced mother who was rehoused on Tyneside with

her child recalled her fearful reception by the lads. 'When I first came to live on my estate I had to take my bairn to hospital regularly, but I could never stay with her overnight: I couldn't leave my house for long – because of the break-ins. My house has been broken into that many times, I've lost count. They took food, ornaments, a television, video. I was not insured because you can't get insurance round here, it's a high-risk estate. The people breaking into houses know that.

'Once I just felt like smashing my house up myself and setting it alight. I couldn't stand it. They threw flour all over everything. At the time I wasn't working, I was living on £32, plus child benefit. However, I had no debts – I couldn't afford to have debts.

'It began in 1988. I came home from my job – I was working in a shop. The bairn was at my mam's, and I found the window put out and the back door kicked in. Everything was smashed up and even the beds were stolen. They took the bairn's school uniform, too. I called the coppers from a friend's house and they came round after about half an hour. The police just laughed. They couldn't believe it. I was so upset I could have whacked them – but then I thought better not because then I would have got charged. After that the bairn slept on the settee and I slept on the floor. It took me about three years to replace the beds.

'I found out why they did it. They just wanted to get me off the estate. No other reason. Apparently they did that to everybody, just to show how tough they really are. It drives you mad.'

Single parents or women fleeing from their husbands are unloaded as emergency cases on the hard-pressed estates where they command no respect, especially from the lads who are their contemporaries. Joe Caffrey concluded that there is 'a real problem about roving boys – nobody knows what to do with them. The youth and community service hardly recognise the problem in most places, so they don't target that problem group. In the Seventies the way the lads targeted their aggression was different; it would be directed somewhere else.

Now they're screwing their own people. These lads gravitate towards the vulnerable young lasses.'

Often the lads become parochial itinerants, going home to change, or to eat, or collect a Giro, while nesting in other women's houses, often those of young mothers whose parental responsibilities exile them from the culture of their own generation, and who are glad of some company. A young woman in the West End of Newcastle regarded a group of lads as her mates. They used to gather in her back garden where they would bring out bags of glue and get high. They more or less moved in. They would come for a coffee, watch television or stay the night on the sofa. She knew that they were into stealing cars and this and that.

A few weeks before the riots she was horrified when one of the lads came round with a ring and a radio – he'd stolen them from one of the women nearby, well known as a nice woman and one of the neighbourhood's active citizens. 'I told him never to bring stuff like that back into my house.' When the neighbour had returned to her house one afternoon with her children following a meeting nearby, she found she had been robbed and rushed into the street to find the culprits. A couple of her friends chased them into a pub: one of them, a man, followed a lad into the gents' toilets and kicked the door open, while one of the women grabbed hold of the lad. Watched by friends and foes, this woman dragged him across the road to the victim's door. One of the friends recalled, 'It had been kicked in – the kids were screaming and the house was wrecked. She had hold of him and made him look. "Look! That's what youse are doing!" she said. By then the other lads had wandered over and they were watching. Usually the lads are not confronted.'

After that incident, the lads still kept coming round to the young woman, though not with the prizes stolen from her neighbours. On the Thursday the riots came to Scotswood, she popped out to the shops with her friends and their babies. Suddenly she heard a screeching car outside. 'I ran out of the shop and collected my child. I looked up and saw a white

Astra speeding up and down, directly outside the post office. There was blue smoke coming from both the front and rear wheels. What he was doing was extremely dangerous – there were several people in the area at the time, including mothers with small children. I was only a matter of yards from where he was performing his stupid antics and the car came to a halt directly adjacent to me.' Later she saw the lads throwing bottles and bricks at the police. She knew them. They were her visitors.

That night one of the roving boys came knocking on her door, hoping he would let her in – he was on a court curfew. She refused. The following day one of them got into the house anyway, through a back window, and left a bag in one of her cupboards. When she looked, she guessed it had been stolen from the post office. In the small hours of the next morning another of the roving boys came knocking on her door, looking for somewhere to sleep. Reluctantly, she let him in. The next morning, one of the lads was banging on the front door. He rushed past her into her house and reported to the other slumbering rover that he had just stolen a handbag and dumped it in the back gardens. Minutes later the police arrived and found one of the lads in her sitting room and the other hiding in the airing cupboard.

Often, women bringing up children alone had to put up with encampments of roving boys outside their homes shouting at them because, unlike this young mother, they would not welcome them inside. One young woman in the West End kept a bucket to store the stones thrown through her windows. If you could not beat them, it seemed, you could not join them either – because you were a girl – but you could let them in. A young woman who moved into Scotswood with her baby had her house squatted, in effect, by the lads. Six or ten of them would 'visit' with a bag of cans, drink, and throw the cans out of the window. 'She really tried to look after herself,' said one of her neighbours; but she could not get rid of the lads. To get clear of them she had to get clear of the neighbourhood.

No one was free from the culture of intimidation and

hassle. Some Meadowell children talked about the things they put up with and the things which would make a difference to their lives:

'It would be better if people didn't fight, if there was no biting or kicking or pushing or strangling.'

'People go away when somebody tries to burgle them. Somebody burgled our house and they took the bread; smashed the window and the front door; they took every single thing out of the house – my computer, the beds, the curtains, all the ornaments.'

'The bad man was in the bushes and went shuffle shuffle. The bad man took our baby away. The bad man said, "Do you want a sweet?" and he said, "Come with me," and where they went he said "You're not getting a sweet, you're getting killed."'

'I saw a man taking a child away because he'd been shooting birds.'

'It would be better if the big lads would not kick or be naughty, and if people talked to each other and you could say, "Please don't nip me" and they would say, "I'm sorry."'

The criminal fraternities were well known on the troubled estates. They belonged to small networks, often only a handful of extended families, fortified by their access not only to an arsenal – guns, crossbows, catapults – but also to a battalion of cousins and uncles, and, orbiting around them, their courtiers, admirers and apprentices. 'Newcastle has always had a reputation for hard crime,' says Elswick councillor Nigel Todd, 'and there have always been West End families connected with crime. But it's changing, it's recruiting more people. It's a business. Young people of sixteen and seventeen can't get social security benefit. They are supposed to be taken on by training schemes, but there aren't enough places, so there is a body of people who can be exploited – they're the criminals' footsoldiers. The way the syllabus works is from joyriding to ram-raiding.' Their alleged enemies were their neighbours, the school dinner ladies, the chip shop ladies and catalogue ladies, the men in the bookies, anyone who might challenge them. 'The lads can control the philosophy of an estate just by intimidation,' said a Meadowell youth worker.

Neighbourhood Watch and community policing rose with the economic decline of neighbourhoods all over Britain, but neither system responded to the impact of that crisis on estates whose social space was increasingly regulated by organised crime and masculine tyrannies.

This has created a crisis of spatial democracy in neighbourhoods. 'The lads thought they *owned* the shopping centre, it was their territory,' said one of the Scotswood women. 'After six o'clock very few people went out on foot, if only just to the chippie. Even the police used to *drive* through.'

There is always a spatial dimension to a power struggle, and here it was in the streets. 'Men and women are only as free as they are mobile,' says a geographer from London University, Bill Hillier, who has definitively mapped the daily movement of men and women across their communities. 'Men are always trying to immobilise women. Women create networks around a landscape: they tend to grow their networks outwards, by movement, by contacts. Men make theirs through formal associations, with rules of entry: you've got to be one of the boys. Men make formal associations, women make open associations.' Having hijacked public space, these local imperialists create lacunae, they sponsor vacant blots which everyone else evacuates. What was once shared space becomes a colony.

Community policing had not risen to this challenge of informal intimidation and spatial tyranny. A police tendency in some of the peripheral white estates has been to maximise the sense of danger to themselves and minimise the danger to the community itself. What they therefore did not seek was a more penetrating but subtle alliance with the community. The aura around these lads misted both their danger to their own kin and their dependence on their community in general and their mothers in particular. 'For every lad who is a nasty little shit there is a mother at home who loves him. So there will be no love lost for the police,' suggested a Tyneside lawyer. 'The reality is that the police find it very hard to make any meaningful links. The police don't think in terms of meaningful communication with the community in this kind of context. They blame the mothers.' The fact that communities and families do not ostracise or evict their criminalised children, or rather their sons, is forgotten in the lament, interminably invoked, that Britain's poor places are impoverished because of the failure of the family. But the failure of both politics and policing to support the mothers leaves them with *effects* of a mode of masculinity promoted by the powerful men in the lads' lives – their fathers, the police, the politicians, the prison officers and the judiciary. Is this what the Scottish novelist, William McIlvanney, meant in *Docherty* when Mrs Docherty muses, 'It appeared to her that the sins of the fathers *were* the sons'? Without any social systems to offer a sources both of support and of challenge, the women manage life for the men.

'These men live in a twilight world,' said one of the men's lawyers. 'They're lying around on the sofa in their boxer shorts, watching videos; they have their tea when it's put in front of them; then they go out TWOCing and burgling.' When the men get into trouble, or when their wives want them out, it is their wives and mothers who make the arrangements. 'The men won't go to their solicitors, they won't liaise with the housing department, they won't liaise with their kids' schools. It's the women who make the appointments, it's the women who call to cancel the men's appointments, it's the women who make the apologies. We have women who ring up saying the men want to know what's happening to their case, or when he's due in court. What is absolutely astonishing about these tough men is that they have to have their slippers under some woman's bed. The men cannot make out on their own. The reality is that children in this community do not grow up seeing men do any of the coping, caring or standing on their own two feet.'

Neither the police nor most politicians challenged this mode of masculinity or the 'philosophy of intimidation' as a message by men to their own community as well as to outsiders. The locals knew just how dangerous life was and that the police, to be effective, would have to offer a protection that matched the power that endangered them. Superintendent John Broughton, who took over the management of North Shields police six months before the riots, sympathised. He was typical of a new generation of senior officers in the constabulary who were trying to confront these difficult and dangerous networks. He recalled that Meadowell felt impenetrable to police officers. 'There was a feeling that we weren't welcome, and a feeling among many others that they had no power to do anything about it, that it was easier to live with the situation than stand up and be counted. From a policing point of view it meant that the very people we needed to help us do our job, the public, weren't helping us in any way, because of the fear of retribution.'

Superintendent Eric Lewis said that before the riots in the West End, 'people didn't like the situation, but they weren't prepared to do anything about it. Well, they did it in their own way, but not by cooperating with the police.' However, the community had tried to organise its own campaign against crime, and in any case, unless the police provided protection, then people had only one alternative to silence – to flee.

Evacuation from Meadowell was the only solution for thirty households facing serious threats – including guns and firebombing – during the year before and after the riots. North Tyneside council's neighbourhood housing office used emergency powers to rehouse them away from the area.

One Scotswood resident complained that when the police came to her home they said, 'If you live in a swamp, what do you expect?' Towards the end of the decade people had already begun moving out of the area and within a couple of years there had been a mass evacuation. Residents were becoming refugees elsewhere in the city, doing anything to get away. In the summer of 1988 there were 2,350 council dwellings in Scotswood and the adjacent Fergusons Lane estate. Of these, 65 were empty. A year later that figure had almost trebled and in summer 1990 the number of empty dwellings had reached 278. By the summer of the riots it was 388. A year later, another hundred dwellings were empty, bringing the total to 488. An even higher proportion had been abandoned in the private sector – a hundred private properties were lying vacant, out of six hundred. Homes valued at between £30,000 and £40,000 were selling at £5,000 or even £3,000 – a £5,000 flat in Elswick was not uncommon. The exodus was caused by harassment, crime and the absence of police protection.

This is the story of a family who escaped from their once-loved home in Elswick's Jubilee estate. It was a family of active citizens who had done exactly what the police had asked of the community.

Their estate was opened, as its name suggested, in 1977. In 1991 a sixth of the dwellings, were empty.

The family had moved to Jubilee from one of Newcastle's typical terraces with a father, mother, children and grand-mother. The mother was a machinist; the father was a ware-houseman. Both were currently unemployed. They had never taken a holiday and wore their relatives' cast-off clothing. They kept their car after the husband's redundancy, however. It was a sign that they were indefatigable. They weren't down and out, they could ferry the children and their grandmother, they could go, go, go. The mother tells their story:

'We were thrilled when we got the house. I'd badgered the council for two years, so I was over the moon. It was beautiful. My big thing was to keep the kids out of trouble, because a lot of the kids were roaming around, into diddling, breaking into houses and flogging the stuff. They were hiding it from their mothers, though some were doing it to their mothers, too. So I kept mine busy.' Every day they escorted their children to swimming baths, jazz gigs and sports centres.

Every week she went to meetings – she was a community woman. She was active in the tenants' association; they got fences put up, shrubs cut down, streets swept, they felt they were the experts on their environment and campaigned to improve it. During the Eighties the money started running out. 'The tenants were getting sick – they felt we weren't achieving anything, and it got to the stage when that was true, we weren't.'

A few Asians lived on the estate. They were beaten up. The harassment seemed to be organised – bricks began to be placed strategically across roads into the estate, cars would be stopped, and if the passengers were black they'd be dragged out and beaten. 'I saw it happen, they'd be booted around. My husband used to go mad with me because I'd swear at them to leave them alone. Asian people had an awful life, but they had to put up with it, they were outnumbered. They just locked themselves in their houses.' In 1992 an elderly Muslim, Khoaz Miah, who lived on the Jubilee estate and who regularly attended the mosque, was making his way home after last prayer when he was attacked by a group of young white men. By the time he was discovered by the police in an alley between the Jubilee and the mosque he was dying. He was never able to describe what had happened. A community march which drew in people from all over the West End took to the streets that month, to mourn and to protest. A large police operation was mobilised to seek his attackers.

The family lived next door to an Asian shopkeeper whose walls were regularly daubed with 'Get the darkies out'. The tenants' association would get the council down to sandblast the walls to clear it off.

Arriving home early one evening in their old banger she and her husband noticed a lad fleeing past their house. 'He was holding what looked like a collection bag from an electric man or a gas man. I watched him run to a car, so I took the number, and then I saw the gas man running, so I asked him if he'd been attacked.' He said he had just been robbed. She rang the police station. 'My husband was playing war with me: he said did I realise what I was doing. The police asked if I'd seen the lad, and I wasn't going to lie. I thought I'd be safe enough, because if I had to identify him it would be behind plate glass, like it was in the films. But it wasn't

like that. I had to be in the same room, and the police said
I had to walk along the line and tap him on the shoulder if I
recognised him. I nearly died. Because, of course, I recognised
him right away. I was even more terrified when I found out
who he was. He came from a well-known family in the West
End.' 'Well-known' meant notorious. The family's pleasures
included playing with shotguns.

Her teenage son was a decorator on the Youth Training
Scheme. Working one afternoon, he saw the works generator
disappearing out of the door. He followed it and saw two men
run away with it. He called the police, toured the neighbourhood with them and spotted the men. A search unearthed the
generator. Yes, he said, he would identify the men in court.

That day changed his family's life. 'All my kids caught
it,' said his mother. 'He was tormented and pestered. My
daughter came home to bloodcurdling threats: the lads said
the girls would be raped. Kids on the estate called my son a
grass and told him, "You're going to get fucking filled in." Our
car got smashed. Eventually my son said, "Mam, I can't stand
it." He went to live with his girlfriend. He felt that every time
he came near the West End he might get killed. If he came to
see us in his girlfriend's car the windows got smashed and the
tyres got slashed.

'The kids on the estate used to say the same things to
me, and my daughters. They broke into my friend's house
and accused her of being a grass. At first I was proud of my
son for picking out those lads, but afterwards I wished he
hadn't, because the police have not protected him, and that
gives no other child any hope. It was total harassment from
then on, every day, several times a day – though they never
actually broke into my house because I kept a dog and they
were frightened of it.

'From then we also knew whenever there was a burglary
going on because they would cut *our* telephone wires – in
case we would telephone the police. One night they broke
into the Asian shop next door. My telephone wire was cut.
A gang of lads were outside shouting, "Grass". We could hear

them banging around next door, so I found one of my kids' old baseball bats and my daughter and I sat at the kitchen table drinking tea with the baseball bat while they robbed the shop next door. They had posted kids next door and outside the shop on either side of my house, so we couldn't get out. I felt that if we left without the dog they'd have us, and if we took the dog they'd have our house. We were prisoners.

'I begged and begged the council to shift us away, but they wouldn't because we weren't injured. One night the lads were kicking our windows. We called the police. They arrived; I told them what happened; the gang walked past and I told the police, "That's them." The lads were shouting, "Fuck off" so I was shouting, "Get away from my door or I'll strangle you!" The police knew we were being harassed, but they told me this was no way to talk to the lads, that they weren't doing anything, there was nothing physical. I began to understand how the Asians might feel.

'It got to the point where my husband actually stopped me calling the police, because the police weren't interested. It got to the point where they wouldn't come on the estate unless it was *en masse*. But we had to live there.'

Her son, on his YTS scheme, was the only person in her family with a job. She, her husband, her daughter – who had left school with half a dozen O-levels – and her brother-in-law, were all unemployed. The family's exodus from Tyneside began when her daughter finally went south and found a job. Her husband followed and found a job, too, and then the brother-in-law migrated and found work with them. The mother reluctantly evacuated herself, her younger children and their elderly grandmother. All of them went south. The family was working at last.

'But you can't expect every family to move out and go to the other end of the country. We were lucky – though I don't *feel* lucky! I was just getting my family out of danger. I didn't want to leave my own mother, my brothers and sisters. It's such a shame, because I had loved it there. I'd fought to get to that estate, I'd thought I was set up for life. The danger turned me out of my home. I hate it in the south, but why should people have to put up with all that crap? I think back and what I remember is lads running round the estate with black plastic bags. They'd broken into people's houses and the next morning the stuff would be on sale. For all the harassment we had, they'd even come to our door selling other people's stuff. That's how they live.

'It needs some sort of community gathering-together to sort it out.'

Community policing was a hybrid emerging from the undergrowth of riots, Tory party conferences, progressive pleas for local accountability, fear of crime and a communal sense of loss, a feeling of being alone with it all. Perhaps it was the atavistic grief of the adult, of being unparented, that was codified in the complaint that there was no access to the one agency that represented authority. All these diverse pressures supported the populist cry for *more* policing. Although in many areas community policing achieved neither a reduction in crime nor any alteration in communities' relationship to crime, it did establish a conversation between the police and the people through the medium of the Community Forum. That was something.

However, it was not the bobby on the beat who could convert a problem to a priority. In Blackbird Leys, for example, the community beat officers' concern about increasingly audacious joyriding was communicated in 1990. During that summer the centre of the estate was a joyriders' circuit and a focus for car theft. But the community officers were powerless to influence senior managers' priorities. The least resourced areas did not necessarily command the investment to match their needs. Elswick had a neighbourhood-based community police service – an experiment which worked. But central government financial pressure left it with a short life – after a year it was withdrawn. In the year after the riots Northumbria Constabulary had to resort to special pleading, regularly, to secure additional funds to support crime prevention initiatives in some of its most beleaguered communities.

Senior police in Northumbria have acknowledged that they had abandoned some notorious estates and one officer commented: 'A domestic dispute on an estate, which can involve a whole street in mayhem, could get a police officer involved. He'd go, give pertinent advice and he'd come back and say, advice given, all quiet. But if he went to a squash club and a man had lost his credit cards there would be a four-page report on it. We can say to police officers, go out and be caring; but the values of our organisation don't reflect that.' The needs of a community overwhelmed by crime demanded complexity and flexibility, said a police manager: 'Community policing demands a whole strategy of service, a management philosophy that has been taken on in industry. But how can I ask my coppers to be sensitive if I treat them like two-year-olds and don't encourage lateral thought, or innovation? We crucify them for mistakes. We force people, in order to be administratively correct, to lie to the organisation and the organisation allows them to do it. So is it any wonder that people are not honest to the people outside when we don't encourage them to be honest inside?'

The police seemed to be the one public service entitled to respond entirely at its own discretion. Unlike social services, the railways or refuse collection, the police were not bound to enter into any dialogue to define *when*, *where* and *how* they might respond to 'consumer' needs. It seemed that the police were cautious about a conversation unless it was on their own turf and on their own terms. The accusation that people living in Newcastle's West End had failed to cooperate with the police excused a withdrawal from the community.

There was a sense of catastrophe in Scotswood. In May 1989, when the exodus from the neighbourhood was already well underway, citizens involved in the web of organisations anchored in Scotswood Community Project launched a campaign called Stop Crime Against Residents (SCARE). They wanted the authorities to deal with a minority within the community who were 'making life unbearable' by joyriding, burglaries and threats of reprisals. People felt that 'the police just don't seem interested in us' and thus 'the overwhelming feeling is that there is now a lack of trust in the police and despair that residents have been abandoned by them.'

Northumbria police responded negatively with the riposte, 'A lot of crime in Scotswood is committed by residents on residents, which is more difficult to detect. We rely a lot on public support which sometimes we don't get.' In May 1989 Chief Superintendent John Hillyer went to a meeting with Scotswood residents and heard about harassment, children being beaten up, bomb threats, bricks through windows, empty houses being left vulnerable to entry, joyriding, police taking two hours to respond to calls and telling victims, 'What do you expect? You're in Scotswood.'

Superintendent Hillyer listened to all this and then told the forty residents that he wasn't surprised at two-hour response times – resources were 'slim'. Most of the estate's problems came from the estate itself, he told them. The police problem was evidence. The residents, not unnaturally, felt that it was the police force's job to find evidence. He urged the residents to give Neighbourhood Watch another try.

SCARE was not welcomed because it was demanding action by the police rather than simply offering support to the police. Its genesis lay in local experience, its template was defined by fiercely-felt *people's* needs rather than *police* needs, and it was autonomous. That made it unacceptable. 'They weren't prepared to do something. Well, they did it in their own way, though not by supporting the police.'

SCARE was naturally no more acceptable to some of the lads in the neighbourhood. Indeed, they made their hostility plain. Anyone walking into the Scotswood Community Project building, home to SCARE as well as to a cluster of other campaigns and services – Newcastle's first Credit

Union, a childcare scheme, a tenants' City Challenge team
– was accused of being a grass, too. When well-known local
activists stood at the bus stop, popped into the chip shop,
dropped into the local post office, went for a bus, or leaned
over their garden fence, they ran the hazard of a personalised
chant of 'Grass, grass, grass'. If the lads were being imaginative
the chant might vary: 'Get back in your cage', or simply, 'Cunt'.

A month after their first encounter, a hundred residents
turned up for another meeting with the police, who told them
that nothing more could be done. A year later, a baby, Richard
Hartill, not yet a year old, was killed in his buggy when a
car driven by lads known locally not as 'joyriders' but 'death
riders' ran out of control. Before the tragedy the community
had identified one of the drivers to the police. More than two
hundred residents blocked the road where the baby had been
killed. It took another year and somebody else's riot before
Scotswood got a traffic calming scheme they had been asking
for.

CHAPTER 9

Boys Will Be Boys

The scale of the pyrotechnics during the riots was, to the places where violence, joyriding, burglary and fires were everyday events, all that seemed to distinguish the riots from the travails of daily life. The riots did not represent revolt, they were simply larger displays of what these neighbourhoods had to put up with much of the time. The tempo of the policing – passive and then explosive – was also just another thing they had to put with from the men in their lives. What none of these neighbourhoods believed was either that they were *supported* by politicians or the police or that they were *represented* by the riots or the rioters.

A conversation with a group of boys and girls in Ely revealed the confusions and crisis of confidence that the riots created in their communities. The teenagers were there, some of them had taken part, but did they know what they meant? As displays of force the riots had followed a familiar format – they were about being hard – but as displays of dissent they seemed to be meaningless. The girls in this conversation watched the riots, the boys joined in:

'Since the riots we've had more police. You feel you are being watched for everything you do.'

'The riots gave Ely a bad name – it was unfair.'

'I was throwing stones at the coppers because it was fun and everyone else was doing it.'

'*Did you want to hit the police?*'

'I didn't care.'

'You can't stop it, can you? People won't listen to you.'

'They'd call you a sap if you didn't do it.'

'I was throwing stones at the police because everybody

was doing it. If it's happening it's worth doing it because you wouldn't want to be called a sap, would you?'

'*What does fighting achieve?*'

'Nothing really, it shows who is the hardest, so you get more respect.'

'*Who from?*'

'Other boys.'

'*Girls?*'

'They don't really matter.'

The legal definition of 'riot' in the Public Order Act is a *collective* disturbance for a *common purpose*. The riots of 1991 were something else: they were a cacophony of dissenting voices – dissenting from each other. What they showed was what divided the communities, not what bonded them. The protagonists were young men whose response to the world they lived in was pestering and predatory. The *places* they firebombed were not icons of public pain and punishment – there were no Bastilles; they were mainly public service buildings or small shops. The flames carried no message except beautiful menace. In a relatively unarmed country, fire had become a ubiquitous weapon. To the fire-raisers it carried mesmerising potency. The motif for media representations of Meadowell's most notorious night became a flaming landscape. The fire-raisers' work was mighty, it transcended the boundaries of Meadowell, and made this place which had no signpost into a place that suddenly did not need one. Its horizon was a sunset where the landscape entered the heavens and expanded into space.

Another tactic was to knock out the street lights or to blow out the power supply. Controlling darkness and light like this implied omniscience. The flame-throwers were like Icarus, boys flying, and that night in Meadowell they could do anything.

'Fire-setters aren't communicators. It's easier to strike a match than talk to someone. It is a very extreme response, of course, and we see it among people who don't think about consequences,' says Andrew Mutley, who works with fire-raisers at Newton Ayecliffe children's centre. Fire has changed its place in British life, with the demise of the cooking range and the open fire in the sitting-room. 'It is in nature, like wind and water, but in modern British culture people don't have access to it, they don't learn about it,' he adds. 'They don't learn that it can be positive. You can cook on it, sing around it, be warmed by it. At one time it was a domestic event. Now people don't have fireplaces.' For fire-setters, however, 'it is the most exciting tool at their disposal.'

'The police and these young men are very close to one another,' reckoned a professional in the criminal justice system who worked with both. She was, of course, referring to their shared predilection for masculine company and mastery, and their compulsion to take control, to overcome.

It was also true that many of the young men arrested in the riots tended to be 'known' – they were familiar to the police because they were already caught up in the criminal justice system. They appeared in court, usually recognisable as the accused not just because they were familiar, or because they were standing in the dock, but because they were the skinny, pale lads who looked, as they used to say, like 'ninepenny rabbits'.

One young man had a formidable record. He had been a burglar; he had stolen cars; he had beaten a man accused of being a grass with a baseball bat. Beautiful, with a blond crop and a thin, statuesque body, he had had a career in burglary characterised by a boldness that was hardly efficient – he kept getting caught. He made no effort to hide himself during the riots in the West End of Newcastle. Indeed, they were a great show. The police had provoked and the lads did their duty.

The West End was this lad's patch. Most of his offences had happened within a mile or so of where he lived. He was on his way home to Scotswood from an offenders' attendance centre in town when he saw a notice attached to the lamppost outside his local pub, the Bobby Shafto, announcing the riot that evening. He was spotted looking at the notice, but any attempt to pin the poster on him foundered – he could not write.

Around teatime he returned to the pub and found a stolen white Vauxhall Nova parked outside, with a group of lads standing round it. It was waiting to be played with. He started it up with a little piece of metal and drove it down to Benwell and back again. The white Nova ended up incinerated. He was part of the group of lads who tried to smash a hole in the post office shutters, who then kicked a door in and shot up to the flat above. People across the road saw these boys throwing petrol bombs at the post office, at the window of the flat above, and then at the stairs as they rushed out and back into the crowd.

He had been released from custody not long before the riots. On most days, his life was lived within a one-mile radius. He went the couple of miles into the city only when his mother took him to buy clothes or when he was due at an attendance centre – an alternative to custody. He never went to the cinema – 'I don't like it' – and he never went to any cafés – 'I don't know any.' He heard about the Meadowell riot when he was at home with his mother, like thousands of other listeners who tune in nightly to Alan Robson's popular local radio show, *Night Owls*. 'My ma said they were daft. I said nowt.' Did he think they were daft? 'In a way, aye, in a way no. Burning everything down was a bad idea. But they did it for their mates, the two lads that died.' He was tried and convicted on charges of firebombing the post office – one of Scotswood's most important economic resources.

When Elswick was set alight the night before Scotswood, he was there. 'All the kids were talking about it so we went up. It was daft because they wouldn't let the fire engines past to put the fires out. They were at the fire engines, not the police – but they should have let the fire engines through because it's their job. Then we just went back to Scotswood. I went to the Bobby

Shafto, as I usually do, sniffing glue with my mates. My mam knew about the glue. She tried to keep me out of it; she kept watching me.'

After he had first seen the notice outside the Bobby Shafto, 'I was talking to my mates for half an hour, then I went home. My mam is always in – she makes the tea. I had a bath, got changed, went back to the Bobby. Around six o'clock loads of people were getting into hoistie cars [stolen cars] and the white van that was full of kids from Benwell was there. About eight o'clock they were flinging the car about and the police started coming.'

When people started throwing the petrol bombs stored behind the kebab shop opposite the post office, he joined them. 'I was high as a kite on glue. It was daftness. Everyone was shouting to the busies [police] "black cunts" because of their uniforms and because of the way they treat us.'

He was throwing petrol bombs into the road 'so that the police couldn't get past, because they would just have kicked us all over.' But there were other people who wanted the police to get through, weren't there? 'Aye, all the women. The old people didn't like it either, and half the young lasses were shouting and bawling at us.' Did he take any notice? 'No, they were just shouting in case they got hurt or their houses got hurt. They were just being scared.'

His route to the riot had begun a few years earlier when he was fourteen years old. He was not very good at reading and writing. 'I packed in school. Teachers asked us to read in front of the class. I cannot. It just showed me up.' Was that why he stopped going to school, because he felt daft? 'Aye.'

'I'd leave the house about nine o'clock, when my mam thought I was going to school – I never told her I wasn't. I'd go down to the park at Scotswood Dene with my mates. We messed about.'

Messing about was a frugal sport. 'We were banging into glue. We didn't talk much.' So who does this young man talk to? 'Just my mam.' What about? 'All sorts.' He tells her things he tells no one else, not secrets especially, just anything. 'I don't know if my mates would be interested.' When he wasn't going to school he was at the dene or 'hanging around the school at the back where everybody went for a smoke – we didn't go in. My mam found out when the school board woman came after about eight months. My mam said I had to go to school! Then she took me to school. I felt shown up. My mates were just laughing. I didn't go back.'

Then he became a burglar, and he had a habit. 'We were all bored. We wanted some glue and one of the lads mentioned burgling a house. It was near where we lived. We kicked the front door in and took the video. One of my mates sold it for about £100, so we all got £33 each.' That lasted for about two days. 'We just kept burgling. I liked it – till we started getting caught. I liked the money.' Hanging around the pub connected the boys to a network of fences who would sell their stolen goods. The lads sat on the front steps of the pub and did business in the back. Passers-by were often the inhabitants of houses they had penetrated and whose property they had pinched. Sometimes these people were still paying off the instalments on items the lads had long since forgotten.

Burgling was a boy's thing. 'It's not a lasses' thing: they go shoplifting.' He kept getting caught. His mother was furious and that bothered him. He loved her, but she was no match for a laugh, for a rave, for his mates. 'I couldn't do anything about it. Me and my mates just had a good laugh, just pinching cars and having a laugh. I got out of my head really. We got glue from the paper shop. I liked the illusions, just seeing things, like trees moving in front of you when they weren't really there.'

When he and his mates began stealing cars he started driving them up the Armstrong Road. 'People used to laugh. I'd have preferred it if they didn't watch, in case I crashed.' It was the burgling and the joyriding that drove the neighbourhood crazy. 'People think we're rogues.' Did he care? 'Sometimes, because you could be walking along the street and they could be saying, "He's a house burglar."' He had beaten up people who had given information to the police. 'Sometimes I think they're just cunts, sometimes I think they're doing people favours to stop people taking property.'

His own property consists of a bedroom with a bed, a wardrobe, a television his mother bought him and a 'ghetto blaster' his father bought him for Christmas. He liked driving cars and doing handbrake turns around Armstrong Road, but he did not care to keep one, have one for himself. 'Didn't matter, I just wanted to have a go in a car.'

He had been locked up four times and spent another four months in cells after the riots. Nothing much made any difference to him. He rarely kept appointments, rarely put in his community service hours or went to his attendance centre sessions. Not unusually for young men, the only thing that began to get to him was a girl. 'Don't know what I'll do but I've got engaged. I'll settle down in my own house, not burgling.' He liked her. 'She's good to be with.' Why did she like him? 'I don't know. She just says I've got to stop burgling. She says it's people just the same as us we've been taking things off. I've seen people whose houses we've burgled and I've seen what they've been like, just upset, going mad.'

This is a young man who is a glue sniffer and petrol bomber, a burglar and a joyrider who takes tea with his mother and tidies his room. He costs his community a fortune. But he has lived his life in an era which disinvested in the social skills he might otherwise have acquired – literacy, work and cooperation. He was capable of deadly dangerousness. He and the lads like him made the difference between a poor place and an impossible one – hundreds of households in his neighbourhood decided that the only way to survive was to leave.

The criminal justice system saw some of what he did and locked him up from time to time.

In the aftermath of the riots and the incremental political panic over neighbourhood crime, a parliamentary consensus in favour of locking up these young men was cemented in 1993.

Lock-up made little difference to this young man. It made a difference to his home – he wasn't there. It made a difference to his community – it gave it a rest. But it made no difference to him. Except that it was just one damn thing after another.

'I feel young men get no respect from anybody,' said one Juvenile Justice worker, who worked with adolescent offenders for many years in a professional culture committed to keeping them out of custody. 'The police treat them like shit, the system treats them like shit. They have no status in society, no respect, and they don't give it to anybody either. Locking them up, beating them up – I've never understood how you can help a person be more caring by treating them in a brutal way.

'I'm not sure they think about what they do, and that's what we try to get them to do: think about it. But this society treats children very badly. They're punished but they get no service. If they go to court and get a supervision order – which means they stay in the community – they will hardly be seen by the system or by social services until they do something else. They go back to court, they get punished, but they get no service. Most of the young men we see in Juvenile Justice have poor standards of education. The kids are blamed, but the education department isn't called into court to explain itself.'

And so it was with this young man. Nothing made a difference, except now and again his mother and his girlfriend. They were the ones who made him get up in the morning and keep appointments and think about something else other than having hallucinations, cars, and breaking and entering.

They, of course, could be seen as accomplices rather than as the one resource that might restore him to a community so hurt by him that it does not want him. The community itself was seen as an accomplice by a criminal justice system that knew, as much as any and more than most, how bad he was, but also knew as little as any about what to do with him. 'Lock him up' was its answer, sometimes. 'Blame the parents' was its rhetoric. 'What do you expect, where he comes from!' The criminal justice system relied on his mother to get him to court and keep him out of trouble. However, she was treated like a problem rather than a resource. Their neighbourhood, too, was seen to be part of the problem, not part of the solution. When the community tried to secure police cooperation in its campaign against crime, the police walked away. 'They burgle from each other,' said the police. That attitude gave them permission to give up.

The men and boys arraigned in Cardiff's riot trials would, in the olden days of the Fifties and Sixties, when their parents were their age, have been wrought in the image of what used to be known as 'the working man'. They might have gone mad on Friday nights, got girls pregnant, got drunk, got into fights, but they would have stayed on the right side of respectability because they earned enough to live and stay legal.

One generation later the men's relationship to the world had changed: instead of being defined by work, it came to be defined increasingly by crime. With alternative sources of employment abolished, scavenging, stealing or redistributing stolen goods were hardly surprising sources of income. One man in his early twenties lost his job after he was arrested during the Ely riot. He was in the streets because he lived there. His presence implied no endorsement of the events, he hated the violence. 'The police should have acted as soon as the crowd built up, but they let it grow, then they got agitated and wanted arrests. I'm absolutely against violence – I grew up with it. My mother is a school dinner lady; she knows I didn't do anything because my father used to be violent to her and I've got a great hatred for him. He knocked her teeth out, he broke her jaw. I used to jump on his back when I was a kid to try to stop him. I'd wake up and hear it, and I used to go out in the street. I wouldn't want any child to go through that. The police came once or twice, but they'd just put him in the cell for the night and then he'd come home. I'd never fight, I'd always talk rather than fight.'

He voted Labour, hated Tories. 'I've lived all my adult life through the Tories and they've done nothing for us.' He thought 'loadsamoney' meant earning £250 or £300 a week, regarded community leaders as posh people, and described himself as 'a pauper'.

Apart from minor motoring offences he had never been in trouble with the law but he lived in constant tension with it. 'I've never stolen in my life. Mind you, I have taken parts off stolen cars to make a bit of money. That's stealing I suppose – stealing by finding.' He was being modest about himself as a mover in Ely's informal economy, but was actually part of the chain in a massive trade in stolen goods, the videos, tele-visions, hi-fi systems, keyboards, car wheels, car seats, bikes, trainers, clothes, stolen cigarettes and drugs: anything useful that could be taken from one place and put in another.

There is a significant trade in small supplies of cannabis, amphetamine and cocaine, sold by young unemployed people who would no more fit the fantasy of a 'dealer' than they would fit the image of a 'worker'. They earned a little, and would hang about at home or in other people's homes. Drugs or drink were as significant a part of their lives as anyone else's. Drugs, drink and video technology domesticated the social life of the young poor.

'The action is in people's homes,' said this receiver. 'You have a smoke and watch a video. People would rather stay at home. They're at home getting block-up, getting stoned. Ely's main problem is money. The council isn't bothered about the place, but then it's short of money. About eighty per cent of the youngsters haven't got jobs. If they have, then the wages are so crap that they can't afford to live.'

Clean, legal, decent families now had their grip on respect-ability, however precarious a grip it might have been, severed by their boys' behaviour. Post-war full employment tended to make transgression sporadic rather than structural but the effect of the economic crisis on these places, and the criminalisation of young men, contaminated entire families and their neighbourhoods. The parents of one young man, yet again supporting him through a court appearance, were reminded of their boy's exile from their own society. 'The judge said, "You will not go to Ely to intimidate these good people", but we live here! We've lived here all our lives,' said his mother.

His family was close and calm but there was little they felt they could do to keep him from the lawless culture of his peers. 'I can't say a lot about the police because my son has been in trouble,' said his mother, 'and if one is in trouble they condemn the whole family. A lady across the road called me over one day, though, when she heard about our trouble, and said, "You hold your head up high, don't take any notice!" Her son had been beaten by the police once and they'd never been in trouble before.'

Her son, a rather serene young man, pretty, who looked like a pale Prince, had worked as a hairdresser, a butcher and then a builder's labourer. He had been made redundant more than once and had already been imprisoned for a series of car offences. He had been arrested when police were moving up streets close to the riot in Ely – he was watching the spectacle with friends. Several of them later made statements repudiating police evidence that he had thrown a stone at a police officer, but none was prepared to appear in court. When he was arrested he was found to have three truncheon bruises across his chest.

'Three times I've been beaten up when I've been arrested,' said the son. 'When the police see us in the street they say "We'll get you." The other day they arrested me and said, "This is one of many: we're waiting for you." So I've got to look out all the time. I'll be standing on the corner, they'll go past and stick two fingers up and if I did anything they'd arrest me. Most of the kids I know have been beaten up when they've been locked up.' Though he had been arrested mainly for car offences, he and his comrades were also using the cars for burglaries off the estate, usually from sports shops and clothing stores in neighbouring towns which they would relieve of their leather jackets, tracksuits, jumpers, 'all the dear stuff that the kids wear.' They would sell it for half the shop price.

His parents' hold on respectability had been attacked not only by the boy's offences, but by police behaviour. 'The police officers are as bad as the boys,' said his mother. 'We were down the road and we heard one of them shout at a boy who is well known for joyriding, "What time are you going out joyriding?" They get a kick out of it as well. They came to arrest my son once for stealing a car radio. They kicked the door in at seven o'clock in the morning. The officer was so wound-up he was kicking the door and dragging my son out. I said why didn't he let the lad get dressed, I didn't want him going out in his boxer shorts. But the policeman went to his car radio and asked for assistance!

'If a police officer comes to the door about my son I invite him in and talk to him decently. But this behaviour makes you turn away from the police. To be honest, I have no respect for them now. I know this is getting to be a bad place, there's such a lot of crime nowadays and the police have to put up with a lot, but all they seem to do is lash out and think later.' It was no use to her that the police behaved just like the boys.

The young men above were imprisoned on charges of violent disorder arising from the riots. They and their peers – including the police – were caught up in popular cultures that chiselled masculinity as brittle, impregnable and volcanic. This insulation is confirmed by friends of some of the rioters.

'This police–criminals thing is massive,' said a Meadowell youth worker. 'They both need each other to get their kicks.' The dominant culture among the young men of the estate provided the kicks. 'There's a glorification of the criminal thing, and there's not a lot of pressure to pull out of it. Age barriers don't matter. The thirteen-year-olds and eighteen-year-olds might be in the same peer group. They might include people up to thirty years old. Maybe that's something to do with the men on this estate not growing up.' So it was more important for the lads to be among the lads, whatever their age, than among their chronological peers, whatever their gender.

A labourer, who was not a criminal but said many of his

mates were, passionately defended brutality as a way of sorting things out. He grieved at his own lack of skills, was fatalistic about change, enjoyed the company of men, endured women. He lived with his mother, paid her £20 out of his £120 wage. 'She says I get on her nerves because I never do anything in the house, but I'm never in. I sleep in different places. I've got a girlfriend and I stay with her about once a week – depending on whether we've had an argument. We argue over the slightest things. I prefer going out with the lads. We talk about football. You don't need to talk about women when you go out drinking. You want to forget about them – you see enough of them to start with.

'I'm not a thief, I never had the bottle. But I stopped going to school when I was about fourteen. I used to go in, get my mark and then jump over the fence and go home. Now I wish I'd gone to school, because I would like qualifications, I'd like to be a decent joiner, but there's no chance. *Definitely* no chance of that. I'm very handy, and they've been talking about jobs at Royal Quays over the road, but I'm not building up my hopes about that. I've been let down too many times. I can't say that was because of where I live. I suppose it was lack of skills.

'What would make it better here? I don't know. It will *never* be better. Anyway, it's canny. There's nowt wrong with it, just a bit run down.' Asked what he thought about lads who were burglars or joyriders, he said, 'Nowt to do with me. I've got nothing against them, it's their lives. As long as they don't pinch my car I'm not bothered. Burgling, that's different, because they're pinching off people like ourselves. You've got to live in a house, but a car is a luxury, it's different. They can pinch as many cars as they want.

'What I like to hear about is the ram-raiders. The two crimes I like are ram-raiders and football violence. They get my adrenalin going. I enjoyed the British fans' violence in Sweden – there just wasn't enough of it. I like to see the fans going mad. It's exciting. I was involved only once. I hit somebody and broke some pub windows. That felt good – I wouldn't have done it if it didn't.'

*

The lads got into trouble and the lasses got pregnant. The one was on the run, the other was trying to make relationships. The one was killing cars, the other was kissing a baby. According to a youth worker who had, himself, been one of the lads, their culture was about 'proving themselves by having bottle, being good drivers, getting into places, looking for fights all the time, being a bit crazier than everybody else, being able to get control of other people.'

Another community worker reckoned that 'by the time the lasses have kids the lads are twiddling their thumbs. They just walk away from it. I've seen it happen for years. They never take responsibility, and then they start having relationships with younger lasses of thirteen or fifteen as if they want to extend their own childhood. Lasses are just bodies to be shagged. Then of course the lads get in trouble: they're racing around in cars, or doing odd "jobs" to finance the booze or the drugs. The lasses have the bairns. The relationship with the lad has broken down, but the relationship with his mother will remain. It's amazing. The responsibility bypasses the son, who does nothing, but his mother will be helpful, passing on a cot, or some clothes. Often the lasses will still go to see his mother, and go round for Sunday dinner. You go into houses to meet the women and you just know that they are coping with *difficult people* – the men go underground. As they get older they don't even meet each other any more. They don't go out, they're these figures who you must not wake.'

The conventional wisdom that the police and the criminals mirror each other implies more than the obvious – that the territory they share is crime – it is concerned with the way both live their masculinity. For the police, their identity as a gender is secured by their employment as enforcers: the institution endorses an identity in its power, its preoccupations, its uniform, its exclusivity. The criminals' empathy with the police, and their envy of police officers, are not so much about an institution as an informal, illicit regime of force.

Among unemployed men – so the argument goes – poverty produces an identity crisis; their unemployment leaves them without a role. Is it a wonder, we sigh, that they turn to crime? However, these conversations with men about riots and crime tell us a different story, one that shows how unemployment *reveals a mode of masculinity* whereas the commonsense notion has been that it *causes a crisis of masculinity*. We know that unemployment and poverty produce a human and economic crisis for both men and women, but that is perceived as an economic crisis for a woman and an identity crisis, a gender crisis, for a man. Yet the masculine trauma lies not so much with poverty as with its assignment to the world of women. Archetypal proletarian employment, no less than the City, the Church, Parliament or the police, has been characterised by sex segregation. Masculinity established its identity by enforcing difference, by the exclusion of women. Unemployment denies that difference its institutional framework. The social space men inhabit becomes solely local and domestic, and that is the space they share with women. Difference is reasserted in a refusal to cooperate in the creation of a democratic domesticity.

In employment, men's exit from the domestic domain was excused – they had to go *out* to work. In unemployment they have no alibi, their existence is domesticated. But their resistance is evident in their emotional and physical itinerancy. As workers, their flight from fatherhood was mediated by their pay packet: men's quest to purge women from the world of work, and their struggle to gain privilege for their own pay packet, at the expense of women, was expressed symbolically in the notions of the 'breadwinner' and the 'family wage'. In unemployment, men's flight from fatherhood has no hiding place, they have children and then leave someone else to look after them. What they all seem to insist upon, however, is that someone other than themselves take care of *them*, too, that someone should take them in. Nothing in the culture these men make encourages them to take care of themselves, to create a domestic domain. Being a man means being not-a-woman. So, unable and unwilling to make homes of their own, they become cuckoos moving between their mothers and other women.

But while the young women are at least trying to *make* life, the lads who are their contemporaries are often living like the Sicilians in Tomasi di Lampedusa's novel, *The Leopard*. They are the ones who 'never want to improve for the simple reason that they think themselves perfect; their vanity is stronger than their misery.'

CHAPTER 10

Freed Up

The police superintendent whose patch included Meadowell, John Broughton, was certain that the way things worked was this: 'The women take responsibility and the men are freed up to do what they like. They are peripheral to what happens on the estate. We have to empower the women to call in the chips on the criminals. There is no reason why they can't start to lay down the conditions about male behaviour.'

The crisis of crime as a crisis of masculinity was an equation that was evaded in the great debates about crime and community in the Eighties and Nineties. Though clearly sustained by *something* in popular consciousness, by a sense that men do something dangerous with their *pain* and their *power*, the political debate resisted that new knowledge and rehabilitated antique moral panics about communities and crime. It went further, it constructed a new myth about children as criminals.

Although juvenile crime actually declined in Britain after the mid-Eighties, and although its decline was beyond the drop in the population of juveniles, children and young people were at the centre of the great law-and-order debates of the early Nineties. In 1991 youth was the focus of riots and by 1993 public attention was mesmerised by *children* as *criminals*. Masculinity disappeared from the debate. In political discourse gender became the unmentionable, masculinity the problem with no name.

The gender contrast was stark in the offences committed by young people in Ely who came before the Juvenile Liaison Panel in the year before the riots – forty-two were committed by girls and 417 were committed by boys. There were thirty-nine burglaries by boys and five by girls. Shoplifting engaged both boys and girls – nineteen boys compared with fifteen girls. Twenty-eight boys committed grievous or actual bodily harm offences, compared with two girls. Boys appeared for fifty thefts from cars. There were no girls. Boys were involved in seventy-five TWOC (Taking Without Owner's Consent) offences. There were no girls.

In the first half of 1991, three-quarters of the young people appearing before Newcastle's Juvenile Court were boys. More than half – 122 cases – came from the devastated West End of the city. Staff working with Juvenile Justice, who were dedicated to keeping young people out of custody (and thus out of the punitive regimes and criminal networks operating behind locked doors) had also noticed a slow but steady rise in the number of boys under thirteen coming before the court. There were more of these very young boys committing offences than all the girls put together. The total number of girls comprised only eleven per cent of young offenders. Boys between ten and thirteen years old made up fourteen per cent. That was a rise of one percentage point on the previous year. Older boys, between fourteen and seventeen, comprised nearly three-quarters of the total.

In Ely during the year of the riots, the overwhelming majority of criminal offences appearing before the Juvenile Liaison Panel in 1990–1991 were committed by boys – forty-two offences were committed by girls, 416 by boys. Even in the crime category thought to be favoured by women – shoplifting – fifteen offences were committed by girls and nineteen were by boys.

In Oxford as a whole, of the 699 cases which went before the courts in the year after the riots, only fourteen per cent involved girls and women. These gender proportions were not peculiar to these places – they were the national picture.

The 1991 riots replied to Superintendent Broughton's prescient question with an answer that illuminated these figures and that eluded all the political commentators in the great debate: the men were freed up to do what they like and the women were defeated.

Neighbourhoods were evacuated by all other sources of authority. The probation service in North Tyneside and the West End was supervising 516 offenders in 1991; only seventeen had a full-time job. Eighteen were on a training programme and fourteen were at school.[1] The rest, more than 450 young offenders, had little or no place to go but to hang around their communities all day, every day. 'Apart from the streets many of the lads would be in some woman's space,' said one welfare officer. 'They'd have a girlfriend or a mother. They don't wander very far, they're very visible, very well known.'

A woman was running around Scotswood in her nightie during the riots shouting, 'Where's my son? Where's my son?' On another estate another night the mother of another teenager went scavenging among the crowds for her son. 'Don't you dare!' she told him when she found him on the edge of the riot watching other kids raiding shops. 'Hey mother, look at that!' he hissed. 'I'm sure if I had not been there he'd have been in and joining them. It was killing him that he couldn't, because he would not dare do it with me standing there, and I kept him with me all night,' she said.

A woman rounded up a couple of teenage lads, her own and her friend's boy, and took them home. His mother had been scouring the streets looking for him, too.

The mothers were all that was between these boys and riotous assembly. Nothing else was there to stop them.

A woman heard a day or so later that her son had been spotted throwing petrol bombs. Although he had already left home, she had been asking herself, 'Where's my son?' and as soon as she discovered where he'd been and what he'd been doing she told the police. She shopped her son. She was not the only one.

In the Nineties the emotion of entire estates was contaminated by betrayal: whether the mothers kept their children's

---

[1] Northumbria Probation Service, *The Tyneside Disturbance of September 1991: A Northumbria Probation Perspective*, 1991.

secrets or shopped them, whether they challenged them, protected them or threw them out, they were betraying their
children, their neighbours or the community. Before, during
and after these riots there were mothers whose sons' minor
and then major transgressions exhausted their affinity and
took some of them to one of the ultimate transgressions:
they wanted their sons – their babies – locked up.

If all the complexities, comings and goings, disappoint-
ments and dislikes that vex family life are also lived in
poverty while others enjoy plenty, then they are endured *in
extremis* and there is little to offset the hazards of everyday
life. The things which other classes can call upon to calm the
maelstrom – time away at work or school, playgroups, cars,
tutors, swimming baths, videos, cubs and brownies, music
classes, psychotherapists, holidays, a new pair of jeans – all
cost money.

'It started when he was about eleven. He would not go
to school,' said the mother of a petrol bomber. 'I couldn't
get help. He was *my* problem. Once I took him to school
and the head said, "Oh, you're stopping," and my lad said,
"No." So the head said, "Out. There's the door."'

Her son had problems and he became a problem at home
and at school. She was a person, school was an institution.
She tried, it did not. 'I learned my son the most I could
– how to read, how to write, how to tell the time. But I
knew I was slowly losing him to the street. We were living
on income support. My husband was working part-time, and
my son would say, "Mam, can I have . . .?" and I would have
to say "Son, I cannot . . ."'

Whatever else she did or did not do, she started with
her own failure. 'He started stealing from shops. I discovered
he had a drink problem because I found cider bottles under
his bed. He started being violent at home. When he started
thieving I tried to stop him, but he'd say, "It's the only way
to get money."' There was nothing she could do about that.
She could put a meal on the table but she could not supply
him with the treats others enjoy. A decade on income support

meant that her own wardrobe was made up of cast-offs from her own mother, or her own daughter.

When her son left school officially, he was already a burglar. It was then that she discovered him in the act of breaking and entering a local shop with a gang of lads. She called the police from a call box. 'They said, "You're shopping your son!" The police picked up the lads and let me know later on that night. "We've picked up your son. Are you coming to see him?" I said, "No, this is the only way I can get help."'

There was no help to be had. He was periodically locked up. After the riots, when he was identified as a petrol bomber, his brothers and sisters discovered that he had been among those setting fire to houses in their neighbourhood. One of them wrote to him while he was in custody and said, 'Why did you do that? It could have been me and my friend and mam's friend' He wrote back and said, 'I'm sorry.'

One of the roof boys arrested in the Tyneside riots moved around his family, from one aunt to another, a silent squatter, on the run from everyone except these women who supplied him with a conversation, a space, some tea, a bed. One of his aunts lived nearby, alongside a road which came to be known as bomb alley, where groups of boys – rarely girls – stationed themselves along the walls and threw rocks or bricks into the road, often at buses. Almost a year after the riots, buses were withdrawn from that route. Coming and going, getting away, just became even more difficult.

Joyriders parked cars inside the estate and torched them, sometimes catching the trees in the flames. 'It's so tiring; people are often frightened to go to sleep. I have visions of a car piling into our house,' said his aunt. 'We are besieged in our own place. The little lads see the big lads doing it, and when they are questioned by the police – who are never here when it happens – they'll say, "What have I done?" The riots missed our estate, but they are slowly destroying it.'

When her runaway nephew ran to her for sanctuary, this sad woman welcomed him. 'I let him stay, of course, but I told him we'd have to tell somebody. I was afraid his social worker would take him away – and me, for harbouring him! But she just asked me to come to a meeting. He would never talk usually, but he said, "You're not putting me away, I'll run away." They said he could stay: he was over the moon. But he was never out of trouble. I talked to him about it but it never seemed to sink in. Then he left my home and went to his other auntie, and he was still getting deeper and deeper into trouble.'

She explained that when his mother had been pregnant with the boy, his father had left her: he did not want to be a father. When the boy was born his mother's sisters moved in for a month to help. His aunt, after being married for twenty-one years, decided that she was better off being both mother and father to her own four children and told her husband to leave. For most of her married life she had moved merely between her mother's house and her own. 'I didn't go out. I thought that as a mother I should be in the house.'

'I sent my husband packing because he was out every night. He had no time for the children and when the last one was born he just didn't want to know. All he did was eat, drink, sleep. He never bathed them, dressed them, fed them, took them to school. So I just got fed up and sent him packing. That was the best thing I ever did. I think men are bone idle.'

Her nephew hated his own father. 'But the people who cope with him are the women in the family. I don't think he realises what he's putting us through.'

Her own son had already absented himself from the challenge of cooperation involved in an institution, where he would have to survive success and failure, engage with others' otherness and endure the effort of negotiation. 'He has stopped going to school now – he's twelve. He won't go because he saw my nephew wouldn't go.' He was phobic about the only institution, school, to which he had automatic access, other than his home and his street. He was another lad who had little to say, it seemed. He had been moving in and out of the kitchen during this conversation. He opened his mother's

purse on the table, pocketed some coins and said he wanted
to go out for chips. It was too late, she protested. He pestered,
she conceded. 'Okay, but be back by ten o'clock.' He was back
in time. 'Good boy,' she said. He stood behind her chair while
she quietly continued her chronicle. Watching me watching
him he raised his fist behind her head, as if it were holding
a knife, and slowly brought it down to her neck. 'Time to go
to bed soon,' said his mother, and he disappeared.

As that child entered his adolescence, what alternative
way of being could attract him? He could not be a *man*
like his *mother*: she could not be his role model, it seems.
Anyway, he was already at war with her. What she did was
take care of people. What all the other men in his life – his
father, his uncle, the brotherhood who threw bricks at the
buses, the police, the court – promoted was what he himself
now perpetrated, simple force.

CHAPTER 11

Grafting is Women's Work

More men commit crime than women and the crimes they commit are more likely to violate their nearest and dearest and their neighbours than the offences committed by women. The great *unspoken* in the crime angst of the Eighties and Nineties was that it is a phenomenon of masculinity. Indeed crime is one of the cultures in which young men acquire the mantle of manhood.

It is now no longer possible to contemplate crime without contemplating gender. And yet, no government, secretary of state or chief constable has stated the obvious: the problems of policing are also problems of masculinised corporate culture. Crime statistics tell a story about masculinity and crime prevention must, therefore, contemplate the reform of masculinity.

This is not to say that boys and men are bad and girls and women are good, it is simply to repeat the obvious, that men and women do something dramatically different with their troubles.

A Home Office study of men and women born in 1953 showed that one in three men and one in fourteen women had committed an offence by the time they were thirty-one years old. These excluded minor offences associated with drink or driving.[1]

However, the justice system's response suggests that a woman's transgression contravenes not only the law but also the lore of femininity: a much higher proportion of women

---

[1] *Criminal Careers of People Born in 1953*, Home Office Statistical Bulletin, issue 30, 1989.

convicted of stealing are sent to prison than men, fifty per cent compared with twenty-seven per cent of men.

Of all the offences committed by women, seventy-one per cent are for stealing; stealing comprises forty-one per cent of all offences committed by men, which are much more likely to involve acts of violence.[2]

Stealing figured more strongly, too, among young women sent to prison than for all women – among those aged between seventeen and twenty who are sent to prison, the proportion convicted of stealing was sixty-six per cent.[3]

A peer of the young men who ran criminal networks in Newcastle was, herself, an exemplar of women, crime and punishment. When she was not in prison she lived in Scotswood. Her record was seen as a series of 'survival offences' by her probation officers who noticed that they always involved acquiring goods which had both a use value and a currency value – she could always sell them. She had been sent to prison eight times for stealing.

Small, dark and handsome – her good looks were part of her cachet as a criminal – by the time she was in her early twenties, her career had established a clear pattern. It was regularly punctuated by spells in prison or at attendance centres, alternatives to custody. She began her day a little late, but it was never a dossers' day: she got going by 10 a.m. 'I've got that much going on!' The first stop would be an attendance centre. 'Then some shoplifting, then visiting friends and after that sorting out my house.'

Her career began when she was sixteen years old and had just left school. 'Everybody has their troubles. I left school, I had no money, I had to survive. Grafting is work to me.

'I drank in the rough bars in town, got chatting. I was

---

[2] *1990 Criminal Statistics, England and Wales*, Home Office, 1992.
[3] National Association of Probation Officers, *Women, Children and Custody*, March 1989.

easily led by Mr X. He said, "Wanna make some money?" I said, "I'm not going on the streets." He had a cheque book, stolen; he gave it to me. He would have had to buy the cheque book – it probably cost about £50. It would have been stolen in a "pop and seize" – a weight on a string, like a conker, break the glass, get in – and we would have made about £800 at the end of the day.

'What I did was go into a post office and cash a cheque, go into Marks and Spencer, buy £50 worth of goods, take them back later and get a refund. It was always a man who got the cheque book, and the man had the car, but I was the person they couldn't do without. Anyway, I used to think, "I do enough running about, you run me about."

'At the time I didn't actually steal anything when I was doing cheques, so I didn't have a guilty conscience. I *deceived*. Even the shops got something from what I took – they got a cheque that bounced.

'Doing cheques is like acting. When I go into a shop I convince myself that I am the person on the cheque book. If the police have been called, I've stood and argued with the police officer that I was the person on the cheque book. Once I've walked away from that counter I've thought, "Yes! I've done it!" It's a performance, doing something that's not allowed, pulling it off. I have to admit I got addicted to that buzz.'

Would she be a burglar? 'No, definitely not. Not my scene. I could not directly pinch from a person. Women shoplift. Most women wouldn't burgle. The rogues' world has different kinds of graft for men and for women. Can you see a woman climbing on a roof and doing a creep, a burglary? In Scotswood they have very old-fashioned ideas about Women's Lib. The men think the women should be chained to the kitchen sink and all that bollocks. The women go along with it because they are scared of men.'

Once she herself was married she, too, had reason to be scared. 'He was bashing me quite a bit. If the men don't do the physical they do the mental harm. All the women I know have been bashed.

'After I got married he barred me from doing cheques.' Why did she let him stop her? 'He'd been in jail for violence and possession of firearms.' She turned to shoplifting. The big stores were the location; expensive clothes were the items, which would then be sold to a circle of customers. 'What's the point of going into a cheap shop? I can sell anything. Underwear is a big seller. I've made a lot off underwear, clothes – especially kiddies' clothes – jeans, ornaments, anything you might have in your house, anything that is saleable. Electrical goods are not my scene.

'If I needed something for, say, £130, then I would have to pinch stuff worth £260 and sell it to make £130. I very rarely buy things, only the things I can't pinch. If I need curtains I make a calculation and estimate roughly what I'd need to pinch to make enough.'

After several stints in prison – the last time for stealing goods worth only £52 – did she consider stopping? 'Could you live on the dole? It explains it all. Could I do an honest-on-the-books job? To be honest, no. Who's going to employ me? I've been for interviews, I've half-lied, I've lied, I've been honest, but I might as well have *thief* stamped on my forehead.' Wasn't she a thief? 'No, I'm a survivor.'

'At least I wasn't going into someone's house. I was taking from a company, and a credit company covered the cheque card. It is companies that I injure, not a person. I couldn't steal directly off you or off anybody else, but I can steal off a shop or a company – God, they've got millions!

'Anyway, what am I supposed to do when I get £47 a fortnight on the dole? It doesn't even pay my bills – and then the court wonders why I steal! The likes of me could never get a cheque book of their own. That's discrimination. You can never beat the system, you can only bend it.'

Her offences operated within a code that put a screen between herself and the victim, which was corporate and distanced. Just as the notion of a fair day's wage for a fair day's work bleached out the experience of exploitation, so her self-defence reinterpreted the panic and pain. Her etiquette operated both as an ethic (much more than simple manners) and as an ideology which cauterised, in the imagination, any connection with a victim or an injury.

Commodities were never simply what they seemed but in her domain, in her system, they were a return to raw trade. To her, the items always had to have an exchange value; they became a kind of convertible currency in a local economy where barter coexisted both with straight sterling and with unofficial exchange rates. Like any other fast and flukey transactions, her activities carried a buzz. They were dodgy and therefore dangerous.

A young woman who quit school when she was fourteen years old in the mid-Eighties, got into sniffing glue and gas. During the day she stole things. 'My thing would be shoplifting and cheques and the lads would burgle warehouses, shops and houses. I used to sneak off with other kids and we'd go shoplifting. We took tops and jeans and shoes. Then we'd sell them to people around, friends, your mam's friends. People asked for what they wanted, they'd say, "Get a pair of jeans size thirty-two waist."

'It was nearly always clothes. Sometimes tea sets from the cheap shops where you could dinner sets or where they had downstairs departments where there weren't any cameras. We put the stuff in black bin bags or carrier bags.'

She was arrested when she was sixteen and cautioned for stealing shoes from one of the big city stores. 'I never kept the stuff. We didn't pinch it to have it, we pinched it to sell it.'

For a couple of years after leaving school she worked as a machine operator and then as a fork-lift truck driver on an industrial estate, taking home £110 a week. But she earned £30 or so more stealing. 'I did shops locally. I'd keep some of the stuff or sell it. You could always sell things, no matter what they were. Or I'd go up to the town for clothes – tops, jeans, suits, children's clothes. You can always sell children's clothes.'

The second time she was arrested it was for stealing jeans. The third occasion she was arrested by CID officers, in pursuit after a call from a shop where she had tried to use a stolen cheque card.

She did not drink, but she enjoyed soft drugs. She did not do break-ins but she had friends who did. 'I once did a house,' said one of them. 'It was my friend's house. We took a video and put it in a shopping trolley and walked it down the road. I just kept it. I've broken into cars a few times. I was with a lad who does it. We did it when there was nothing to do and we wanted a frisk.'

These girls' adolescence and ambitions had been framed in an era and an area where street culture was dominated by being hard. These girls were gay. Though their values were honed in the streets, the city clubs and among each other, they were defined neither by the lads with whom they kept company nor by their heterosexual contemporaries who were joining the community of mothers. Their sexual orientation meant that they were neither controlled by men nor pestered or protected by them. 'They can't be masterminded by men who draw women into cheque books,' said a Newcastle probation officer. 'And unlike other women, whose crime is motivated for their family and is about getting food and clothes, their offending is about a different kind of gain or survival, their own.'

A mile or so away lives a grandmother with a record. Her career is cleaning. The photographs of ten grandchildren are everywhere in her home, all over the mantlepiece, the living room and the bedroom. Every week she cooks Sunday dinner for a dozen children and grown-ups.

Her first contact with the police and a court was during her divorce. Her husband was a miner. 'It was rough. He nearly killed me. Look at the scars on my legs – he hit me with the poker, he kicked me with his big boots.' Her life was lived almost entirely at home in a mining village. 'It was twenty-four hours a day, living like a slave. You did what you were told or you got a hiding.' He also used to throw her out of the house. 'Sometimes I slept in the outside toilet.' After several attempts to leave, she went to the police, who found her a haven in a Salvation Army hostel. This was in the early Seventies, the era before battered women's refuges.

Two of her children were still with their father. She next heard from the police when her husband had belted and bruised their daughter. Her new life was lived with her children in the city where she worked as a part-time cleaner. She also claimed social security. She was caught. That was her first offence.

Her second was a year later after the electricity in her home had been restored and a metre had been installed. By then she was living with a man as well as her children. He, too, was unemployed. 'It was him, he broke into the metre. We took the money. I was desperate. I had no money. I called the police to say that the metre had been robbed. But when the police came they said they couldn't see any evidence. There was a broken window, but they said it had been broken from the inside. They said, "You've done it yourself" and then of course I started crying and said yes, I'd done it myself.

'The electricity board weren't going to replace the metre then, but I promised I'd not do it again and I paid back the money we'd taken.' She also lost her rebate.

For that offence she was put on probation for two years. Apart from the Salvation Army the probation service was the first to do something really useful: it gave her a holiday with her children. 'I'd never had a holiday before. Actually, until I lived in Newcastle I'd never even been to the city before.'

It was not until many years later, when she was a middle-aged woman, that she committed any further offences. One of her sons was, by then, leaving school. But because he was under eighteen years old he was unable to claim unemployment benefit. Her household was in great financial difficulty. She took a part-time cleaning job in a city store. There were a dozen women doing the early shift. After she arrived for work at 6.30 one morning in 1990 three officials swept from the shadows: 'We hadn't seen them, they appeared from nowhere. One of them tapped me on the shoulder and said, "I'm from social security and you have no right to be working." Apparently they'd been watching us for some time. I was really humiliated, I said, "You should have come to my home." There were three of us being caught. We tried to run, but there was no way we could get out of the building.

'When the social security official said, "Why did you do it?" I said, "Could you manage on what I get?" I'd got kids to support. I got no money from their father.' She stopped claiming benefit and kept up her part-time job while she was on probation.

Two years later she was claiming social security and doing an evening shift in an office block. One morning a social security investigator knocked on her door. 'We have reason to believe you are working. You can be identified. You might as well admit it,' he told her. When she was interviewed by the investigator in her solicitor's presence he explained, 'You think I'm nasty, but I'm only trying to help . . .' She was charged with fraud and deception and given eighteen months' probation.

She was fifty-one years old and she had been earning £20 a week while receiving £55 social security benefit.

At the beginning of the Eighties a domestic worker in a London hospice was on the move, following her husband to his new job in the North. He had been made redundant by a menswear shop. He was soon to be made redundant from his job on a building site in the North. After 1982 she never found work with a wage again.

At the beginning of the Nineties when she was forty years old she was arrested by a detective who knocked on her front door and charged her with fraud and deception. When she was convicted, 1,444 offences were taken into consideration.

Her recruitment into a crime syndicate was nothing if not a story of her time: she was a respectable woman fallen on the hard times of the Thatcher revolution, targeted by a scout who reconnoitred the neighbourhood for desperate women, and recruited into the only career she had been offered in years: crime.

The story started when the family left their London council flat in 1982. It was a bad year, when the Government assiduously rallied its arsenal to defend itself against opposition within and without, when it saw the total unemployment figure heading catastrophically towards three million.

This domestic left her much-loved job in the hospice to take her three children to join her husband, in a caravan. 'At the time I didn't think it was too great but I look back and think it was heaven.' It felt like liberation for children who had grown up in London but it was cold at night, cramped. And the sojourn was cut short when her husband was made redundant again. The family moved back to Tyneside, home territory. They were swiftly allocated a council flat.

Her people had been formed by the industrial crucible of the North East – shipbuilding – and her father worked as an engineer in the shipyards. He never failed to get to work – even during a bus strike he walked to work. Her mother was a model of respectable wifehood; she polished the front step, she baked every week, she brought up nine children. Her brothers were skilled workers, all union men. Her sisters worked in shops and for the Provident, as debt collectors.

After the husband's redundancy, there was no employment for the couple. 'My family would drive up to our door with black plastic bags of clothes. My mother baked on Mondays and gave us food. On a bad day I'd get an inquest: what was I doing with my money? It sounds ungrateful, but they wouldn't be worrying about the next slice of bread. I was, all the time. I'd be thinking there are so many slices of bread to last so long.'

Every fortnight the Giro arrived from social security. 'I'd work everything out, the bills, and there would be almost nothing left to last through the two weeks. This went on for for ages. It seemed like a lifetime. All the time my marriage was getting worse because my life was getting worse.

'I carried the whole burden. The kids didn't say, "Dad, I'm

hungry," they said, "Mam, I'm hungry." He watched the telly and read thrillers borrowed from the library. He didn't do the washing. He didn't tidy up. He didn't clean the house. Only occasionally he cooked. It was only me doing anything. I felt like a human hoover.

'I didn't go anywhere at all, except to my mother's. I went from my house to her house and nothing in between. I hadn't gone back to square one, I'd gone further back than that. To be honest I began to feel that it would be better not to be here at all.' This went on until 1988. By then her children were teenagers, the marriage had collapsed and she'd asked her husband to leave.

A woman in her thirties had moved onto the same estate. They got to know each other a little and the woman came up with a plan to make money: 'We could go out with some people and cheque books and get things and sell them. The cheque books would be provided – the woman said that people broke into houses or got them from cars. I knew it was illegal.

'At first I thought I'd do it for a bit until I'd paid everything off, until *my benefit was my own*. I'd do it until I was on my feet – Utopia! It was just the thought of going to the post office and cashing the Giro and not having to give anybody any of it. Little did I know then to what extent I was going to get involved.

'I can still remember going shopping with a cheque book – stolen – buying a load of shopping worth about £40 with a cheque, and it meant I had something to eat for every day of the week.'

She was the shopper in a system worked with militaristic precision. A stolen cheque book could cost about £75. She knew none of the cohorts in the syndicate beyond her immediate contact, the supplier of the cheques, and her driver. The night before a day's work, a cheque book was delivered and she rehearsed the signature. The next day was spent buying goods up to the cheque card's £50 limit, all according to items on a list, which specified the make and the size. Typically, the list included children's clothes, sportswear, pots and pans, crockery, shoes. On Friday she did half a dozen loads of food shopping, one for herself and the rest for the syndicate. Sometimes she saw a pair of trainers she wanted to buy for one of her children. That would be her payment. Otherwise she earned about £15 for a day's shopping passing between eight and ten cheques, enough to cover everyone who had a stake in that cheque book. She could spend a maximum of about £1,500 with a reasonably packed cheque book. But the most she would be paid for a week's work would be about £60, plus a supermarket shopping.

The two women met the driver, they went into town or sometimes to other cities. Her contact followed her into the shops, or waited nearby with the bags. 'We always had a list. I've gone into Argos with a list including the stock numbers and the exact price from the order form, or the catalogue.

'One of the popular things was the Eternal Bow dinner service. It's beige with flowers. People want everything to match, from the dinner service to the pedal bin, the utensils that you can hang on the wall and even the electric kettle. It could take six or seven trips over a period of weeks.

'Once I had to get a new teapot and I went to a store with my daughter to buy one. My daughter picked up the Eternal Bow and said, "I think that's lovely." I said, "No, pet." Maybe the woman at the counter had served me – I reckon I put about twenty of the sets together.'

Once in, she felt she could not get out of the system. Her contact regularly appeared with bruises or bleeding after a beating or clumps of hair missing. Her condition was a warning. 'She knew who *they* were. I asked, but she said best not to know. At the same time *they* knew who I was. I was told once to change my mac, to get a dark-coloured raincoat from one of the cheques, because *they* thought I was too visible. So *they* knew what I looked like and the coat I wore – so, I'd ask myself where they hell were *they*?

'It was when I realised that I couldn't say I wasn't going that I realised what I'd got into. It really hit home when I got caught. I was in a store and my contact was in McDonalds waiting. The cheque card went through the machine and it went off. It was making this noise so I ran, I got to the glass doors but an old lady was in front of me and a security guard was behind me. So I stopped. While we waited for the police I thought, thank goodness it's over. I wasn't thinking about what was going to happen, I was just feeling relief.'

She was charged and allowed out on bail while she waited for her case to come up at the magistrate's court. Her contact appeared from time to time for the news. She finally went to court and was fined £100, to be paid in weekly instalments of £5.

'I thought, "Lovely, I'm out of it!" Within a week I was at it again. The contact appeared with a cheque book and told me if I didn't do it then my house would be turned over. She said they would pay my fine. They didn't. They were very heavy people. And she did some terrible things. If she knew a woman who was a single parent who was doing a part-time cleaning job on the side, she'd tell the social security. She would put women in a situation where they needed some source of income.'

In the second phase of this criminal career she worked four days a week. Cheque books would be brought to her home during the evening so she could practise the signatures. 'Liberty depended on being very skilled at it. Occasionally a shop would want authorisation, then you knew to run for it. Of course you lost the cheque book and on the next occasion you had to pay off the lost cheques before you earned anything.'

For more than a year after her first arrest a secretary in the fraud squad was beginning to recognise her handwriting on the stolen cheques being processed by the police. It was the secretary who then amassed the volumes of cheques she had signed and it was this vigilance that brought detectives to her home sixteen months after her first arrest – the secretary had recognised the way she wrote F and Y.

The fraud squad arrived at 8.45 one summer morning, a few weeks before the riots. They searched her home but found nothing. However, by then they had her fingerprints, and sightings of her recorded on shop video cameras. They told her they had a lot of evidence. When they took her to the police station to be charged with fraud and deception, she was shown the evidence – files full of cheques all over the room. She was asked to identify what she thought were her cheques and she spent several hours trawling through the documents, often recognising the signature of an unknown person whose name, for a day, had been her own. Her cooperation stalled when they asked for names in the syndicate. She named no one. However, before her trial in November 1991 she received a warning. One Friday night she took a walk with her dogs down the path behind her house. Three men sprang out of the bushes, punched her in the face, kicked her to the ground and beat her. 'Just very quietly they whispered, "Don't mention any names."

'That secretary did me a favour,' she said. That was the end, because from then, of course, she was no use to the syndicate. However it was the beginning of a process that would end in prison and expose the paradox of her life as a law-breaker.

Her trial lasted less than a couple of hours. She pleaded guilty to fraud and deception involving cheques to a value of £63,000. The court took 1,444 offences into consideration. She was sentenced to eighteen months in prison.

When she was finally undone she was struck not by a crisis of respectability, but a crisis of responsibility – who would now do what she had done? Who would do the *work* of looking after her family?

'My first thought was my daughter, and would my husband look after her. He'd never taken responsibility before. He was a man who had never done anything for himself. He'd had a mother and then a wife to do everything for him. We had been married for nineteen years. We had grown up together. He couldn't believe it at first, he thought I was a survivor and now I'd toppled off the pedestal. Never in our married life had I said *I want.*'

Before her trial she left a schedule of instructions posted up about how to run the home. Washing instructions were attached to the cupboard door. Her husband did not know the washing machine's setting instructions. 'First the whites,' said her guide, 'towels, socks, underwear, sheets. Set number three, place soap powder in the middle section . . .'

Her relatives discovered what had happened through the debt-collecting grapevine – her sister was a Provident collector around her estate, and heard the news. 'They'd known I was doing something, but no one had ever asked before.' It was her mother's reaction she feared most. 'I was thirty-nine years old, in prison and dreading a letter from my mother!' When it came the letter was tolerant and contained a stamped addressed envelope for her reply.

During her imprisonment she was encouraged to do catering work. Catering was what she had been doing all her life. But at least she got a certificate inside that she could use outside. Her prison officer was an affable woman. 'Her husband used to bash her. "Never mind," she said to me once, "You'll have a lovely holiday when you're out. You must have stashed a load away." I told her that she censored my letters and therefore she knew that my husband had had to get an electricity meter installed. We couldn't pay by waiting for the bills. She didn't believe it. After a bit she came back and said she had read my case notes. She apologised.'

She was released on parole after six months. During her time inside her daughter had stopped going to school. 'My daughter had been shocked, but the thing she was really frightened of was whether the school would find out.

'I thought I'd done everything my mam had instilled in me. I had been a good mother, a good wife, but I had been to prison, so who was I to tell my daughter about right and wrong? Like me, she'd made her own web and she couldn't get out of it. Maybe my daughter thought I wasn't woman enough to tell people where I'd been, but I was.'

When they went together to meet the child's teacher, she asked the child whether she knew any other children with parents in prison. No, said the child. Well, there were several. No one ever found out from the staff.

This woman, who had always seen herself as nothing if not a good mother, re-entered the world with a new nomenclature – she was a criminal. Her career in crime was not a rebellion, nor was it a thrilling transgression. It was private and it brought her little pleasure. However, even amidst her fear of the syndicate, and her assignment yet again to a reluctant and subordinate place amidst the mysterious and the powerful, she recovered a crucial confidence that she was once again doing what, as a daughter and then a mother of the skilled working class, she had always done – she was taking responsibility for *everything*. Her life crisis was an effect of a national economic crisis. Her family's history, economically and culturally, was the history of the English industrial revolution. Her crisis was its crisis.

This woman's dependence was only ever economic. Everyone in her family expected her to keep their lives going, and she did. By the end of the Eighties she and her family had looked for work in three counties. Now her robust respectability worked not to keep her legal, but to keep her decent, out of debt and independent. The fortitude of law-abiding virtue that was inscribed in her class transferred itself to law-breaking only as a mode of survival. Unlike many of the young men whose law-breaking happened in a culture that *made* them into *men*, her criminality was not social, it was a secret. Publicly it was perceived as an affront to her identity as a woman; economically she had perceived it precisely *as a woman's obligation* to keep the family going. In the olden days she might have been a woman who baked and cleaned the front step, like her own mother. Nowadays, being a good woman, like her mother, had dispatched her to prison.

These women's work was not work like any other; it was graft, the work of the ghetto.

CHAPTER 12

Community Politics

C ommunity is dead, long live community politics. Just
as the very notions of neighbourhood, collectivity, class,
consensus and solidarity were alleged to be waning as the
organising principles of British progressive politics, community was reincarnated by liberals and radicals and conservatives
alike after the Sixties as a political constituency. Community
politics appeared like a golden egg, immaculately conceived,
small and perfectly formed, bringing classes together, reforming the quality of life within the neighbourhood. For progress-
ives the promise was of a politics made in heaven – a carnival
of convivial campaigns that would re-engage the people in the
political process.

This fantasy was the heir to the fallen idols of twentieth-
century modernism and the metropolis, and it was at its best
when it rehabilitated confidence in the benign chaos of the
complex city, the cooperative discipline of *social* space and
of local society.

Community politics was a celebration of civil society and
it could be no coincidence that its reincarnation was most
marked in the poorest parts of the cities, where it embraced a
commitment to cosmopolitanism on the one hand and a critique of the entire political system on the other. Community
politics was solidarity against the state. Its success, however,
was contingent on much more than critique. It demanded
the party-political system's recognition of autonomous movements and initiatives outside the party system. This never
really happened in Britain. In the Seventies, Labourism jealous-
ly guarded its municipal fortifications against the challenges

of tenants. In the Eighties the Conservatives smoked out the space of citizens' activism. Just as the collapse of the Eastern European states at the end of the decade exposed the brittle and often brutal temper of local life when starved of the means of organisation, so the exhausted estates on the edges of British cities exposed the poverty of politics, and its estrangement from society. There were communities, but there was little or no politics.

After the riots no political party sponsored any discussion in any neighbourhood about what the people had lived through and how they would recover. At most, the political parties sought to explain the riots, or rather explain them away.

In Ely it was the resourceful Community Education centre at Trelai Library – little more than a community shed – that called in anyone and everyone who wanted to be debriefed about what had happened and talk about how to reinvigorate the estate. Community Education, which sponsored not only classes but also a radical retirement culture among those citizens over fifty, became the first focus for a strategy to staunch Ely's decline.

In Newcastle's West End, political debate was stifled. There was a plethora of neighbourhood structures, venues and meetings through which a review might have been aired. But debate was closed down. 'We were instructed not to talk to the press,' said a Labour councillor, Nigel Todd, who had spent the night of the Elswick riot on the streets and visiting the vulnerable.

Politicians, both Labour and Tory, in Ely, Blackbird Leys and Tyneside, condemned the criminals and reiterated propaganda about the potential of these territories in the hope that inward investors would not be too dismayed. But the practical process of recovery was organised through the medium of community politics, by activists who suddenly found themselves no longer shunned, but now part of the business of bidding for funds for their communities in the Government's City Challenge lottery. These activists then became a resource, not a problem.

But the concept of community assumed there were homogenised neighbourhoods with universal interests. All that was burned out in the riots of 1991 because, in each location, neighbourhoods witnessed their own combustions as both an effect and a cause of conflict *within*. Meadowell was the paradigm, a place where community politics was shellshocked by poverty, internecine harassment and lack of support from the political system beyond its boundaries.

However, Conservative condemnation of 'criminals' on the one hand and radical critiques of law and order on the other, could not conceal the evidence finally exposed during the riots of contradictions, of heroic endeavour and blithe destruction within these small places. The decade between 1981 and 1991 in Meadowell witnessed the renaissance of militant self-help as a response to economic crisis. The rise of cultures of crime, both organised and spontaneous, was the shadow of that movement. So, there was both a community activism and a criminal response to economic catastrophe, and these two tendencies were also inflected by gender and generation. They existed in a constant tension that was dramatised in the destructive spectacle of 9 September, in milk bottles filled with a pint of petrol.

Meadowell's entry into community politics began with the creation in 1969 of the Community Development Project, a Home Office initiative based on a dozen neighbourhoods and designed to 'find new ways of meeting the needs of people living in areas of high social deprivation.' Tyneside was already the poorest metropolitan area in the country and it became home to two CDPs, one centred on Meadowell, and the other in Scotswood. The CDP local teams embarked on the first part of their brief, research into and action on de-industrialisation, bad housing and low pay. They sent detailed reports to Westminster. 'They waited for a response. Nothing happened. Central Government departments were either hostile or, more often, uninterested.'[1]

Soon, the other part of the brief, mobilisation of community self-help, 'began to bring out the real contradictions at the heart

---

[1] *Gilding the Ghetto: The state and the poverty experiments*, Community Development Project, 1977.

of the CDP notion.' As soon as the teams began in earnest to work and organise with local tenants and action groups, 'they found themselves drawn into direct conflict with councillors and officials of the local authorities – the very people who, in part at least, were their employers.' That conflict consumed some local projects. It was, of course, in the nature of community politics itself – challenge was not welcomed either by local or by central government. But the clatter of the conflict between the locality and the local state drowned the sound of the conflicts within the community – between the community and the criminal responses to their difficulties. That internal conflict went unnoticed by the CDP tradition. This was all the more ironic since CDP was a Home Office initiative that was concerned with the connection between poverty, children and crime in the community. 'The origins of the CDP suggests that its concern was not in poverty itself but in the consequences of poverty – specifically the rising crime rate and, in particular, the rapidly increasing rate of juvenile crime.'[2] The radical researchers saw this orientation, however, as a device 'to develop a wider sense of responsibility for keeping children under control.' Because neither gender nor crime was high on its agenda, the CDP tradition either missed or misunderstood some of the most active and the most destructive agents in their territories. The CDP's final report is explicit: 'Many CDPs were approached by the local constabulary with offers of assistance and cooperation in their early days. The North Shields CDP, for example, in addition to receiving frequent informal visits from local police during its first year, also received specially compiled monthly lists of indictable and non-indictable offences reported in the project area. It was some time before the police realised the project was not using the information and stopped compiling it and sending it.'[3] No one was to know then just how devastating the consequences of that indifference were to be.

[2] *Ibid.*
[3] *Ibid.*

*

Meadowell estate began life as The Ridges, the creation of
Tory Tynemouth, a borough that was absorbed into a muni
cipal fiction, North Tyneside, after the 1974 local government reorganisation. Tynemouth acquired land from the
Duke of Northumberland and built The Ridges using the 1930
Housing Act, which facilitated slum clearance. To this
enclave were sent refugees from pre-war private rookeries
whose new homesteads were to become post-war municipal
slums.

By the time the CDP had established the first advice centre
on the estate in the early Seventies, the northern half was being
modernised and residents were being uprooted and rehoused in
the interim. Networks of neighbourhood representatives were
generated by CDP community workers seeking out tenants
who would speak up for their own street. 'We opened minds,'
recalled former CDP director John Foster, who was later to
become a senior officer in North Tyneside council.

'We certainly increased the aspirations of a lot of *women* on
the estate.' A measure of the challenge which that represented
was the response of the men who lived with these women. 'At
some point all the CDP workers were threatened by the men,
because of the changes in the women. You'd get blokes saying,
"What are you doing? My wife is never in!" I used to say to
the team, "Don't be frightened of using the local facilities,"
so people would go to the local pubs and clubs and the men
would be there. They knew that what the women were doing
was good, but they didn't have the energy or the capacity to
involve themselves. They would also say things like was their
lass "up to something with them community lads" [the CDP
workers].'

Foster was candid enough to admit that these thoughts
on the women's situation enjoy the benefit of hindsight. At
the time, the CDP's priority was to engage men, or rather
the men's movement – the Labour Movement. The movement's history in the North East's mining, maritime and
engineering industries had been a classic case of men's politics

masquerading as class politics. These working men's economic self-defence against their employers in the pits, the shipyards and the engineering factories was organised not only at the expense of women, but to the exclusion of women. The history of the colliers, shipwrights and engineers was a story of men's crusade against women's right to work with them. The Labour Movement had, therefore, never represented the whole working class, and rarely strayed beyond the boundaries of the workplace into the domain that men shared with women and children – the neighbourhood and the home.

Not surprisingly, the CDP's efforts to engage the Labour Movement in a community coalition concerned with the politics of housing did not work. 'We tried to target groups like the trade unions, trades councils, organisations on the economic and industrial side. We got involved in them and we sought out shop stewards, but there was only a handful of them and they got involved a bit, but not much.'

There was an industrial dispute at a ship repair yard and CDP used the occasion to service the workers, both to be useful and to encourage reciprocal support for the community. 'We set up an advice centre for them and hoped to unite the community and work locales,' said Foster. But that did not work either. 'The old Labour Movement structures were not particularly relevant on the estate, and most Tynemouth Labour Movement activists did not live there.'

The people who did connect with CDP, however, were women. 'Women became very active, and in fact most of the community organisations were created by women,' he added. 'For me that was the fundamental thing that happened.' So, even though they were not its first choice, its prime targets, women became the CDP's allies, and the CDP was the first agency with any authority that lent its support to women in Meadowell.

The CDP focused on modernisation of the estate. That galvanised the neighbourhood networks, which then supported the advice centre, set up by the CDP, when it was threatened with closure in 1978. A six-week sit-in secured its survival for another five years and in fact it endured until the year before the riots, when activists again occupied the centre to save it from closure.

A culture of active citizenship was emergent alongside the CDP. A configuration of communal solidarity spanned several networks. Some were doing some straight talking with the council and campaigning against the Government's crusade, after 1979, against public housing and poor people. Some were creating local utilities to encourage independence.

Meadowell showed the need for politics in the decade that saw the decline of Socialism, the death of Communism and, some would believe, the demise of radical politics altogether. Community action provided access to self-discovery and a social world. It connected people who lived on a jagged edge to national cultures and movements. The place was never seen as doing this, of course. Meadowell was not seen as inventive or generative.

In the Meadowell estate what was at stake politically was the reform of relations between the citizens, as tenants, and their landlord, one of the most powerful influences on their everyday lives. Community politics also created modest democratic enterprises to mitigate an economic state of emergency on the estate. It had yet another dimension – informal initiative on the street: a party to celebrate the wedding of Charles and Diana; baking and bingo to raise cash for children's holidays; a food co-op.

The CDP and the advice centre which survived the Project's demise in 1978 did not please the local authority. They were absorbed in tenants' troubles and their priority was to challenge the council's management of the estate's affairs. Therefore, 'we were seen as the enemy,' said John Foster. Some of the 'enemy' were the women who organised the estate's recovery after the riot. Their political prescience had not been respected enough to pre-empt the explosion of the riots.

John Foster's belief, as a senior bureaucrat, that the women constituted the core of the active citizens, and John

Broughton's conviction, as a senior police officer, that 'we have to empower the women to call in the chips' attracted little or no institutional investment in the Eighties. By the Nineties the women were asset-stripped.

One of the activists was Margaret Nolan, who grew up in Jarrow, the Tyneside town that became an icon in the history of the Great Depression. Her married life was spent in Meadowell, which, unlike Jarrow, made its mark not as a home of tragic heroes but as home to the wild boys, or as they say on Tyneside, the radgy gadjes. Jarrow was the starting place of the most famous and the most conservative of the Hunger Marches, which tramped from the Distressed Areas to the capital. The Jarrow March, its genesis and culture, were intensely gendered – it recruited among the workless men whose street-corner languor was one of the motifs of England's Hungry Thirties. The men's enforced indolence was public. Their wageless women were hidden. They were working – at home. The Jarrow March adopted a discipline inherited from the First World War. By modelling its style on military manners it condensed several virtues of soldierly sacrifice, war and work into an image not of the whole community, but of masculinity and martyrdom.

Jarrow occupied a sentimental place in the history of the Hunger Marches, not because it was radical or ingenious – the earlier marches organised by the National Unemployed Workers Association were more inventive and audacious. This was the Labour Party's march. It was engaging not because it was challenging but because it was pacific and pleading. Jarrow also framed the memory of the Hunger Marches by giving to posterity some heart-stopping photographs of the bonny lads, young fathers hugging their children as they left for their great adventure, reminiscent of the jaunty tragedy of the 'tommies' departing for the Great War.

Margaret Nolan was born into that history. She was a grammar school girl but said, 'I left school at seventeen under great pressure from my father. He was a labourer who said it was a lad's place to get educated and a girl's place to get a job

and have a family. He didn't feel that supporting me at school
was worthwhile.'

She was a good Catholic girl who married a good Irish boy
and within four years had four children. In those days, in the
Sixties, the Meadowell was still known as The Ridges. It was
a shoddy suburban colony to house the poor who had formerly
sheltered in the Bankside, where the Tyne met the North Sea.
'I moved to the Meadowell because it was the only place I was
offered – at that time people with problems were put there,
and the problem the council said I had was children. I was
frightened for my life when I was put there.'

By the time Margaret Nolan's fifth child arrived she had
made five moves in five years. Her husband had worked with
the Co-op Dairy until he was made redundant – one of many
redundancies during his working life. She worked as a hospital
cleaner and went to night classes. She was not seeking out
political activism then. 'With all those young children there
was no way I would have been looking for it.' Neither did she
respond when the CDP began putting leaflets through doors
inviting people to take part.

Her first participation in politics was provoked by the way
families received social security: in cash over the counter, to
the men. 'On Friday afternoon they'd get paid at Borough Road
in North Shields and come home via the pub and the betting
shop with whatever was left. I was one of those who used to
get what was left.' She protested to social security. 'I objected
to the way it was handed to the men when it was supposed
to be for the women and children.' By the mid-Seventies she
was the breadwinner, working nights as a nursing auxiliary
in Newcastle. Because it was she who was working and her
husband who was unemployed, her family forfeited the income
support to which they would have been entitled had she been
a man.

Margaret Nolan and her friend Maureen lived opposite
each other; they both had five children around the same age.
They shared the cooking of their Sunday dinners. One or other
would make the Yorkshire puddings, and they went back and

forth with vegetables. Sometimes there was a joint, otherwise there would be sausages or corned beef. 'We'd go all out on Sundays and my friend Maureen made rice puddings, and her mother-in-law made scones, so we shared them as well.'

So Nolan's life as an organiser began with Sunday dinners. It entered the public realm when she and her friends organised bingo sessions to finance treats for the children during the summer holidays.

During the Eighties she became a street representative in tenants' campaigns, she helped to found a Credit Union – a poor people's savings bank – and a food co-op. After the riots she campaigned for funds from City Challenge – the Environment Department's local government lottery – to rescue the estate.

Before the bingo began, Margaret's and Maureen's coming and goings, back and forth with Yorkshire puddings, were noticed by a neighbour thirty years older than both of them, Nancy Peters, who was in her seventies when she watched the riots. She had arrived in Meadowell twenty years earlier than Margaret Nolan, after living, like her, in a private rented slum in North Shields. Both came from immigrant folk. Nolan was white, Peters was black. 'There were no other black people on the estate who I connected with. I'd only think about it if anyone harassed the children and called them a nigger. Once my daughter came home and said a teacher had called her a cannibal. I went up there right away and asked him if he had any connections with cannibals, whether he knew what they were and whether they were any particular colour. That was the only time I went to the school as a parent.'

She worked as a hospital cleaner and brought up ten children alone after her divorce. She brought her weekly groceries home in a pram. She worked, baked, brought up children, read books. She lived a little, local life. She noticed Margaret Nolan and her friend in the street, and watched their Sunday comings and goings. 'She used to look at me and I would look at her. I was a bit shy. She looked at me as though she wanted to speak.' Eventually she did, and Nancy Peters joined the bingo.

Behind Nancy's house was a corporation depot which was also used as a dump by people from as far away as Whitley Bay and Tynemouth. There were reported to be rats, bedsteads and even a dead baby. One day, 'I was up to the teeth in flippin' anger and shouting and bawling about it to a neighbour.' She was overheard by the advice centre worker who was leafleting the street, who suggested she stop shouting and go along to the centre and do something. She did, and while she was there she made another suggestion: 'The kids have nowhere to play. Why can't we have a park?' So began her career as an active citizen.

Molly Woodhouse was rehoused on the Meadowell in 1981 because her husband was terminally ill and they needed sheltered housing. She worked as a buyer with the North Shields department store, Walker's – 'the house of quality' – until it closed down in 1985 when she was seventy. Her husband had worked in the shipyards as a riveter and had always been a strong union man, in the boilermakers' society. He was a member of the manual élite, the labour aristocracy. When she retired she began doing voluntary work and in 1983 turned up for the first meeting of people interested in establishing a Credit Union, at the Cedarwood Centre, which was a Church of England resource on the south side of the estate. There she met Margaret Nolan. The Credit Union was formally launched a year later at the advice centre, with a dozen members all saving £1 a week each, which constituted its only capital. Members could then borrow twenty per cent above their savings and arrange their repayments with a loans committee – members like themselves – according to their obligations.

By 1991 Meadowell Credit Union had about four hundred members. It evoked a tradition of radical cooperation previously long gone but which had enjoyed a serious revival in the Eighties. It allowed people who lived in one of the Brazils of Britain, where the economy was defined by debt, to realise their imaginary selves, to glimpse self-sufficiency.

The union was the first agency to attack the fiscal haemorrhage from the estate. In 1985 the organisers surveyed debt in a couple of streets and calculated that an average of £10 a week was leaving each house in repayment of debt at rates of interest that varied between thirty-three and one thousand per cent. The Credit Union interest was one per cent. 'We assumed that about half of people's repayments went on interest. That meant an average of £5 leaving two thousand households, fifty-two weeks a year, on interest alone,' said Margaret Nolan.

The Cedarwood Centre housed washing machines and a drop-in centre. A group of men organised an Angler's Club and a group of women set up a Wellbeing Group: the centre was where they enjoyed themselves, keeping fit, or going out for a meal or to the cinema. A local branch of Church Action Against Poverty had a Women's Issues Group, and this came up with the idea of a food co-op. In 1985 the co-op began going weekly to the cash-and-carry, bringing back what basics they could manage and selling them.

Molly Woodhouse had been a wage-earner for forty-five years. She was a family woman who had no friends beyond her six sisters and six brothers. She ran her own car and her own home, and was a redoubtable member of the respectable working class. She was shocked by what she was seeing. 'I was so sorry. The food co-op started because of poverty. I'd had no idea what poverty was. Whatever I had, I'd worked for. I thought I was poor. But there was a difference between being poor and poverty – and this was poverty here,' she said.

FOOD CO-OP was inscribed in a modest but glittering mosaic on the walls of the Cedarwood Centre – the only art to decorate the estate's walls apart from graffiti. The food co-op waned towards the end of the Eighties, exposing the fragility of organisations founded on so few resources. It tried to encourage healthy eating, which cost more money and lost the co-op some of its stalwart customers. Meadowell gave birth to Britain's first estate-based group in MIND, the mental health movement.

All these endeavours represented a renaissance of militant self-help which were shadowed by Meadowell's increasingly sinister decline. When riots razed all the community's food

shops in 1991, the Credit Union became the banker to a food
co-op re-established by the women in response to the new
emergency.

Of the groups focused on subjectivity and self-development,
rather than rights and self-help, the most spectacular success –
both in stamina and public productions – was a writing group
which ran in the second half of the Eighties and was supported
by the writer Kitty Fitzgerald. She was a Writer in Residence
in the North East and a member of the Amber film collective,
part of Newcastle's rugged realist tradition of cine and stills
photography based in the Side Gallery.

Fitzgerald spent an evening with the writing group, and
another and yet another. Meadowell expected groups to come
and go, live and then die, especially those with a personal
rather than a public focus. But this relationship lasted several
years, generating first of all a volume of life-story writing
and pictures, *Mixed Feelings*, and later Amber's feature film,
Dream On, which emerged out of writing and improvisation
by Amber actresses and writers which engaged the Meadowell
women and came out of their experience. *Dream On* – sinister,
witty, surprising – was screened after the riots and revealed
what the riots did not: what people had to put up with, or
rather what women had to put up with from men.

The destiny of the old corporation depot behind Nancy
Peters' house was emblematic of the way things were to
go. It had been earmarked as a car park or an allotment
ground in the early Eighties – it became neither. Nancy
Peters' 'shouting and bawling' had triggered the creation of an
alliance between children, adults and the advice centre. They
surveyed the residents and found that eighty-eight per cent
supported a play space. They launched a campaign. Schools
supported them; a group of girls designed a model of what
they wanted. Eventually the council put up £140,000 for a
glorious playground, well equipped with sturdy playground
furniture, a playworker's hut, and all of it surrounded by a

wall. The ribbon was cut just before the summer holidays in 1986.

But children also had their own list of priorities, and at the top was a 'parkie' on the play site – a keeper to keep it safe. They knew they would need protection. No money, said the council. So, every day, on a rota, residents opened up the playground and every night they locked it up. Every Sunday they cleaned up the site, and every Monday morning they discussed with the council 'workie' what needed to be repaired or replaced.

After a year they were tired. 'We felt we were being taken for a ride by the council,' said Nancy Peters. Suddenly they discovered that the council was about to employ a play worker. There had been no consultation. Although the worker would be an asset, they felt hurt and snubbed. This was a place full of pain, with a collective ego that was alert to all disrespect. The council tried to patch it up but the residents were hurt. They backed off, the Sunday clean-up stopped, the Monday repair session ended, the treasured play site deteriorated.

'It would now be seen as a disaster, but it was a classic example of what happens if you don't work with the people,' said Margaret Nolan. 'It won't work.'

The play organiser who had stumbled into this storm was Keeks McGarry, a young man whose professional survival was initially a struggle against daily destruction. He was severely tested at the play site. He started by playing it cool, being almost no more than a 'parkie', hanging around, getting to know people. Then he began organising sessions to the swimming baths, campaign weekends, parachute games, competitions. Older children tried to push Keeks and take the territory. They set fire to his hut, stole from it, stole from him. 'They were testing me,' he said, 'but they wore down when they knew I was there to stay.' The play space was not there to stay, however. Having spent what seemed like a fortune to build it, local government was not prepared to spend another fortune to support it and defend it against the attrition of the angry young kids.

Community development worker Denise Riach said that in the Eighties, and even the Nineties, 'You could often still get the money for a new project, but what you could not get was the money to maintain it and to protect it.' The tragedy of the play site was that it had been built out of an organic movement, it had been nurtured by a network in the neighbourhood – but there was no *institutional* strategy for its survival.

After the lads had torched Keeks' hut he moved into the hinterland of the estate where there were other outposts of community action. There had been a sedate local library in Avon Avenue on the north side, which had been revitalised in the mid-Eighties with new, popular stock, a café and a new name, the Book Centre. Keeks persuaded the council to give permission for painting sessions during the winter twilight hours, between 4 and 6 p.m. It became a very busy place. But the Book Centre was finding it difficult to withstand not only the kids' wear and tear, but also harassment and violence. It was finally defeated by a combination of the poll tax cuts and children's destruction. In 1990 the Book Centre closed. By 1991 Collingwood Youth Club, on the south side, had lost most of its staff. The youth service on the estate had all but disappeared. In its absence, the regime of the angry young men held sway.

By the end of the decade Meadowell was going mad. 'We began to notice it in the resource centre,' recalled Denise Riach. 'We started to suffer constant harassment from kids. We'd had the general burglaries before that, but that was normal. In 1989 and 1990 it became horrific. We had to keep our building locked up while we were inside. We tried talking to the kids about our work, but that bore no fruit, and in fact it created more problems. It made us even more of a focus.'

'We kept telling the council that something was happening,' said Molly Woodhouse. 'We could feel it. But they didn't want to listen to us.'

'They said we were paranoid,' added her friend Nancy Peters.

But the women were experiencing the consequences of the estate's crisis in their own lives. During the Credit Union sessions, twice a week at the resource centre, Molly Woodhouse said that 'We used to get locked in. The kids used to pull the shutters down. We had no telephone, so people would be locked in for hours because we couldn't telephone out for help. Twice a week we'd have to call out the security men about the shutters. Kids would shout through the letter box, "You can't get out unless you pay us £10." The estate was petrified, young and old, because of what was happening with these kids. For two years we lived with boarded-up windows.'

Many of the activists marked the beginning of the end as the legislative aftermath of Margaret Thatcher's third General Election victory in 1987, when the impact of the Tories' remarkable triumph began to be felt. In 1988 the Government implemented one of the most drastic changes in social security legislation since the Beveridge plan for the welfare state was introduced after the Second World War. This left forty-three per cent of the poor worse off.[4] The effect on an estate where almost every household depended on some kind of state benefit was palpable. The abolition of discretionary emergency payments, to cope with crises and catastrophes, dead refrigerators and disappearing beds was disastrous in an area as volcanic as Meadowell.

The new Government launched a Housing Act designed to alter the architecture of public housing management, by separating councils from council housing. The act generated a new nationwide tenants' movement to defend municipal ownership, the first to enjoy the unreserved blessing of Labour councils. Indeed many Labour councils sponsored the setting-up of tenants' associations on estates where there were none. When the poll tax was introduced in England and Wales at the end of the decade it was met by almost universal opposition. It had a ready-made infrastructure of resistance in the new

---

[4] Carey Oppenheim, *Poverty: The Facts*, Child Poverty Action Group, London, 1990.

tenants' movement, but also attracted an unusually hetero-
geneous coalition of rebels.

Meadowell Action Group was a tenants' movement that
mushroomed after 1988. It sent a coachload of residents to
the great poll tax demonstration in Trafalgar Square, where
they found themselves among 250,000 people. It was bliss. 'It
was brilliant, I'd never experienced anything like it,' said one
of them – even though the bloody mess at the end of the demonstration left them lost in London, scrounging lifts home to
the North East through the night. The action group was busy;
its meetings were big. It overran the resource centre and at the
end of the decade rented its own place from the council – the
MAG House.

Full of good intent, the Group hoped to entertain elderly
tenants, and to intervene against neighbourhood terrorism by
offering space to young people. It was a disaster. 'It became
really frightening,' said Linda Craik, one of the organisers.
'They thought they should have the place all the time. It's
true they were bored, they had nothing, but they couldn't let
us have it in peace.'

In short, they would not *share* space. 'One night we were
having bingo for the pensioners. The lads kicked off by putting
the boards on the windows through, then they started charging
the windows. I got an old door and put it behind the heating
pipes to jam it up against the window. That still didn't work.
The lads were throwing concrete slabs through windows. We
tried reasoning with them, we could see everything getting
worse, but it didn't make any difference.'

When the lads were in the building they robbed it, they
threw its vacuum cleaner out of the window, set fire to the
door. They became unstoppable. 'It wasn't the residents' fault,
they were *devoted* to doing what they could. It was the workers,' said Denise Riach. 'We were naive, we allowed anarchy.
We gave too much and the kids didn't earn enough.' As in
many other community spaces, users had to lock themselves
in, to keep the lads out. They learned to do that after the lads
locked them in and would not let them out.

'Apart from people's financial problems – finance is a killer here – they had to put up with eleven-year-olds terrorising everybody,' said Denise Riach. 'Nobody knew what to do because they were frightened of them. The kids got high on it, and people couldn't stop them. Why? It was fear. Tenants' groups discussed it. We considered going *en masse* to their houses to talk to their parents, but it never happened. We could never get enough people together who were prepared to withstand the consequences – if you confronted people you got your windows smashed.'

Another professional who worked on Meadowell reckoned, 'It is easy for people who don't live here to say, "Stand up to it!" But you might get your house burned that night. The intimidation was really powerful, yet it was something that was often denied, because to admit it was like grassing on the whole place.'

The lads' piece-by-piece destruction of the MAG House humiliated the women and became a community legend. It made people feel that nothing was sustainable, nothing was safe. Years after the event, people still recalled the time when one of the old people playing bingo had a coronary attack and the ambulance was called. The lads started bricking the ambulance and the police had to be summoned. 'We don't dislike the old ladies, it's not personal,' they would say. 'When they broke into the Credit Union, they said, "It means nowt to me." Negative aspirations became the aspirations to have,' explained a youth worker.

The effect was exhausting. 'You just get into the habit, you barricade yourself in. You get used to locking doors when you're *in*,' said one woman. 'If the lads are around, you lock yourself in and you stay in. If they're not around, you heave a sigh of relief. So, you are governed by the boys. It's easier to lock the problem out than deal with it. You can't get on with your work when you are constantly harassed. They're intimidating not because they're big but because they prove time and time again that there is nothing they won't take if it's not nailed down.'

Once when someone forgot to lock the resource centre some young men wandered up into one of the offices where a group was working, occupied it, threw stuff out of the windows at passing cars and boasted about who they had burgled. They needed to say no more. Cedarwood's Wellbeing women's group bought exercise equipment – a treadmill, a rower and a bike – and kept it in the building's secure room. Once when it was empty a hole was hammered through the wall. Everything went: exercise equipment, typewriters, kettles, photocopier. Thereafter Cedarwood was kept secure by a volunteers' sleeping rota. 'The place was under siege, it was broken into daily,' said Molly Woodhouse, one of the volunteers who slept there several nights a week for a year.

Nowhere was secure – everywhere could be broken into and entered. There was always an alibi, poverty made theft predictable. But there was something else active here: it was also in the conquest of space, other people's space, that these boys were constituting themselves as men. The modelling of their masculinity was frenzied, obsessive; it knew no boundaries. They could penetrate anything while they themselves remained impregnable. What they admired and serviced was the criminalised brotherhood; what they harassed and hurt was community politics. It was an entirely and explicitly *gendered* formation.

A voluble woman active in the Credit Union went into the youth project, a reincarnation of the old Book Centre, and was greeted by a cold chorus: 'Fucking whoring cunt . . . fucking twat . . .' A youth worker remonstrated gently; the chorus ignored him and continued. She left, thinking to herself, 'I don't have to hear this,' but staying silent. She never went there again. The boys' power was a rehearsal. It was more than negative aspiration – though in truth they did their worst – it was also personal and purposive.

The angry young men victimised the women, the neighbours, the community. Nothing stopped them. That gave them permission to riot, and then to represent the riot as the community's dissent.

The unruly women had done something different with their troubles. They had done their best. They had had babies, made relationships, put the food on the table, they had cooperated and organised and created community politics. They found no support from the police, the party political system, the state or the criminals – presumably because that demanded something too difficult: that they empathise with the *other*, the women. All these forces either failed to offer them protection, or punished them. That was why, despite the scale and stamina of community politics in Meadowell, it could not become hegemonic. That was why there was nothing to stop the riot.

In 1990 the uneasy truce between the council and the resource centre was finally broken. In September that year North Tyneside council had its level of poll tax capped. Having survived Central Government cuts since 1985 by plundering its reserves, the council now felt it had no room for manoeuvre. Among the new cuts, £90,000 had to come from the community services sector – the four advice and resource centres were targets. Instead of distributing the pain across the sector, it found two-thirds, £67,000, when it felled Meadowell resource centre alone by cutting its grant altogether. The centre was given twelve days' notice. The web of groups wrapped around it found itself with the bills and workers' redundancies to deal with. 'Local people with no experience were left in the lurch to pay off workers,' said Margaret Nolan. 'Nobody from the council came and offered to help us through a traumatic time – I expect that was for their own safety.' This was the council's response to the poll tax.

Eighty-five per cent of the national population were passionate in their opposition to the poll tax. They organised their dissent in many different ways, from complaining about it at the bus stop, shouting at Mrs Thatcher on television, failing to fill in the forms, filling in the forms and failing to send them off, marching, lobbying, and rioting. Meadowell

residents were the same as everywhere else. As in other poor
places they mostly did not pay. The tax was the one issue upon
which the council and the tenants might have been expected to
agree. But now the council and its tenants were not only not on
speaking terms, they did not speak the same language. Their
local difficulty was replicated all over England and Wales:
popular feeling unsupported by any strategy or resistance
from the major opposition parties. Indeed, non-payers became
their public enemies. As political parties they had no *modus
operandi* outside the state. They, therefore, identified their
interests with those of the local state.

Poll tax *resistance* took as many forms as there were
people, they were abandoned by Her Majesty's Opposition
who subordinated politics to government. The Opposition's
ideology was framed by the institutions it inhabited; it felt
naked outside them. What it presented to the people was that
it *needed* them to pay up, not that it shared their protests and
problems. That was no use to the people of Meadowell.

Allegations about the influence of the Trotskyist sect, Militant, were behind the real rationale for executing Meadowell
resource centre. It was seen as an anti-council hive of Militant supporters because of its association with the Federation
of Anti-Poll Tax Unions. The centre was not part of the
federation, though the MAG was active in its advocacy of
non-payment of the poll tax. The tenants' complaints were
heard not as a legitimate lament, but only as 'anti-council'.

In any case, Meadowell's activists were eclectic in their theory and practice. Margaret Nolan, for example, would not shun
a Militant supporter: 'Some of the things they say I wouldn't
disagree with, but you only see them when there's disputes,
whereas I want to be part of something that is positive and
there isn't anybody I won't talk to. I'm part of Church Action
Against Poverty. I can't say that I haven't bought the Militant
paper, but I also buy the *Catholic Universe* and the *Sunday
Sun*.'

The blow to the resource centre was aimed at the 'enemy
within', but was seen as an attack on the entire estate. 'That

loss was really significant,' said the Reverend David Peel, who ran Cedarwood during the Eighties, 'because it was so many people's sole source of help.' In 1990, the council's instructions to change the locks were never enforced after old trade union connections were called in – the workers would not do the deed – and the women squatted the centre during the following year, until the riots.

So, the social scaffolding of Meadowell was being dismantled, despite the best efforts of this coterie of active citizens, all of them poor. Harassment contaminated all social relations. It was almost inevitable: Meadowell had two magnetic fields – community solidarity and crime. By pulling away from the former, the state and the political system abandoned Meadowell to the latter.

The redoubts of active citizenship on these estates were run by women whose improvised self-help systems denied their reputation as lairs inhabited by an inert underclass. In Blackbird Leys, one of the active citizens began her life on the estate as a newly divorced, single parent. 'The only way I could get my kids back was to get a place to live. I was told Blackbird Leys was the largest estate in Oxford, that was all. So I came here. I knew nobody. My parents were abroad. I was absolutely alone. My husband stopped paying maintenance. I had no money. I'd never heard of income support,' she said. When she arrived at Blackbird Leys she delivered her children to school and went to buy a newspaper. A young woman noticed her. 'She told me I looked lost and invited me for a coffee.' That was her first friend. In her desperation about money she went to the estate's neighbourhood advice centre. 'They told me everything.' In return she began helping out in its coffee bar. She then began to help out with advice sessions, managed to get a Manpower Services training job for a year and then trained as an advice worker. She became part of a coterie of community activists who raised over £100,000 for a purpose-built adventure playground on the estate.

Another of the Leys' activists suffers from agoraphobia. Her family ventured south from Scotland to find work during the Sixties, and although she had 'a wee job' she had to be transported in her daughter's car. Generally, she could not get beyond her garden wall.

'Everybody was having the day off for the Jubilee in 1977. There were a lot of kids around so I suggested that if one of them would come round the houses with me and collect money I'd put a party on.' The street party was a triumph, and launched a regular collection for treats, parties and trips to the seaside. 'For five years my dinette was the committee room,' she said, while a group of parents endlessly raised money and ultimately secured a grant and a piece of land from the council. By 1983 the network had put up a prefabricated community centre. 'I loved doing it because of the challenge – I'd never done anything you could say was anything.'

She was still afraid of going out and had no telephone, 'I can't afford it, not on a pension.' But she had a passion for politics. She had Chris Mullin's *A Very British Coup*, borrowed from the library, on her coffee table. She never missed television broadcasts of Prime Minister's Question Time, or *Panorama*, *On the Record*, *A Week in Politics* or *Newsnight*. 'I feel very connected to the world because of it.'

The community centre attracted new members and new challenges. 'I remember walking in to a committee meeting with my friend and I heard this man saying, "There's three cunts we want rid of." My friend handed in her resignation there and then and he said, "One down, two to fucking go." So I picked up everything belonging to me and left.' Nothing in this man's political environment had disturbed his confidence in his raw misogyny. No one challenged his assault on these women, nor his prospectus for the place. It became a drinking club.

'It took me until I was thirty-five years old to discover that I had been made to feel like a crappy person,' said another of

Tyneside's community activists, who, typically, got involved in politics because of her children. Her political career began when her doctor referred her to a women's group for depression. 'I'd count the days until the next time we met. It was the first time I was able to talk about how I felt and the first time anybody wanted to listen – in my whole life. It was the first time I felt people liked me.'

Ten years before the riots the woman got past the pain, took responsibility for her neighbourhood and then found herself navigating storms at home. 'The men never, never say they are proud of us. My husband says, "Who do you fucking think you are, Jesus or somebody? You think you can walk on water! You just do it so people will think you are wonderful. But you are just a fucking cunt, you neglect me, you neglect your kids, you neglect the house. If you were a decent woman you would stay at home and look after me." I get this all the time. But he doesn't do any of it. He complains about the bills. They're *my* bills, he says. I say yes, they are mine, I use the washing machine, I use the iron, I use the cooker. And then when the riots happened and we were frightened he blamed me.'

Ely's early political world, formed in the Thirties, and characteristic of South Wales, was sustained by proletarian institutions: the Co-op, the Chapel, the Communist and Labour Parties. Among its community activists then was Lil Price, a woman who had been imprisoned for riotous assembly in 1932 in Bedwas – a mining village which made history during a Herculean contest between radical and independent trade unionism, 'The Fed', and company unionism. In 1932 the Bedwas pit owners organised a lockout at the pit in Rhymney village and in February, during a demonstration against 'scabs', she was arrested and sentenced to four months in prison. Her husband was locked up for six months and her small son was cared for by her sister. The neighbours looked after her chickens.

Of the 1932 incident, Lil explained: 'The riot was because the women were demonstrating. They went down to meet some of the scabs coming home. My neighbours were trying to stop the scabs breaking the strike. The pit was the only work, there was no other.' Lil Price moved with her young family to Ely, where she was an active member of the Communist Party and the Women's Co-op Guild. Still an active reader in her eighties – she was reading the latest biography of George Orwell in 1992 – she entered the last decade of the century, after the demise of Communism, in a fury.

She and her lifelong friend, Kate Walters, were among the dozens of women who were Ely's active citizens and, in their case, were mainstays of the estate's Communist Party before and after the war. They used to call her enclave in Ely around the northern end – where the riots broke out in 1991 – 'little Moscow'. Every Thursday Kate Walters used to go to Lil Price's house, where she would often be polishing the stair rods, and team up with her to go to the Women's Co-op Guild, which was the spine of the women's Labour Movement in the first half of the twentieth century. None of this infrastructure of activism remained at the end of the century. By the Nineties there was no women's wing of the Labour Movement. There was a tenants' association, sponsored by the council to protect municipal tenure of the estate, but there was no party-political organisation concerned with the collective will. 'Labour has always been an insignificant group of very few members. People vote Labour but they are not particularly interested in organised politics,' said the local Labour leader, the Reverend Bob Morgan.

One of the most potent presences on the estate was outside politics: it was Community Education, one of the most affectionate and enterprising local initiatives in the city, which organised holidays, health classes, education courses, a community festival, plays and pantomimes – a recent star was a seventy-year-old Cinderella.

The other supportive presence was Barnardos. In the Nineties many estates in Britain were being galvanised not by political parties but by traditional charities which were modernising their social base and their professional practice by breaking away from their role as rescuers of the perishing. Several were filling the space left by the political vacuum. Barnardos had built Ely's most modern building, a family centre, where it also sponsored one of Ely's community enterprises, a nappy co-op. It was run by women who joined a mothers' group after Barnardos leafleted the estate. They worked out how they might make a modest difference to their own and other women's conditions of existence: packs of Pampers disposable nappies were expensive and only available from supermarkets off the estate. Their cooperative association bulk-bought and sold the nappies cheaper and in any combination that matched a woman's needs. 'A woman can come in here and buy just one disposable nappy if that's what she wants to do. Sometimes she's run out of money and that's all she can afford,' they explained. The co-op expanded and housed shelves of baby products and racks of second-hand clothes.

One of the founders recalled her first hesitant day in the group. 'I went feeling very nervous. I'd never been to a meeting before. I thought what would they think of me, what would they be like? I thought they might be snotty or stuck up.' But they were not, they were just like her, young mothers on a council estate. Like her, several had been battered. 'The group was quite good, I felt better, as if I was useful for something.'

When she left school she worked packing frozen food, got married, had a baby. Then it all changed. 'He'd be out all day, but he wasn't working. If I asked where he'd gone he'd say it was none of my business. He wanted to be one of the boys, so he would then bring his mates round, and they'd be there all day, smoking ganja and drinking. He liked to show me up. "Do this, do that," he'd say in front of them. He was stealing, though I didn't know that at the time.' Her husband was 'one of the lads' on the estate.

'I was his ammunition. He knew he could hurt me if I

said anything that would cause an argument, and I'd get a good hiding. Eventually I told him a few home truths and he belted me, so I went to a solicitor and she told the police who took me to a refuge.' He sold all her house-keeping equipment. He chopped up the bed and threw it outside. She started her life over again with what was left: her children, her house, 'the suite, the fire and the pictures on the wall.' According to conventional wisdom, however, this woman was the paradigm of Ely's problems, a single parent, impoverished and punished by a young man who wanted to be master. The Reverend Bob Morgan, Ely's gen-ial political mentor, repeated the 'common sense' thesis that the decline of the estates was commensurate with the rise of the lone mother. 'One of the biggest problems is one-parent families with the attendant problems of poverty and disci-pline.'

During the debates about the meaning of the riots in 1991 the spectre of the 'problem family', the demise of the masters and the rise of the lone mothers was constantly invoked. Implicitly, if not explicitly, the mothers, but not the men, were scapegoated. No political commentators alluded to the resilience and ingenuity of single parents, or to the capricious and often cruel culture created by the men who abandoned and harassed them.

Elswick's former councillor, Mo O'Toole, reckoned that the women on the estates and within city politics had access neither to the resources of the political system nor to cham-pions within the system. Their networks had no access to the great and the good, the powerful people or the police. Not surprisingly, the political system's estrangement from everyday life, and its targeting of these poor women as the problem, meant that politicians did not know what they were dealing with when they encountered these active citizens. These were the people who sustained the *only* solidarities that did not endanger their neighbourhoods. But neither the police nor the political system knew what they were made of, where they got their ideas from, or what they had to put up with. It was and is foxed by them, can't fathom them, and ultimately is not interested in them.

That crisis of empathy is a clue to the political system's culpability for the catastrophes of 1991: it did not know how to support the women and it did not know how to challenge the men.

CHAPTER 13

Joy of Driving

The driver was dressed, the car was ready, the time was right. It was ticking towards eleven o'clock and the fortified police carrier with a dozen officers aboard was pulling out of the Blackbird Leys 'arena' when the hooded driver, known as the Don, revved a stolen two-litre Maestro and skated past the police and a watching crowd at 60 mph. This was the most audacious incident during the Oxford riots, when the Don drove into a square recently cleared by riot police.

This master of joyriding did indeed bring great joy to his audience, who savoured the chagrin of the officers doomed to do nothing but watch man tango with machine. Rude and red, the Maestro was a perfect dancing partner for the mystery man. This was not a star among cars, it had been selected from the common chorus, but it was strong, it could swing. It was also utterly recognisable as a mainstream motor – and that made the performance witty as well as piquant. The Don made the car *more* than a Maestro when he tossed it into an immaculate handbrake-turn, hit the horn and swept into the wings, to safety. It was not the car's status, it was the Don's performance that mattered.

'It's like driving a motorised bicycle; it's a surprise. The status was in the *doing* of it, in saying to the police: you are *impotent* and I'll rub your nose in it,' commented a consumer psychologist who specialises in cars, John Armstrong. The Don was a chic dude, a man who wore ironed tee-shirts with a sharp crease in the sleeve, never a wrong wrinkle, who wore trainers and had electronic accessories – a phone, a sound system, a camcorder. He was the acknowledged king of the road.

'That Maestro! In front of all the TV and the riot police!

That was to show that we ain't skinning teeth, we're not fucking around, we're doing what we want!' explained the Don. 'That is the attitude: we're doing what we want no matter what they do. The most the police can do is come down and arrest someone and lock them up.'

He got into cars because he simply loved driving. 'It wasn't the speed, I just wanted to be in a car, driving. My thing was driving around and nicking cars. I was nicking Mark II Ford Escorts first. They were great at the time, and it was just great driving till all hours with the lads.

'I did it several times a week, regularly. We never took cars from Blackbird Leys, never took one from our own manor. We'd go to another estate or another county. Sometimes your mate would drive you there, it would depend what crew you were with. For me it was always at night. Then when we were finished we'd park up and leave it.'

The genesis of the display lay in the discovery of a specific manoeuvre, the handbrake-turn. 'The handbrake-turns started in 1989. I thought, I'll have some of that, that's what I thought. It's good, young lads up at the shops doing handbrake-turns. There's no way I'd miss a display if I knew it was coming. You hear it on the grapevine, you get the news. Certain people will always get to know what's going on. They're what we call the spectators.

'Then it became pure display. That is the whole point, there's no use doing handbrake-turns down the A34 because there's no spectators. Where the crowd is hanging out is where the display will be. By the shops is good because it's wide and it's the main bit of Blackbird Leys.'

There was an informal but highly regulated hierarchy among the young men – always men – that separated functions into that of performers and that of providers. The drivers did not steal the cars, that was done by the thieves, who were the labourers, the apprentices. They knew what cars to steal – the souped-up versions of the most common vehicles, the Vauxhall Astra, the Montego and the Maestro.

The division of labour happened 'because there were too

many people, everybody wanted to have a bash,' said the
Don. 'There's certain people who we describe as the drivers,
and there's another sort of person who goes out and maybe
spends all day looking to get the cars. Ten times out of ten
the man who is driving is not the man who got the car.

'We don't do it at three o'clock in the afternoon, because that
would be dangerous, but we do it any time after ten o'clock.
Anyone who came into Blackbird Leys after that would know
that as soon as they hit the shops they had to beware, because
a car could pop out from anywhere. It's not a no-go area, it's
just that people know they've got to be careful and that the
driver is the one who's calling the shots.

'The people who nick the cars get a buzz out of watching
it,' explained another major driver, Paul. 'It's because people
want to see the display that they nick them. They come out
to the shops and they say, "There's a car parked," and you
say, "Okay, I'll display."'

It would not be cool to be keen; hanging around doing
nothing, preening, accumulating an audience would be the
prelude. 'There's the man who nicked the car. That's as far as
it goes for him. He'll find you, they always find you, but they
never tell you where it is – they don't want ten men to know
where the car is! Then when the man is ready they go and get
the car. The man might say, "Yeah, okay, I'll display," and
that's it. He'll come out when he's ready, say eleven o'clock.
He can sit out there, and the police can come out there in force,
but he can sit there till two or three o'clock in the morning and
then he can come out and do what he's going to do,' said the
Don.

After the spring of 1990, when the night boys gathered
regularly by the shops in the small hours of the night to watch
each other, the performances became ritualised. Although
joyriding in Britain has been associated with white boys,
here the performers and the audience and their critics were,
like the rest of Blackbird Leys, both black and white. For a
long time – more than a year – the police did not respond.
'They let it mature nicely,' said the Don. 'They were taking

no notice.' But drivers' taunts and public pressure produced a police presence, and that dramatised the displays. 'At the end of the day there is no one who goes out to display who does not believe, in themselves, that they will be getting chased. If you go out there you have to expect to get chased. It's an educated risk.'

By 1991 the displays were being designed not only for the drivers' fans, but for the police, and it was a measure of the drivers' confidence that this freedom was about *control*. They could guarantee a police presence because, in the end, they felt irresistible. 'We'd just stay there till they came.'

Joyriders' communication systems were built around the community on the one hand and technology on the other – their personal networking was intimate, informal and often intuitive. Radio scanners gave the joyriders greater knowledge of police manoeuvres than the police could reciprocate. Police communications systems were exposed because they were institutional, formal and electronic. Eavesdropping was easy once the joyriders had access to the radio technology. 'We had our scanners, so we knew what was going on,' said the Don. The main thing is to get in there and have one over on the police.' In time, then, the necessary audience had expanded from friends to enemies.

The arrival of the camcorder on the high street in the Nineties produced another revolution in the art of watching. Just as the domestication of the means of visual reproduction revolutionised the production of pornography, so it occasioned another metamorphosis in the witnessing and worshipping of the car and the joyride. Blackbird Leys created its own samizdat system of videoing and then distributing cassettes of the displays; it generated a new dynamic between the displayers and their audience – or rather their audiences. Videos produced a proliferation of constituences within the community, and inspired a newly rewarded narcissism. The night boys who loved being seen, who needed to be seen, could now see themselves. 'It gave people more incentive to go out; it made it more exciting to watch themselves. People really wanted to buy that,' said the Don.

It also domesticated the audience – people could watch the sport in their own homes, and circulate prized videos around the estates. The new technology carried commensurate dangers. When one of the major drivers was videoing a friend doing a display he was caught by the police; his video was confiscated and used in evidence against the other driver.

The joyriders explain their commitment to the cars in the nonchalant vernacular of car salesmen, in the understated and unexplained tones of trainspotters and the helpless compulsion of the junkie. 'When you get in the car you're hyper, hyper. You can never say when you are going to do it, or when you are not going to do it. You don't know that you will *not* take a stolen car,' said Paul. 'You might see a car and you just want to be in it. You get the urge, you get hyper, you don't know why.'

This exemplifies the rendering up of joyriding to biology, to instinct, in which the rider is both master and victim – the victim who cannot stop himself, and the man who has created mastery in his addiction. 'You see a *bad boy car* and you say to yourself, yeah, yeah, I'll have some of that,' said the Don. 'I'll say to myself that if the police come they can't catch me. If I'm in a stolen car the police have to be fucking good to catch me. The police have chased me on many occasions.'

Walking in the street and stopping at the lights, he spots a black sporty item. He watches it; in fact he can't concentrate on anything else but traffic, his eyes tracking, scavenging the street for the sight of something lovely. He's thinking about it all the time, he thinks of not much else. 'Cheeky,' he says, smiling at a black Astra. 'You cannot come down Oxford in a black Astra and expect to see it there the next day!'

Hanging about in the grounds of the Blackbird Leys leisure centre he sees another black car, a Golf GTI, incitement on wheels. 'No justice being down here. That should be on the M40,' he grins, but he can't take his eyes off it. 'They got no manners coming down here in that.'

*

At first it seems that these young men are anthropomorphising the vehicles, as if the car itself is animated, challenging, seductive. However, in their preoccupation with the vehicle, they seem to treat it as an object existing only to be captured and controlled. Both these young men stole and drove cars purely for pleasure; that was their ideology and it was their motivation. Tyneside's illegal car culture, on the other hand, ranged from an industrialised car trade, in which stolen cars, particularly very fancy cars, were refashioned in garages across the region and resold, to an informal trade in stripped components and an incendiary pleasure in extinguishing car carcasses.

Between 1982 and 1991 the number of vehicles set alight in Tyne and Wear increased by almost four hundred per cent. In 1991 alone 2,355 cars had been deliberately torched, an average of ten cars being set alight in the county every day. During the months before the Meadowell riot there might be two or three cars being stripped down daily on land beside Smith's Park metro station or Collingwood youth club.

One of the major movers in that informal economy was an industrious young man who lived with his mother and father and siblings – all on the dole – and began truanting school when he was about fourteen, despite his mother's best efforts. 'I started stealing cars when I was fifteen. Before that I used to go in cars with my mates. We would go into Newcastle, to the posh areas like Jesmond, because we knew that was where the decent cars were – you could tell by the posh houses. We got there in a mate's car; he had his own although it wasn't insured.'

The cars they prized were Ford Orions. 'We could get £150 for a good set of wheels at the end of the Eighties.' His network was a group of lads who would steal a car, 'with a screwdriver in the keyhole on the door. We'd shake it back and forward and up and down and then it would click open. Pull the door open, rip the casing off the steering column, find the silver barrel of the ignition lock and snap the barrel with a fifteen-inch wrench. There's a square groove, so you'd stick the screwdriver in and the car would start straight away. Snap the steering wheel lock and drive off.'

They would get it into the sanctuary of Meadowell, leave it for half an hour, then strip it of everything that moved: 'We would take out everything that was worth anything – tapes, radio cassette – then we'd stick it in gear, and the wires would burn up in fifth gear, hoy a brick on the accelerator so that it would blow up.' Once it was ablaze they would sometimes call the fire brigade.

'Then we'd hang around with the lasses at the bus stop. Or we'd talk to people on the wall. We just used to be a gang around there, sitting around by the bus stop or the wall or the youth club.'

Car theft in Britain began to worry the police not long after there were cars to steal. By the end of Margaret Thatcher's reign as Prime Minister, thefts of and from cars made up nearly a third of all recorded crime.

In the Twenties when city streets were congested with horses and carriages they were hardly commodious for the car. Owners were not allowed to lock their cars, rather they were expected to guard them. In the Thirties, when there were about one million private cars and vans in Britain, that ban was withdrawn. But it was not until 1949 that Chrysler introduced the key-starter and it took another twenty years for that to be a legal requirement in all cars. Ten years on, most cars were to be fitted with steering locks, which produced a brief decline in car theft. But after that respite, car theft resumed its rise. However, the pattern of car crime began to change. There was, according to Home Office research, an 'astronomical growth' in thefts *from* cars.[1]

The object that excited this meteoric increase was the miniaturised radio cassette. It was first introduced by Vauxhall

[1] Barry Webb and Gloria Laycock, *Tackling Car Crime*, Crime Prevention Unit paper 32, Home Office.

as a standard feature in a mass-market car, the Cavalier, in 1981 and in less than a decade was fitted automatically in almost all new cars. The most dramatic increase in the following decade in theft from cars was of vehicle accessories and parts (a rise of a hundred and forty-three per cent) compared with other personal items (a rise of forty-three per cent).

The function of joyriding also appeared to have changed during the Thatcher decade. Theft for temporary use – just for the hell of it, the pleasure or the use of it – declined as the dominant feature of the statistics. Nearly ninety per cent of stolen cars were recovered in 1970, whereas that was down to sixty-six per cent in 1990.

While TWOCing became most visible and vexing, at the turn of the decade, the phenomena remained as opaque as ever. Home Office researchers found that there was either a decline in police efficiency – they were finding fewer cars – and thus in the statistics *taking* a car appeared as *theft*[2] or that the nature of TWOCing really was changing. Maybe taking cars was, more and more, becoming theft. Maybe what had been an expediency, a habit or an addiction, was becoming a career, a source of income.

The car is an unusual commodity when it comes to crime: it is probably the only mass, movable object which is, technically, typically *borrowed* rather than *stolen*. The having of a car does not necessarily mean the owning of a car. The difference between borrowing and stealing created a specific offence, Taking Without the Owner's Consent, which was introduced in the 1930 Road Traffic Act to address the phenomenon of cars recovered within forty-eight hours, extended to a month in 1960.

The offence illuminated not so much the difficulty of stealing a car – clearly it wasn't *very* difficult – as the difficulty of possessing one. Ownership is surrounded by obligations and legal requirements. Like house ownership, car tenure is clothed in an armour of regulation, but unlike

[2] *Ibid.*

house ownership, car ownership is concerned not only with the advantages of security, or value, or shelter, but also with the responsibility for the vehicle's safety and its *dangerousness*. The TWOCer challenged the state's regulation, not so much of ownership but of responsibility. He engaged only the visceral pleasures of pushing a car to its limits, by speeding, crashing, dumping. Passing a driving test, owning a driving licence, paying motor insurance or road tax are all immaterial to the will to drive.

TWOCers were unburdened by responsibility for maintaining or fuelling the car by simply taking and leaving it. They escaped everything that made car ownership a social responsibility as well as a private power. TWOCing meant only a drive, a performance, a journey. What this highlighted was the paradox that the commodity most strongly suggestive of *individual freedom* was also a public danger and thus the subject of rigorous *collective* regulation.

TWOCers, who were usually represented as alien and atypical drivers because they were driving other people's cars, because they did not *possess* their own, actually illuminated the contradictions embedded in the car as a commodity. TWOCers refuse the disciplines that demand social scrutiny: safety, roadworthiness, reliability, of both car and driver. The TWOCers' relationship with the car is unmediated by social duties and therefore there is no distance between the driver and driving. The joyrider shares the mainstream fantasies that animate the typical motorway speeder and lays bare the principle of driving as a dialogue with danger, the car as a lethal weapon.

This is illustrated by a comparison with the kind of person whose social class would be closer to that of the TWOCer than of the owner of the cars he would be stealing – a man of a certain age whose cars are always introduced to his nearest-and-dearest with the words, 'It's got a few things wrong with it.'

'You can't ignore what is going on in the car, in its gurglings,' he said. 'You have to fret about it. The dilemma is between flogging it and nurturing it. But if it's not your car you can afford not to worry – the car's only meaning is its capacity to be thrown about. But for me its meaning is: is it legal, have I the right to drive it, can I afford to drive it, and will it survive what I want to do with it?'

If the 'old banger' man was the TWOCers' *alter ego*, then the ego targeted by motor marketing during the Eighties revealed the alignment of the TWOCer with the mainstream motoring man – the TWOCers shared the same desires as other drivers. The clues to their compulsion lay not in crime, as such, but in car culture.

Car advertising during the Eighties unabashedly celebrated danger, irresponsibility, excitement. 'One of the things we know a lot about is men and cars,' said the marketing manager of one of Europe's major car manufacturers. 'The Eighties had a very macho background, it was about very exciting driving. But we are starting to see that as a negative thing, that we shouldn't be buying into irresponsible values.'

According to the consumer psychologist, John Armstrong, when men step into a car, 'they step into a private world in which they feel invulnerable. They feel grander, more power-ful, they have no feeling of their own vulnerability, and so there is nothing to stop them doing what they do.'

One of the emblematic advertisements of the Eighties was a straight-in-the-vein Peugeot 405 fantasy, with the car flying across big country, leaving a trail of blazing cane fields behind it, to the echo of a woman singing 'Take my breath away'.

This was Marlboro country, a brilliant pastiche of fire-power. According to one of the consultants engaged in the preparation of the advertisement, 'It was not trying to do anything except build an image. There was nothing rational about it. It was for people who were on fire in their lives. There was a demand for excitement, and fire was atavistic, basic, frightening – it would excite people and frighten them. It was an advertisement for people who wanted to be asser-tive, progressive and ballsy. It was the fire that did that.' It was also suggestive of the elusive flight of the driver – this was a getaway car, a runaway driver; it left only destruction, it could not be caught.

The advertisement spoke right into the fantasy and the reality of the joyrider who became the escape artist of the motoring fraternity as well as of the criminal justice system. 'These young men are clearly saying something to us,' commented a specialist working with young men charged with serious offences. 'Some of them are sexually turned on by driving fast motorcars. They know they'll never earn enough to have a fast car of their own but they are doing everybody's dream anyway, they are making it happen.

'Sometimes you feel that they are almost suicidal. They think so little of themselves that they are not too worried about themselves or anyone else.' They were hooked by a culture that could kill – certainly it killed the joyriders Dale Robson and Colin Atkins near Meadowell on 6 September 1991.

Joyriders were nothing if not creatures of the car culture. Their favoured vehicles were the top end of the mass market, Fords and Vauxhalls that commanded seventy per cent of the market share. In the Eighties they loved the Ford Escort XR2, a model which was not common, but which evoked the commonplace and at the same time triumphed over it. 'They went for the car that the other Escort owners would aspire to,' explained Peter Wells from Cardiff University Business Research Centre.

In the advertising *milieux* these cars are also suggestive of roots and identity. They are in the mass market, and although the pleasure associated with joyriding was special, the cars were not. 'They're about the world they live in,' said Adam Lury, one of the partners with HHCL, a pioneering firm of progressive advertising men. 'They are also about anonymity. A Ford is not a big statement about yourself, your individuality is not revealed.'

Lury wanted to go beyond the association between men and their masculinity and cars as the feminine. 'The parallel between sex and cars is secondary. The real thing is the exertion of control. That is what is at the heart of dream driving.'

That was why the Marlboro legend, the cowboy in the big country, came to mind. 'It's about the cowboy *controlling* the animal, *controlling* the environment. Joyriding is like the bravura of the rodeo rider,' said Lury. The parallel between cars, cigarettes and sex is precisely that they are arenas in which power is pleasure.

Paul the joyrider is unequivocal. His relationship to his woman and to his world is about power. 'I've told her that I'm wearing the trousers; I'm the man in this relationship; that I say goes. Everybody wants to be the boss of something, don't they? I want to be the boss of Blackbird Leys, only I can't.'

The joyriders' penchant for 'British' cars is more than a matter of availability. Lury saw their predilections as rooted in control over their environment. 'Being British, or what appears to be British, is important because the car is demonstrably part of the community – they are controlling part of the community.'

The police, of course, were captivated by the same car culture and the same quest for control. Why else would the police forces have brought Ford Cosworths in the Eighties? The Cosworth was an immensely powerful machine with an excessive engine: it is a high-performance sports car. When it was taken over by Ford, the engine and the badge were transplanted into the standard Sierra body. So, the *company car* bought into what Wells called the 'ludicrous power' of the Cosworth, a car that became, by the early Nineties, virtually *impossible* for an individual to own, because it was virtually impossible to insure.

Cosworth was a ram-raider's car *par excellence* – with its extraordinary acceleration, 0–60 mph in 5.9 seconds, it gave a driver-on-the-run more than speed: it provided the technology to manoeuvre at speed, to get the driver *out* of situations. It was used in one of the most audacious raids in the North East in the year of the riots. A piquant marking of the anniversary of the 1991 confrontations between the lads and the police happened in the North East during the summer of 1992 when a Northumbria police Cosworth was stolen from a police compound by a very cheeky joy-rider.

In the aftermath of the 1991 riots the Home Office was under pressure to do something about car crime which, by then, was a £1.2 billion phenomenon. A car was being stolen about every two minutes – that meant more than a quarter of a million cars a year. Early in 1992 the Home Office was seen to be doing something when it launched a £5-million advertising campaign for Car Crime Prevention Year. 'The scavenging must stop,' said the Home Secretary, Kenneth Baker, when he introduced a new face on the hoardings, the laughing scowl of a hyena. 'The new face of car crime,' it said.

The nationally-networked advertisement, screened endlessly on television, opened with a long shot of the victim – the car – alone in the blue shadows. It was then pounced upon and pawed by the predators, hyenas slithering around the paralysed, gleaming *body*work. Eventually the animals entered the car and hauled out ... what was it? A body? A jacket? Money fell to the garage floor. The car was raped.

This repeated the fantasy of the car as *woman*, and yet refused the humanity of the perpetrator as a *man* by re-inventing him as vermin. That, of course, underlined the tendency to bestialise offenders, to deny them their contradictory connection with their community and their victims, but it also represented the car thief as someone outside culture, as other.

Given the intense gendering of the car cult, the campaign's refusal to engage masculinity at all rendered it invisible. To whom, then, was this film addressed? It was not speaking to the perpetrator, save in the sense that it was speaking into his desire, savouring the assault on the victim. Nor was it speaking *about* the perpetrator, because his desire for the *object* was less significant than might be imagined. It is the desire for the *experience* that powers joyriding. Thirdly, the film did not address the victim because it conflated the subliminal gendering of the car with the gender of its imaginary owner – the car was feminised in its victimisation – whereas joyriders typically stole company cars, souped-up, powerful cars – men's cars.

The hyena campaign was political propaganda; it was nothing to do with crime prevention. It exposed the paralysis surrounding joyriders as perpetrators. Certainly it had learned little from the longstanding experience and expertise of West Belfast, where joyriding has persisted despite massive community opposition and disapproval. In Northern Ireland the militarisation of civil life is mirrored by the power of the paramilitaries, who substitute for the police in some neighbourhoods. Communities have appealed to the paramilitaries to resort to the most stringent measures against joyriders, some of whom have been kneecapped at the request of their own neighbourhoods. But being shot in the knees often proved to be no deterrent. West Belfast learned long before mainland Britain that joyriding was not like burglary or computer fraud, it was a powerful and personal addiction. The criminal justice system, however, treated the perpetrator as a person to be punished, not as a person to be understood. It had no strategy for the remorseless commitment to car crime among young joyriders.

After the riots, senior police officers routinely accepted that the problem was, as one superintendent put it, 'a macho status-seeking thing'. But police forces were no more engaged with masculinity as a problem in joyriding than they were focused on mainstream masculine culture as the context for burglary. Gender, palpably, was not addressed as a *problem* in the propaganda. When asked about how to communicate with the community about car crime, police officers routinely argued, 'We need parents to have ownership of the problem, to know what their kids are up to.' Parents, predictably, had been invoked as the scapegoats in the panic about joyriders. But the Home Office research among the offenders themselves showed the powerlessness of parents; it revealed that it was the peer culture and economics that kept them in car crime.

Only five per cent said that they would have been affected by parental influence.[3]

During the Eighties it became apparent from the workings of the criminal justice system that there were staggering levels of recidivism among joyriders. 'It is no good asking why they do it, because they will happily tell you where and how but not why,' said one prison probation officer. 'We don't really see the significance of it in the probation service because it is what *they* do all the time and it is what they think about all the time.'

For young men whose self-esteem was already in crisis, whose joyriding was perhaps fearless to the point of being suicidal, the criminal justice system offered little or no challenge or threat. At worst it was felt to be disrespectful or humiliating, which confirmed the commitment of many workers in the juvenile justice system to work tirelessly to keep young men out of prison. At best, court became part of the young men's social life, part of the circuit of visibility from the street to the court house, another public appearance where what mattered to them was not that their behaviour was perceived as *wrong* but that it was seen as *important*.

'They love the court,' commented one social worker working with young offenders. 'That's where they meet all their mates.' The probation service was so overstressed by the end of the decade, so understaffed and so overwhelmed by new requirements for paperwork which kept them desk-bound, that many probation workers felt they were hardly in touch with their charges. In any case, they were never given the time to do searching work with their clients. 'I only ever meet the boys at court or at the police station. We never get the time to do proper work,' said one. Another expressed the almost universal sense of triumph on getting a lad to keep an appointment. 'We worry all the time about keeping them out of custody, we think of all sorts of schemes to put to magistrates, so you end up spending a year getting the boys just to keep appointments. They don't

---

[3] Webb and Laycock, *Tackling Car Crime*.

have much investment themselves in staying out of custody, though.'

In the absence of any challenge to the connections between the car cult, the potency of its pleasures, and their very identity as men, the criminal justice system was unlikely to impinge on these young offenders. Many of its liberal practitioners acknowledged that it did not make any difference whether the lads were locked up or let loose upon their neighbourhoods. The awful truth was that *nothing* made any difference to the TWOCer, no intervention deterred him from his simple desire to drive. Why would it?

CHAPTER 14

All Dressed Up

A dozen defendants from Meadowell sat in the dock at the back of a cool, white courtroom. The judge sat opposite them. He wore a wig and a purple, red and black gown made of silk; they wore tee-shirts and three of them wore Berghaus jackets. Had the judge been a mountaineer or a skier he might have aspired to Berghaus, too. Tynesiders beg, borrow, buy and steal Berghaus sportswear. In London the Chevignon and Chippie labels are treasured, in Glasgow it is Armani and Paninari: whatever style is adopted on the estates on the edge of Britain, it marks another revolution in the etiquette of respectability that once ruled working-class dress.

Casual style is abhorred, of course, by style magazines like *The Face* and *Arena*. Class contempt for both the poor and the petty bourgeoisie, enshrined in the shell suit and Essex man, became cool. Clever grammar school boys who had never graduated beyond denim, had their revenge against the gaudy of the class they had evacuated. As worn by the young working class, however, the shell suit was a complex fashion statement about the content of a day, about comfort and the local embrace of a larger Continental culture. Berghaus make specialist sportswear which is a passion among Tyneside teenagers – it links them to a smug, healthy, European upper middle class. In the Nineties specialist sports shops on Tyneside are ram-raided for Berghaus jackets, their green-and-purple colour combination a ubiquitous livery seen on the streets and playgrounds – as seen on Everest and as worn by television war correspondents. Designer clothes stores are being ram-raided in Glasgow. Teenagers are turning up in London boutiques team-handed simply to steal the clothes they covet. People are being robbed for their trainers on the tube. A fashion writer finds a brick through his car window and all that is missing is his new Chevignon flying jacket. Merseyside football fans pinch European teams' ski hats during away games abroad and wear them on the terraces like tiaras. The cults generate a massive informal, illegal economy fuelled by ram-raids and by counterfeit manufacturing.

All over peripheral estates across Britain teenagers were wearing designer casuals that signified their refusal to be peripheral, to be on the edge of everything. Doing a body-swerve on the southern centralism of Britain during the Eighties, their fashion statements represented a commitment not just to a style but to connections with Europe and America that transcended their economic and cultural isolation. According to Steve Redhead, a passionate writer on football's fashions and popular culture, the phenomenon is consumer-led, not designer-led: 'It is not inarticulate, it is not just a look, it represents a real kind of modernity. It is about not being backward, saying, "We are at the sharp edge of fashion." People living on far-flung estates are refusing to be peripheral. The most important thing that the clothes were saying was, "If you can't beat 'em, look as if you can."'[1]

Vital to all this was the label, the mark of money. The desperate communities of the riots refused to be deprived of display, young people exercised a consuming passion for clothes cults. They were worn by the defendants in the subsequent trials. While the older men in their forties wore any old thing, the young men and women were wearing a casual uniform that told its own story about their subcultures as a different mode of engagement with, rather than a flight from, or imitation of, the mainstream. The necessity of labels – Berghaus, Gore-Tex sportswear, and Chevignon flying jackets are obsessively labelled – suggests a serious shift in the way that young subcultures are making their mark.

Heavy-metallers and hippies, despite their adherence to the

[1] Steve Redhead, *Football With Attitude*, Pluto, London, 1991.

ubiquitous Doc Martens and bikers' black leather jackets, are down-dressers who are less interested in the manufacturer's mark but are dedicated to a *look* that also evokes a life and a culture. The casuals, just as determinedly, assert themselves in the adornment of their persons in designer duvets: they are *having* the best of cosy clothes.

The passion for the label suggests aspiration and ambition rather than rebellion, and yet within that style strategy they are breaking the boundaries of work and leisure, respectability and relaxation – the very frontiers that these same commodities would have asserted for another class who move in everyday life between home and work, public and private, those spaces which are defined by dress codes: people who are going places.

In another era, working-class fantasy dressing, of *passing* among men – in the mohair suit or the camel coat – would have promised the ability to *enter* any *occasion*. But the rise of the casual implied something else. Stuart Cosgrove's brilliant essay, 'The Zoot Suit and Style Warfare', on black boys' extravagant appropriation of killer-diller drape coats, argues that the style was 'an emblem of ethnicity', a way of negotiating an identity, 'a refusal: a subcultural gesture that refused to concede the manners of subservience.'[2] Among the young people of the Nineties on peripheral estates, the appropriation of the fabric and form of leisure wear likewise supported an attack on all those demarcations that are represented by clothes – of function, of money – that separated the privileged from the poor. Casual could be worn anywhere at any time: at school, in court, at the chip shop, in bed. Berghaus, by catalogue, by ram-raid, by spending your savings, was a class revolt by poor young posers which borrowed rather than repudiated the insignia of privilege. The way they wore them, their long, lithe shapes encased in perfectly engineered body bags, burst the boundaries between occasions which, by

[2] Stuart Cosgrove, 'The Zoot Suit and Style Warfare' in Angela McRobbie, ed., *Zoot Suits and Second-Hand Dresses: An Anthology of Fashion and Music*, Macmillan, London, 1989.

contrast, defined the days and seasons of the privileged.

Kids who were 'doing nothing' were wearing the gear that people who were always doing something – Alpine adventures or Californian surfing – were wearing when their leisure was time out from their work. The kids were wearing trousers and jackets to school that cost more than their teachers could afford, and which, because they were practical and sporty, could not be dismissed as frippery. 'Casual contributes to the erosion of the school uniform. School is a very important arena of display,' says Stuart Cosgrove, and because casual is neat and sporty, 'it is very difficult for the authorities to take offence, because it isn't scruffy.'

Within its relentless conformity, however, there are roaring nuances of revolt – it is the *colour* that challenges uniformity and the frightened, subdued monocolours of modern men's traditional dress. During the Eighties and Nineties it was colour that separated casual from chic – the revolution in synthetic fibres during the Eighties launched conventional Essex man into shell suits of many colours.

Sport-style resurrects the anorak – an item which the forty-something generation might have thought was as dead as flares, or as unacceptable as a car coat. The coveted garments are not the sculptured tailoring of Euro-chic, they surround the body in baby-gro. At the same time, their allure comes not just from comfort and colour but also from sport. The poor have claimed for themselves the gear associated with striding, racing, jumping, climbing. 'It's about being ahead,' says Steve Redhead. It is also about being hard, being survivalists in a brutalised, gendered, conservative culture dominated by the rigours of bullying, hierarchy, and aggression. Casual style brings the genders together: they wear the same stuff and the same colours, jeans and jackets and trainers. 'It is associated skinhead and football subcultures that involve a conservative, heterosexual reiteration of gender relations, of old roles,' says the feminist fashion writer, Caroline Evans.

But it is the girls who manoeuvre around the culture's sexual conservatism, with their own assertion of 'hard', and who express the mobility of modernity in the way their own identities slip between girlie gear and the identikit anonymity of casual style. It falls to the girls to mark their difference by what they wear in their hair – boys' hair is cropped, conservative; girls wear their hair long, in elaborate frolics up top – or by what they add to their inventory, or by what else they wear.

'Very few girls have trainers as their *total* footwear repertoire,' says the design consultant, Peter York. The emblematic item is the trainer, not the trainer as sportshoe, but the trainer as architecture or aircraft, not as footwear but footpower. 'Trainers are like cars for the carless,' says Peter York. 'They're not really footwear. The way they present themselves is as if they were seven-league boots: you are a magic person the minute you put them on. They're important for the poor because it's maybe all they have.'

There is another connection in his mind between wheels and feet, cars and trainers. 'You are what you wear and you are what you drive. If you can access the *wear* but not the *drive* then you want to get the first and trash the second.' So, it is no surprise that boys wear the trainers and burn the cars.

CHAPTER 15

Strangers and Conquerors

F ire-raising and glorious car chases were celebrated in
the genre described as 'kind of a guy thing' by Mel Gibson
in a spoof line in *Lethal Weapon 3* – a movie monument to
mindless violence. Saturation action is the only *narrative* in
the action genre, which generated some of the most watched
movies in the Western world: the *Robocop* series, the *Terminator* series, the *Lethal Weapon* series. They are nearly all
series, these man-made movies, repetitions of men wearing
their testicles on their torsos, their pectoral bosoms round but
rock hard, their biceps bulging as they take aim and ejaculate
bullets and flames. A young man arraigned in one of the riot
trials cited as his alibi an evening spent watching *Robocop* and
Scarface with his girlfriend.

This is not to insist that the violence of these films
created the violence of the rioters, and it is not to suggest
that the lads *are* the videos they watch, rather it is to say that
their values and pleasures – disavowed and yet reiterated in
political rhetoric – are celebrated in the mainstream movie
market of their time. The video hire shops – the modern library
– find that young men like the 'action' and 'adventure' as their
main course. For pudding they enjoy non-violent comedies, the
amiable, easy-viewing categories that appeal to younger view-
ers, what used to be called 'family entertainment'. Women,
young and old, like 'a good story'. The men don't watch what
the women watch.

The action genre, like the Western and the Forties
film noir, wrestles with images of masculinity endlessly
under threat and yet finally triumphant. The culture that the
riot boys respected and reproduced in their own territory is

neither strange nor surprising – it is the same popular culture consumed by police officers and men in prisons. That is why the action genre illuminates the pleasures and ethics of many young men in an era during which, more than in any other era since the Second World War, the Government has talked the language of force – their forte.

The thrill of chaos and combustion and the pleasure in masculinity without the impedimenta of women or society or complexity, are what animate action-man. Like the Western and the *film noir*, the action genre is obsessed with gender; but unlike its predecessors it is unashamed in its narcissism and its pleasure in the fragile force of a man's body. *Robocop* and *Terminator* are reincarnations of an earlier 'imaginary man'. He is to be found in fascist fantasies which express the 'conservative utopia of the mechanised body.'[1] Although often located in a time and place beyond the here and now, as a parable about an impossible future, the contemporary action-man genre pushes and plays with the limits of masculinity.

It portrays a mode of masculinity which is pre-social: it has no manners, it is not house-trained or domesticated, it has no social skills of negotiation and conciliation. It belongs nowhere because neighbourhood and home are places that real men *leave*. The moral centre of *Robocop* is agnostic. It is mobile and promiscuous because it responds to provocation and it is moved only by *force*. Robocop is neither good nor bad; he is freed from any ethical problem because he is only an enforcer. *Robocop* and Arnold Schwarzenegger's *Terminator* are like Clint Eastwood's Westerns, films in which audiences are allowed 'to indulge every wish-fulfilment fantasy of supercompetent heroism without having to believe in the hero.'[2] Robocop's only popular presence is the police department, not particularly because it has right, if not might, on its

[1] Klaus Theweleit, *Male Fantasies*, vol. 2, Polity Press, Cambridge 1989.
[2] Richard Combs, 'Shadowing the Hero' in *Sight and Sound*, British Film Institute; London, October 1992.

side, but because its virtue is its class. The cops in *Robocop* are the black and white men and women of the raunchy but respectable working class. They do not represent force so much as the humane, oppressed but resilient toilers, the proletariat, in a landscape divested of any evidence of work. The cops' class position is confirmed in the film by their strike against corporate and city bosses, who appear as corrupt, or crazy. The police people are taking *industrial action* in an environment without employment. The urban landscape is uninhabited, a cityscape bereft of people, or indeed places. It is already a phantom, vacant space, where the working class is extinguished. The hired hand is here a hired gun. The landscape could, of course, be imagined as the wastelands of the Western economies, beyond the Cold War, after the end of history. They are places perceived as empty of social relations, where the only congregation is confrontation, where no one puts tea on the table, does homework or aerobics, washes hair, babies or clothes, makes cars or cakes or computer systems. All that emptiness liberates the landscape from work or children, much like the Western film where people are strangers in their own land and where real men establish themselves by conquest rather than cohabitation.

These representations of the city give permission for the havoc introduced by Robocop, whose only manoeuvre is: to Move! Fire! Now! What is striking about the genre – particularly for a viewer who likes a story – is that it carries no critique of mayhem as a way of sorting things out. Entirely explosive, hyperactive, not to say hysterical, one confrontation after another frees action-man of the problem of contemplation, of tactics, and fills the spaces where there would otherwise be a fundamental lack – lack of strategy and lack of a story. What is at stake in the narrative is not the preservation of law and order, though that may be the alibi for the confrontations, it is enforcement, the goal of dominance amidst disorder.

Where the 'frontier' of the Western lies in the prelude to social order, to society itself, so the 'frontier' of the action

movie lies in the aftermath of society. The bodies of the
protagonists are in a regime of destruction where all that
matters is survival. Frank Krutnik suggests, in his study of
gender and genre in post-war Hollywood, *In a Lonely Street*,[3]
that the city shadows of the thriller and the territories of the
Western are worlds where violence and lawlessness are dominated by 'masculine figures of self-appointed authority', where
aggression is legitimised 'in pursuit of his mission to establish
a regime of truth'. But the thrust of *film noir* narrative is 'the
affirmation of the hero as an idealised and undivided figure of
masculine potency and invulnerability'.

And so it is with action-man, whose militarism is informal
rather than institutional. Although connected to a group or a
corpus or lived for a cause, he is always loose, semi-detached.
His potency represents a return to a primitive, visceral masculinity, muscular rather than mental. His identity is therefore
entombed in the body, a perilous place. The biofantasy of
Robocop and *Terminator* revolves around the problem of
fragility, which is the source of uncertainty that haunts
the hard man in the *film noir* – that is what makes *film noir*
such a compelling genre for audiences of both men and
women, because it is an *argument* about masculinity. It is, as
Krutnik suggests, 'evidence of some kind of crisis of confidence
within the contemporary regimentation of male-dominated
culture'.

Robocop and Terminator offer a different resolution. They
are the prototypes of a new mode of masculinity; they are
both sub- and super-human. They are steel, micro-circuits and
mercury under the skin – flesh is merely camouflage. Like the
steel soldiers of fascist fantasy, their bodies do not contain visceral feeling; they are a control, a defence 'against threatening
feelings and against thinking'.[4] These figures are not the sons
of mothers, and therefore they are absolved from the crisis of

[3] Frank Krutnik, *In a Lonely Street: Film Noir, Genre, Masculinity*,
Routledge, London, 1991.
[4] Klaus Theweleit, *Male Fantasies* vol. 2.

gender – they don't need to repudiate women in order to be men; they never risk the feminine, because they have no fibre of feeling. These are men who have no mothers or fathers; they are not born, they are made. Their masculinity is an excess, it is a stereotype so overwhelming that it is a slogan. These men are machines, they are almost human, they are both more and less than human, more and less than men.

It was *Terminator 2* that showcased the frontiers of state-of-the-art special effects, generated by computers which allowed live action and digital effects to combine in the same shot. The company that created *Star Wars*, *Industrial Light* and *Magic*, drew a grid over the body of the actor Robert Patrick, the film's chilling T-1000 character who metamorphosed from man to metallised blob, covered in a gorgeously liquid 'chromed' skin. Computerised 'morphing' transformed him from tiled floor to prison guard to stepmother. In *Terminator 2*, the special effects ensure that no one is what they seem, and the male and female principals are allowed to move across the boundaries of gender. Arnold Schwarzenegger is both mother and father to the child of the Cassandra character, a woman who is muscular and wise and deemed mad. She is a mother and a warrior. However, she is all too human; her mission as saviour and her tragedy as she-who-knows-too-much make it impossible for her to behave as a mother. She wears the uniform and has the temper of a soldier. She is in a hurry. She must save the world and she can't afford the high price of feeling. She is, therefore, a mother like a man, who makes no concessions to tenderness. She is an honourable brute. But she also expresses women's disappointment with men for their massive, epochal failure to be reciprocal parents, to be fathers. The hard labour of saving the world and her son falls to Schwarzenegger who, as a man-machine, dares to be the universal parent. She says of him that 'of all the would-be fathers, this thing, this machine was only thing that measured up.' In an insane world, he is the only one who will not cease, who will not leave, will not shout, get drunk or say he is too busy. His care takes the form of courage and kindness; he is a Teutonic mother whose faculties as a parent are only permitted because he is an alien.

In *Robocop* and *Terminator*, masculinity is redeemed because it is, at last, transcendent – the protagonists are compulsive killers. Robocop and Terminator are allowed to expose the limits of their gender, their manly foibles, in the metaphor of the machine. It is their identity as machines that restores to these more-or-less-men their right to the difficulty of being human. The machine-man is programmed, and that means that although he has to be taught how to be human, the dilemma of deciding who he is and what he does is resolved. He does not think, he cannot feel, therefore he cannot fear. He can only overcome, that is his *raison d'être*.

PART IV

A NECESSARY EVIL?

The challenges of lawless masculinity

During the spring and summer of 1992 more estates in the heartlands of England became household names, in much the way that small towns whose only claim to fame is a team in the football league score a place in the national consciousness. Weeks of repetition brought the names of Wood End, Hartcliffe, Ordsall, Brackenhall Stoops and Hargher Clough to the tip of the tongue. There they stayed. They were places, presumably, with a story to tell, but the record of their troubles during those months offered little sense that they had a history, or little idea why they might be telling us something bigger than themselves, something about Britain.

What brought these estates to national attention was, again, riots. They were all tournaments between two groups of young men – residents and police officers. But the reports of these riots, and the response to them within the political domain, quarantined them as incendiary episodes that were never used to illuminate the environments in which they arrived as a catastrophe. Stories of sleepless nights, of streets of neighbours left feeling powerless, of blazing businesses, libraries and community centres, of deaths, all simply met with political *ennui*, fuelling a fatalism about society itself, as if riot was like flood and hurricane, a 'natural disaster', but committed by people who were themselves disastrous.

The triggers were diverse, but the 1992 riots shared a similar context: endemic economic decline, epidemic unemployment, suburban housing estates, dependence on chaotic and capricious government funding, long sagas of bad blood between young men and the police, young mothers barely surviving, young men in the shadows. All the riot areas were again characterised by the disengagement of the political parties from local society.

CHAPTER 16

Return to Routine

The new riot season began in Coventry's Wood End estate where the riot was detonated by police, who had long tolerated an infuriating sport – lads illegally riding off-the-road scrambler motorbikes across the estate's many expanses of vacant grass. There had been no municipal sponsorship of the sport that might have corralled it within a safe space. So the lads sped across the estate's verges, laying claim to the terrain they shared with their parents, neighbours, girlfriends and children, to the annoyance of everyone but themselves. Some people avoided going out during the boys' time. One verge that particularly attracted the scramblers was about a mile long.

Residents' long serial of complaints to the police were, according to one resident, 'usually met with the argument that the kids would always be at it and they couldn't be there all the time to do anything about it.' There had been many letters and even petitions to the police complaining about the hazard.[1] There was an occasional police blitz.

On 12 May, at 2 p.m., the police suddenly launched a crackdown on the riders. The operation did not seem, however, to be sustainable: an attempted arrest of one of the boys resulted in a forced retreat by police officers. Three hours later boys were stoning passenger buses making their way around the estate. Bus services were suspended and the police returned with reinforcements. But they could not prevent gangs with bricks and stones congregating, looting a local store, setting

[1] *Coventry Evening Telegraph*, 13 May 1992.

fire to the local infants' school, where a brand new library was gutted by the flames. At 4 a.m. half a dozen youths were charged with violent disorder. Solicitors and residents were later to criticise the police for going over the top in their response to the riders.

Running battles with the police were mobilised for the next four days, and spread to other estates. Boys threw a petrol bomb into a crowded fish and chip shop; petrol bombers destroyed three businesses, including a pub and a barber shop, and threw bricks and petrol bombs at the police.

'Mindless hooligans,' said the police; 'people who impose fear,' said the local councillor. 'Give people jobs,' said the local MP. 'Provide a bike track,' said estate workers.[2] In fact, the only initiative to engage the boys' craze for the motorbikes had been set up by the National Association for the Care and Resettlement of Offenders. There had been no rearrangement of the landscape to discourage dangerous driving. Nor had there been a dialogue between the police or the local authority and the boys themselves to see if they could sort something out.

There was no debate in the local media about why the boys seemed so impregnable – and so successful. 'There is a hard core of youngsters who, you could say, are terrorising the neighbourhood,' said Superintendent Miles Cadwallader.[3] Was their behaviour so banal as to be beyond analysis? Certainly, the local press did not seem interested enough in these scrambling boys actually to talk to any of them. Nor was there any local or national inquiry into why police action against the problem failed to protect three estates from several nights of war between lads and riot squads, several petrol bomb attacks on buses, businesses, and community premises. The question was not asked: why did a public order problem of ten years' standing become a major public order crisis?

[2] *Coventry Evening Telegraph*, 2 June 1992.
[3] *Coventry Evening Telegraph*, 13 May 1992.

*

The prelude to riots in Bristol a few weeks later was the Government's rejection of a £37-million City Challenge bid for three of the city's poorest housing estates, Hartcliffe, Highridge and Withywood. The first families moved into suburban Hartcliffe, on the edge of the city, in 1953. A third of its 3,500 homes were owner-occupied by 1992, though that provided no clue to the wellbeing of its 14,000 inhabitants. Indeed, indices of its decline could be found in the closure of the last bank in Hartcliffe, in unemployment and crime figures which were higher than the city average – though by no means the highest – and in higher infant mortality rates than elsewhere in the city. Hartcliffe was home to more children than anywhere else in Bristol. It was a hard-pressed place providing homes for a growing presence of hard-pressed people: two homeless families a week were moved into Hartcliffe.

The City Challenge bid would have brought investment of a massive £180 million to Hartcliffe and Withywood, had it been approved by the Government. It was rejected. This was the second year running that the Government had thrown out the city's submissions to support renewal and attract investment. On the day of the bid's rejection, national unemployment statistics rose to the highest point in five years.

That was Wednesday, 15 July 1992. On Thursday a police officer's startling 1,000 c.c. BMW motorbike was stolen from outside his home. On Friday two young white men, Shaun Starr, aged thirty-two, and Keith Buck, aged eighteen, went for a spin on the bike in Hartcliffe. Shaun Starr was well known for riding around on stolen motorbikes; the woman he lived with did not like it and had a row with him when someone delivered the bike to his home in the early hours of the morning. Around midday the two riders were spotted by one of the police officer's colleagues and pursued. Both young men died as a result of the ensuing chase.

In an action-replay of Meadowell, shops and community services on the estate were petrol-bombed and looted. The baker where Keith Buck had worked for five years was burned out two days running. A hairdressing business, formed by two women with grant aid, was bombed. A dozen shops were damaged by rioters. A job centre was ransacked. A library was torched on Thursday night and about a hundred young men attacked fire-fighters, who radioed police for help. A solitary police van went in and a group of officers in riot gear charged the crowd, who retreated and regrouped while firefighters arrived, escorted by more police.[4] There seemed to be a pattern of people setting fire to cars or buildings to attract the police and then attack them.

The riot exposed the raw divergence between different groups, or rather genders, in their grief. On Friday night Shaun Starr's sister, Lorraine Townsend, had been keeping a vigil by the spot where her brother died, when she heard the sound of fighting. She addressed the crowd five times through a loud hailer and urged them to go home. She was defeated, and in her tears she told them, 'We have made our protest and what we are seeing now is devastation. If you keep this up Hartcliffe will be totally ruined. You are making it worse for the families. It has been terrible for us, but this is making it even worse.' Women began to move away, but the skirmishes did not stop.[5] In the small hours of Saturday morning Shaun Starr's lover, Sadie Davidson, tackled stone-throwers, in vain. The men's mothers also made statements. Keith Buck's mother, Jeanette Buck, said, 'Please stop. I don't want Keith to be remembered in this way.' Margaret Starr said that her son had been scapegoated: 'A policeman hasn't even come by to say sorry.' England, it seemed, had not yet learned the power of grief, ritualised in the funeral, that had become such a significant feature of dissent in Northern Ireland, South Africa, and other grief-stricken countries.

*

[4] *Bristol Evening Post*, 17 July 1992.
[5] *Western Daily Press*, 18 July 1992.

Ordsall in Salford was an inner-city estate of high-rise blocks, but like Meadowell it was on the edge of a prestigious docklands redevelopment, Salford Quays, and like Meadowell lived in economic extremity. It had no tradition of community politics and no tenants' movement until the Nineties. New community initiatives had met with the aggressive indifference of the criminal fraternity and the aggressive pessimism of the police, whose disposition was expressed as 'you're wasting your time with this lot round here, it'll get wrecked.' The estate had a tough coterie of criminals and a tough record of policing which subjected young men, whether they had a record or not, to the kind of treatment that had alienated the community. 'The police were heavy-duty and inefficient, and law-abiding people had lost confidence in the police ability to perform their public duty. There were always allegations of brutality around,' said one Ordsall man.

On 1 July 1992 Ordsall was the victim of a trail of a dozen arson attacks which struck at the heart of the neighbourhood's efforts to renew itself, a tenants' cooperative in Coronation Street. A day later another fire was started at the Carpetworld showroom just before midnight. A crowd gathered to watch, among them a sales executive from the *Manchester Evening News*, Ian Kearney. 'There were lots of people around but it was very peaceful. Suddenly, just after midnight, eight vanloads of police arrived and started wading into the crowd, telling them to get back even though they were not in danger. One man sitting on his fence was coshed in the face and fell. I have no doubt that if I had not moved I would have got a baton in my face. There was no riot when the police arrived. I am convinced they started it.'[6] Then people in the crowd began attacking the police and firefighters. Police denied that the attack had been provoked by the menacing behaviour of the police. 'It was not at all unusual that night; a number of unruly youths caused mischief by throwing a few stones at the firefighters.'

Ordsall residents believed that what was going on was

[6] *Manchester Evening News*, 3 July 1992.

not a riot but a set-piece confrontation between the police and organised crime which people just had to put up with. The arson attacks were regarded as a plan to embarrass the police: 'They were making a spectacle of the police. They were designed to draw the police in and show them up. It was a way of saying, "You're useless and this is what we can do! So start behaving!" That was it, definitely.'

Over the next few weeks community buildings were torched elsewhere in Salford, but on 6 July the war between police and the lads was pushed over a fearful frontier when gunshots were heard: a job centre was torched in Ordsall and when firefighters turned up their engine was the target for gunshots. Three bullets hit police vans. Armoured police vehicles stocked with weapons were then brought into the area. Salford's former police chief, Jim Tunmer, urged the neighbourhood to take on the coterie of criminals who dominated the estate. 'There are hundreds of able-bodied, honest men in Ordsall and it may be time for them now to say, "enough is enough" and stand up to be counted – even if it means their windows are broken.'

This was widely regarded as a provocative reaction that exposed profound pessimism about policing. Ordsall was not alone with the feeling that it was not receiving a proper police service – Greater Manchester had more 999 calls than any other force outside London. Its antiquated telephone system had to process 1,500 calls a day – often calls were left unanswered for twenty minutes. The conurbation was only recently emerging from Sir James Anderton's authoritarian and whimsical stewardship which, as on Merseyside, had tested to the limits the powers of local democracy in determining policing practices.

Salford's veteran MP, Stan Orme, called for an inquiry into the problems of the estates. But neither the Home Secretary nor his Minister responsible for Manchester thought it worthy of an official investigation that armed men on both sides of the law were patrolling the streets of Salford.

Britain's first community pub opened on 21 July 1992 in

Brackenhall, an estate in Huddersfield with a well-established black and white population.

The Phoenix had been an empty building for eighteen months. With the help of the Tetleys brewery it was reopened by Brackenhall Community Council, which sponsored a web of local enterprises, including a credit union. The organisers were taken aback. They'd expected the pub to be popular, but nothing like this: customers were crammed into every corner. BCC's business manager, Kate Zamir, went outside to catch some cool air. The car park was packed with people, too.

The following evening Kate Zamir was driving into the estate at about 9 p.m. She noticed riot police clustered in one of the side streets putting on their helmets and collecting their shields.

On her way towards the Phoenix she noticed pockets of people lining the streets. 'It was as if a parade was coming through but instead of waving plastic flags they were holding stones and bottles.'

These enigmatic assemblies were explained when she got to the pub. The police had raided the car park. Their targets were drug dealers. They had arrested five men. Two were charged with possession of cannabis. Three were released without charges. The operation netted no charges of dealing. 'It was not a great success in terms of drugs charges,' acknowledged a West Yorkshire police spokesperson, 'but we were faced with a choice: it had become clear that people who had ruined the trade at the pub, before it reopened as the Phoenix, were around again – it was like a time warp – so we could wait and see what happened, or nip it in the bud. Police officers can't just turn a blind eye.'

Inside the pub, the first the publican Chris Green knew about what was going on was when 'some young black men came rushing into the pub and approached the two community police with the intention of a confrontation.'

The community police officers were in the bar. One of them was a policewoman who had been involved in the preparations for the grand opening of the Phoenix, and who disclaimed responsibility for the chaos. The raid had been launched without consulting the Phoenix managers, or the BCC's managers Kate Zamir and Ron Bennett. It had also been sprung on a community which had already laid down its own law in an agreement with the local dealers. Their trade in soft drugs had dominated the reputation of the Phoenix in its earlier incarnation. The deal was: no drugs at the Phoenix. It was a pact that was to be vigorously policed by the BCC, the pub managers and the dealers themselves.

Someone had planned the raid, however. Ron Bennet knew who – he had found himself, by mistake, stumbling in on a meeting to plan the operation between a white community activist and a community police officer the afternoon before the car park was invaded. He was sworn to secrecy. 'I didn't tell anyone,' he said. 'That was a mistake.'

The community police officers in the bar insisted that the commotion was not their fault. True or false, it hardly helped. The affable alliance between black and white customers, the community and the police was bust.

The publican looked outside: 'I saw various police vehicles, vans and dog vans.'

The Phoenix was stuck with the unwelcome officers. The officers were stuck in an angry place. Young black men were coming in and out with reports that the place would burn. It was no longer a safe space.

Zamir got the officers out of the bar, got them a drink and got them to call an inspector at their headquarters. Concerned to get his people out, he heard Zamir offer to drive them to safety. Too dangerous, headquarters replied. 'I said if we got the two officers out would the riot police go away,' said Zamir. 'He said yes.'

They made a plan: the Phoenix staff would get the two police officers over the back gardens to a road running parallel to the pub and the police would send a car to pick them up. The Phoenix and police headquarters kept the line open while Zamir warned some of the men moving around the pub that they'd have to get the officers out safely or the riot police would move in.

Two men stood by, ready to create a distraction. There were sentries, a man watching the back door, another man watching the front door. The landlady posted herself by one set of doors and another woman was poised to open a second set of doors when the officers appeared. They all waited for the community police officers. Time passed. Nothing happened. The officers were waiting for the word from headquarters. Young men began wandering in and out, wondering. Finally the word came. Zamir led the officers out of the opening doors and over the gardens.

'Someone shouted, "They're out!"' recalled Zamir. She heard the sound again: 'It seemed to echo, but then I realised I had heard, "They're out!" shouted three times.' The two police officers kept running over the gardens. I stood still – suddenly these figures appeared in the darkness, like organs on hydraulics coming out of the pit at the pictures. The figures stood up together, coming out of the ground as if they'd been squatting. Then I realised what they were. They were the riot police.'

From then on she felt 'no confidence that at any point would I know what was going to happen.' The police had broken their promise. 'They were yelling and swinging their truncheons over their heads, like a charge. I ran back to the pub and told my colleagues the police had lied, that there were riot police on the estate.'

The betrayal placed the Phoenix in double jeopardy. It was a community pub with black clients. The police believed it harboured drug dealers. The clients now believed it harboured police traitors who had lied about the raid and then reneged on a deal to keep away, after securing safe passage for their own people.

While riot police were running around the estate, at war with an estimated three hundred youths, young men menaced the Phoenix itself. 'Burn the pub down!' they shouted. 'Why?' people shouted back. 'It's our pub.'

Zamir had taken a sweeping brush outside the pub and began encouraging people to clear up. Coteries of young black men men were hanging around, blaming the pub for calling in the police. One spat in Zamir's face. Another wiped her face clean. One grabbed hold of her. Another freed her. Nothing and no one was what they seemed. A cool black man, streetwise and serene, Alva Rowe, took her to one side. 'You're white . . .,' he said. 'They don't know you.' They wouldn't listen to her. He then moved among the men, explained that the Phoenix was not to blame, and the mood went quiet.

Suddenly a helicopter appeared and riot police began another wave of charges up and down the streets, banging their truncheons on their shields. They did not appear to be doing much other than running up and down.

A stolen car was being rammed up against the wall. Zamir was frantic – she'd heard that her daughter was driving to Brackenhall to take her home. Was this her? 'It's stolen,' they reassured her. 'The police have sealed off the estate, no one can get in.'

Another car was ablaze. Some shops were being raided. But still the riot squads were running past the pub. 'We in the pub decided something had to be done and done quickly,' recalled one of the women working in the pub. A deputation went out to talk to the young men. A little later as closing time approached the police fanned out across the main road by the pub. The deputation, which included the Phoenix manager Chris Green, BCC manager Ron Bennett and Alva Rowe, went out again and sought out the officer in charge of the lines of riot police, in the hope of negotiating an end to the fighting.

When they found the officer in charge, Rowe was introduced and took off his glove to offer his hand to the officer. According to a record written by the publican later – several of the people trying to protect the Phoenix that night wrote down their exieriences in their effort to make sense of what had happened – the officer's first reaction 'appeared to me to threaten Alva with his truncheon which was already in his hand. It was a gesture that could only be described as an

instinctive reaction, but it still appeared to me as a threat.'
The deputation protested and 'the officer apologised, which
we accepted.'

The group explained that Alva Rowe had been protecting
the pub and trying to control the young men. 'Can we work
together?' the group offered. 'The people won't go home until
you leave,' the police were told. What was the point of running
up and down, they said. What would it take for them to leave?
'Either the crowd or the police will have to do something different.'

The police agreed that Rowe would be safe from any police
action while he moved around the crowd and tried to persuade
people to leave. When the publican mingled with some of the
crowd, 'I found that the rumours were that I had organised the
drugs raid, with the help of my wife and the police. I told the
people around me that the rumours were untrue.'

The police continued their charges up and down the road.
The publican again urged the police to withdraw and let locals
try to calm things down. He himself renewed his appeals to the
people in the street. 'The next thing that happened was the
police began charging up the road again and I had to jump into
a garden for my own safety. I have to say that I was shocked.
The same thing happened again after about fifteen minutes.'

After closing time Rowe went back into the pub and while
he was telephoning the police to report on the situation in the
streets, a woman inside collapsed. The police were alerted:
a woman was going to hospital. The description of the car
which would collect her was telephoned over and the police
were asked to let it through. The confrontations between the
young men and the police carried on into the small hours.

The Phoenix did not close its doors that night. They
stayed unlocked and at about 4 a.m. a posse of protectors
bedded down for the night inside. Alva Rowe reckoned the
streets were safe and at 6.30 a.m. the landlord and landlady
stretched out on a bench, head to head, holding hands in the
dark, hoping to sleep. In her exhaustion and fear the landlady
dreamed she was dead.

Alva Rowe walked home with his dog. He was picked up by the police and several witnesses still up and about saw him being hit by police officers with truncheons. His dog was also beaten and left, limp, in the street while Rowe was taken away in a police van. He was kept overnight in a police cell and charged with offences under the Public Order Act.

A police spokesperson explained that these events provoked profound discussion and 'a lot of soul-searching among police officers'. For some, the sight and sound of trouble produces a singular response: 'You've got to stand your corner.' For others, the events seemed to confirm their view that the trouble could have been staunched had the police agreed to withdraw: 'Sometimes if we just get out of the way then people often settle down and leave – because then there is nobody to argue with.' The notion that the police were giving a firm message to the crowd to disperse had clearly not got across.

'Several people came forward and said to the police that night, "We can get these people to go," and they really did!' said a police spokesperson. 'If nothing else, that night brought the most unexpected people out to cooperate.' That cooperation was to continue and it inaugurated a new era in local liaison. 'It turned out successfully in that it produced good cooperation between the community and the police,' said Inspector John Boothroyd, the Huddersfield Community Liaison Officer. There was still a feeling of bad faith to be discharged, however.

On Thursday, police managers and politicians and public servants came to survey the Brackenhall scene. The Huddersfield Labour MP, Barry Sheerman, reckoned that in the context of the summer riots the police should have been more sensitive. 'People on this estate are very unhappy that only hours after this new community pub opened there should have been such a strong police reaction to what appears to have been a minor incident involving drugs.'[7]

One of Rowe's friends, Errol Pusey, who had been trying

[7] *Huddersfield Daily Examiner*, 23 July 1992.

to calm the crowd, said, 'I do not particularly like the police, but we need them and until last night I respected them. But last night people were treated like animals, like dirt.'

Kirklees Council's Chief Executive, Robert Hughes, whose authority had responsibility for the estate, dispatched staff to Brackenhall to offer help. Apart from its more orthodox duties – swiftly clearing the streets of the bricks, broken glass, the relics of stolen cars – the Chief Executive's office facilitated negotiations with the police. 'The future is in their hands,' said Robert Hughes. 'These young men have got to be supported and allowed to take the lead.'

Senior police managers arrived at Brackenhall and entered into negotiations. No one wanted another night like 22 July. Everyone expected that 23 July would be bad. The police asked the community activists and several of the streetwise men who had defended the pub the night before, who made an offer: let us protect the estate. The police agreed.

Alva Rowe arrived back on the estate that day with a cut above his eye and bruises around his neck and chest. Errol Pusey and Alva Rowe were back on the streets, organising. They tried to keep the gangs of lads attracted to Brackenhall to the edge of the estate.

That night the estate was full of spectators – elderly women in their nighties sat on their walls by hip dudes plugged into their personal sound systems.

The police agreed that if they received emergency calls they would check with the Phoenix. The pub would then check with the lads whether the police were being enticed into an ambush. All were agreed – their problem was the young lads, who were beyond the reach of their streetwise seniors, the older residents and the community activists around the Phoenix. For two nights running there were occasional outbreaks of petrol-bombing and looting. But there was no riot. Kate Zamir didn't go home. She stayed at the Phoenix until Sunday. Her children, both almost grown up, brought clean clothes and sought reassurance. Alva Rowe had become a negotiator and patrolled his neighbourhood to keep the peace. Witnesses signed statements to challenge the police case against him. The charges were dropped.

On the longer term he became part of a new axis on the estate together with Errol Pusey and Tyrone Lyburd, when they formed a new black community group, Tomorrow's People, in an environment that had been dominated by white politics. They teamed up with police officers a couple of weeks later to visit Middlesbrough where a community-based security firm operated on several estates, providing services and employment to locals and linking up with the probation service to work with prisoners before they re-entered the community.

The community beat officers were not allowed back to Brackenhall – it was discovered that they had participated in the planning of the drugs raid that detonated the disturbances. Indeed the operation had been mounted with the knowledge of one white community leader – who had been discovered discussing it with a community police officer – but without the knowledge of the community pub. This had destabilised the delicate protocols of local alliances. More than that, it had brought bad faith into the exercise of policing by consent. Brackenhall Community Council colleagues discovered that the community beat had lied about their part in the raid and about the determination to bring riot police into the estate.

The new relationship between the police, the BCC, the Phoenix and Tomorrow's People which endured after the riot was mindful of the crisis those few days had created for the whole neighbourhood. As far as Inspector Boothroyd was concerned, 'It was a catalyst, it accelerated work on the estate. I feel that Brackenhall as a place is an eye-opener, it is pleasing, it makes me enthusiastic, it makes me want to go and help. I don't mean that in a condescending way, I mean that the people there are proud, they want to do things, and I want to support them.'

The Phoenix was a packed and popular place. It was as nice and naughty as the community itself, its survival was always going to be precarious. But the police operation against alleged drugs dealers had echoed so many disastrous public order crises caused by action that purported to be criminal investigation. Had the raid really been conducted, as Scarman had counselled, with the community's consent? And why had it ignited such dangerousness and such damage? During those days, people were left wondering who could be relied upon to create disorder or to keep calm.

At the same time as there was uproar in Brackenhall there was a week of street war among young men in Blackburn, Burnley and the border town, Carlisle. Huge gatherings of young men, ranging from eight hundred to three thousand, were mobilised with bricks and petrol bombs in Blackburn that week. A fight between two boys became a confrontation between young Indian and Pakistani men. Both communities, mostly Muslim, had lived uncomfortably together in Blackburn's Whalley Range neighbourhood for more than twenty years. A dispute over a young woman's relationship with a young man grew into a larger conflict that was driven by differences over a defence of tradition, over Muslim fundamentalism and young Asians' own navigation through an inhospitable white culture. Gul Khan's café, a popular Pakistani rendezvous, was petrol-bombed in the dispute. The heavy police response escalated the dispute into running street battles between the young men and the police.

Stolen cars were habitually dumped and torched behind the Community House on the Raffles estate in Carlisle, the mellow Cumbrian county town. During this riot season the Community House itself caught light. Fire engines were stoned and there were running battles in the street between people from some of the estate's 'well-known' families. It was all put down to family feuds but the city was not surprised that the Raffles was its link to riots in the national news. Regarded as 'rough', the estate's local culture was familiar with poverty and an illicit economy. But by the Eighties its poverty entered

a different dimension: 'We have children here who don't go
to school because they haven't got shoes,' said one Raffles
woman. The small, semi-detached dwellings in cul-de-sacs and
ample avenues had been refurbished in the village vernacular
popular in the Eighties, but there was no plan for economic
rehabilitation: 'Nobody has a strategy for this place. People
don't acknowledge desperation if it doesn't occur in high-rise
flats,' complained a community activist. The Raffles' fleeting
claim to fame happened during the Eighties when its only
medical practice withdrew because the NHS doctors could
no longer make a living from treating its people.

Young men and police on primarily white estates in the
old Lancashire textile town of Burnley – the Stoops and
Hargher Clough estates – went to war with each other at
the same time as the riots were flaring in Blackburn. On
20 July the street lights were smashed at Stoops and in
the small hours of the morning a motorbike was roaring
around the suburban semi-detached estate, high on revs,
low on courtesy. At 3 a.m. a Ford Escort was dragged into
the middle of a road and torched. When the police arrived
they were battered by bricks and petrol bombs. It looked
like an ambush. A second night of fighting began despite
a police presence throughout the day and the routine was
repeated in running skirmishes for another four nights. Riot
police stormed houses in the neighbourhood searching for
petrol bombs, including one household whose front door was
kicked in by mistake. More than ninety people were arrested.
A few months later, in September, young men attacked again.
They torched cars and felled street lamps in Hargher Clough's
Melrose Avenue, leaving the street in darkness. By midnight
cars were being set alight and lampposts were being attacked
by boys with sledgehammers.

The *Lancashire Evening Telegraph* tracked the July disturbances. With splenetic shock and horror, the paper responded to
the violence with a verbal violence to match. It editorialised

on 20 July: 'It is a symptom of something sick and evil in our midst. Something that must be rooted out and crushed.' The police should make an example of the ringleaders of 'this anarchic plot.' This purple local-press prose went on all week. But the paper at no point asked the question: Why has all this happened? What did everyone think they were doing?

British society had settled so deeply into decline that after more than a decade of the New Right's moralism and monetarism these volcanic eruptions came to be seen not as a failure of the most authoritarian Government since the Second World War, but as the necessary evil that sustained its paranoid political project. In other words, the riots did not disclose a social problem to be solved. Nor did they engage the interest of the Opposition, because they happened so far beyond the pale of respectability that neither the rioters nor their victims could be represented in the political domain. They just did not not even enter society's argument with itself. Britain already seemed so enervated that the riots appeared as just 'one damn thing after another', a 'midsummer madness' that was easily and summarily dismissed as the pathology of the poor. But the political lacuna at the heart of these events was teaching Britain something about itself, that firebombing and rioting were the way that young men in cities all over the country chose to communicate with each other. As their neighbourhoods approached the end of the century no one could imagine even a minimal mitigation of their actions in the way they lived, the way they said things and the way they were answered.

CHAPTER 17

Theory and Practice

In 1992 a BBC radio reporter returned to the scene of the 1991 Tyneside riots and ruminated on the remarkable absence of men from the medley of community initiatives towards renovation. It was not that they were not there: they lived there; it was not that they lacked the time: they had all the time in the world; it was that they lacked the commitment, he said. His discovery suggested a fresh discourse in the debate about the riots. Or rather, it should have prompted a debate. An embarrassed silence surrounded the events of September 1991, as if they were best left, like sleeping dogs, to lie, undisturbed by too much inquiry.

The riots had barked at ideologies which they confounded and confirmed at the same time. The theory of the *underclass* and that of *defensible space* in urban design, two theories which came together to describe junk people and junk places, appeared to be vindicated by the routine rioting of the early Nineties. After all, they had happened on *estates*, in *class communities* overwhelmed by *unemployment* and *crime*. These were all key terms in the theories of the underclass and of defensible space. But in the becalmed British politics of the time, no one stirred. That was partly because the riots invited no reply, no conversation, only slogans and stereotypes: 'unemployed . . . hooligans . . . single parents . . .'

Behind these were the external themes of discipline and punishment, and sexuality, legitimacy and wedlock – or, put another way, motherhood and the fatherless family. Neither sexuality nor style created mass unemployment or the so-called underclass. They were not to blame. But in the mind of the old respectability and the New Right it was not mass unemployment that was to blame for the underclass, it was manners and mothers. If the New Right ventured into the estates and saw the streets captured by thin, pale boys, it did not see the menacing response by men to the abolition of work, nor the street megalomania of boys trying to be men; in short, it did not see a *masculine* response to an economic crisis – it saw instead the failure of the *mothers* to manage the men.

The argument of this book is that neither manners nor mothers are to blame, but that there is an economic emergency in many neighbourhoods where the difference between what women and men do with their troubles and with their anger shapes their strategies of survival and solidarity on the one hand, danger and destruction on the other.

The era of the New Right did not stall the revolution in popular manners, but its economic policies did create a culture which celebrated the separation of acts from their consequences. 'If it isn't hurting, it isn't working' became one of the political legends of the time. That notion was expressed in the seismic shift in employment ideology: full employment had been sacred in postwar Britain until Thatcherism created levels of mass unemployment unseen in the postwar era. Millions of young people without work or wage became as familiar as traffic lights or *Neighbours* or beggars in *fin de siècle* Britain. In the early Eighties the creation of three million unemployed was presented by the Government as the voltage of its economic shock treatment. By the Nineties the prospect of four million unemployed was what Britain was learning to live with.

All the estates that witnessed riots in 1991 had been living with permanent high unemployment and decline, while they were encircled by evidence of prosperity and renewal. The newly-built Culverhouse Cross roundabout on the edge of Ely estate is a retail extravaganza dominated by large chain stores. As soon as news of the new stores reached Ely, the estate's Community Education redoubt, based in Trelai library, set to work to persuade the companies to offer jobs to Ely, an estate the size of a small town. Among the new stores, Marks and Spencer officially opened in 1992, and more than five hundred people applied for work. A hundred received an offer – all of them were part-time jobs on sixteen-week contracts.

In Oxford in 1991 there was a total of only ten vacancies for school leavers.

Meadowell, where in some streets unemployment was about eighty per cent, watched the creation of a new environment literally across the road. A new road was built around the boundary of the estate, running into the Royal Quays riverside redevelopment. The local authority had hopes that the Tyne could be modernised as a northern port, preserving a maritime tradition and links with the seafaring cities of Northern Europe and Scandinavia. This was not to be. The Enterprise Zone, Royal Quays, offered instead some industrial relocation, some new housing and a proposed water sports centre.

No one from the estate was employed to help build the road. A shield of trees was planted on the Royal Quays side of the boundary. No one can be in any doubt therefore that Royal Quays is not Meadowell. No one from Meadowell was employed to plant the trees. New houses and business premises were erected in Royal Quays. No one from Meadowell was employed in their construction. A new Twinings tea-packing factory was relocated in Royal Quays from another Tyneside site – old jobs in a new place. A year after the riots eleven workers from Meadowell were given jobs in Royal Quays.

Over in the West End of Newcastle, where there were twenty thousand workers in Vickers Armstrong shipyards after the Second World War, there were now only three thousand. Regional Aid strategies always supported the traditional but declining shipbuilding and heavy engineering industries, rather than investing in a new economic base.[1] Vickers and

[1] Fred Robinson, *Post Industrial Tyneside, An Economic and Social Survey of Tyneside in the 1980s*, Newcastle, 1989. Fred Robinson, Colin Wren, John Goddard, *Economic Development Policies*, Oxford University Press, 1987.

Swan Hunter had always been cushioned by their heavy stake in the arms industry – the Armed Services were stable, loyal clients, and the international arms trade was a vital market for the remnants of British engineering.[2]

The Gulf War was the beginning of the end for state-subsidised arms manufacturers. The Middle East was the largest single arms market in the world, and UK arms traders had enjoyed a privileged status among the Middle Eastern princes. All that began to fall apart in the international realignment after the Gulf War, when the Saudi and Kuwaiti regimes preferred to look to the US rather than the UK for their military reconstruction. The first victims were British Aerospace and Vickers.

Thatcherism had pledged an end to state subsidy for the regions and ailing industries. The North East's shipyards closed down. By the end of the decade there was barely a shipbuilding industry left in the region. The residents of the West End watched Vickers close its two factories in the West End and along the river shipyards shut down. But with lavish state subsidy the arms manufacturers opened anew in a long, gleaming grey shed in Scotswood, in an Enterprise Zone appointed at the beginning of the decade by the Environment Secretary Michael Heseltine. Enterprise Zones are mainland tax havens. No one knows the cost to the taxpayers of the city, or the benefits to the companies which settled within the zone – all that is secret.

Looking across the river from Scotswood, the residents see another miracle of the Enterprise Zone, the £200-million Gateshead Metro Centre, Europe's biggest retail park, which was built on 115 acres of derelict land, and was fuelled by tax allowances and an exemption from rates until 1991. It provided a crêche for customers, but not for its projected four thousand workers. Looking like an eyeless fortress, topped with stiff plastic flags around its periphery, the Metro Centre is a cornucopia of pastiche – customers walk around two million square feet

---

[2] *The Defence Converter*, National Trade Union Defence Conversion Committee, Newcastle, 1992.

of retail space down colour-coded routes, along 42nd Avenue, or around the Grecian Terrace, or through the Victorian arcade lit darkly with a night sky all day long. People go for the day to the Metro Centre; they have been seen with flasks and sandwiches as if they were on holiday. The Metro Centre is a shopping resort.

The hegemony of the theory of the underclass in the Nineties is one of the triumphs of the New Right. Even amidst Britain's nemesis it still owned the ideological initiative.

The underclass theorists appeared to offer, if nothing else, a *name* for the people causing all the trouble in Britain during the Eighties and Nineties. The underclass were represented as the people with nothing, without employment, without credit and without culture. The notion of the *underclass* displaced the *unemployed*. They therefore had *no* class. It was a notion which had a long life in socialism, liberalism and conservative ideologies alike. During great economic depressions it was mobilised afresh to distinguish between 'the people' and 'the poor', the worthy and the unworthy. We have already seen that it is a definition that objectifies 'the poor' and renders them a homogenous lump because it fails to see the spectrum of subjectivities, it does not discern the diverse repertoire of responses to poverty within the wageless working class.

Nonetheless the persistence of the theory deserves some attention. The theory of the underclass is rooted not in economics but in morals, manners and style. Typically, it is sustained in the traditional distinction between the rough and the respectable. This great divide described part of the architecture of attitudes to be found in every working-class street. The scaffolding around respectability was always shaky: as Moll Flanders' saga shows us, it could be lost and gained by a whim, by luck or a legacy, by a death or a birth.

By the Sixties the cement of respectability – sexual manners – was under siege in all classes. The challenges, the formalities, repressions, and chauvinisms found a political language in the new egalitarianism of the Sixties and Seventies. In the Eighties the cultural revolt acquired an inflection specifically of sex and style. Although the icons of the Sixties, the pill and the mini-skirt, implied relaxed sexual manners, the stamina of respectability was evident in the persistence of births within wedlock, despite the popularity of sex outside it. The Sixties icons were displaced by the condom and the shell suit. Neither the pill nor the condom did much to change sexual mores – responsibility still seemed to lie with women – but the transition from mini-skirt to shell suit and leggings marked a major shift. The shell suit was the tinned peas of its time, the clothing of convenience. Leggings did what the mini-skirt could never do; they were body-hugging but not revealing. The shell suit and the Lycra revolution were the emblematic items: they diminished the dress distinction between going out and staying in, between public and private, between work and leisure and between men and women. However, these totems of mass style were not read among the opinion-formers for their strengths, their flexibility, their colour, their convenience and comfort; they were read through the filter of snobberies rooted in respectability, in rigid demarcations between work and play, men and women, formality and informality. Their cachet did not lie in tags of privilege; on the contrary, they were the antithesis of the power dressing that in the Eighties anchored style to corporate culture rather than to popular culture.

The underclass theory effectively re-established the mentor of Thatcherism, Sir Keith Joseph, who in the Seventies had embraced the theory of the 'Cycle of Poverty', which proposed a circuit of self-reproducing degeneracy. Joseph spawned research projects costing nearly £1 million in the hope of vindicating this cycle-of-deprivation theory. It was a vain enterprise, showing the resilience and ingenuity of poor people's efforts to survive disadvantage.[3] It showed that half the

---

[3] M. Rutter and N. Madge, *Cycles of Disadvantage*, Heinemann, London, 1976.

children born into disadvantaged households did not take the legacy of disadvantage into the next generation.

The renaissance of moralism and moral panic was evident in the theory of the underclass. Indeed, one of its proponents in England, Professor Ralf Dahrendorf, Warden of St Antony's College, Oxford, exposed its mood of paranoia when he explained: 'My profound conviction is that the argument for doing something about the underclass has to be moral . . . It is morally unbearable to have a category or group of people who have no stake in the prevailing values of the world in which we are living.'⁴ This was a class characterised by apathy: 'We are not talking about a potential political force', by 'the one-parent family phenomenon', by 'an accumulation of disadvantages, almost a cycle of deprivation.'

The theory had enjoyed several reincarnations and most recently was recycled from the US, where one of its exponents, who was promoted in the UK, is the American sociologist Charles Murray. His ruminations on the British underclass were published in the *Sunday Times* in 1989 and later by the right-wing Institute of Economic Affairs under the title, *The Emerging British Underclass*. Like Dahrendorf, he appeared to be immune to the disarray left by Joseph's theoretical caprice.

Murray spoke straight into a rugged common sense ingrained in grammar-school consciousness that distinguished between the *economy* of the poor and the *behaviour* of the poor: they created their own poverty, he said. Indeed, Murray could not bring himself to refer to unemployment. In the manner of the New Right's redefinition of the homeless as the 'rough sleepers', he referred instead to the 'failure to work'.

Murray's thesis is also intensely gendered. He is the scourge of the mother-scrounger and therefore speaks directly to a *moral minority* which, despite its marginality in popular culture, enjoyed a place in the sun of Thatcherism's 'rainbow coalition',

---

⁴ Ralf Dahrendorf, 'The future of the underclass: a European perspective' in *Northern Economic Review*, no. 18, Autumn 1989.

which united liberal monetarism and illiberal moralism.

Murray's thesis was candid in its prejudice. Given the preponderance of white people in the habitations of the new poor, he could have cited whiteness as the main characteristic. He opted instead, in his search for the predictor of 'an underclass in the making', for 'illegitimacy'. Until the Seventies – and through the purportedly naughty Sixties – British respectability was remarkably successful in keeping 'illegitimacy' rates low by international standards. However, it was during the Eighties, in the very period that synchronised with the Government's raucous endorsement of 'family values' that respectability was shredding. Britain's 'illegitimacy' rate rose from 10.6 per cent to 25.6 per cent by 1988. That cultural revolution was taking place across all classes, though Murray fixed on its prevalence among the working class.

'In this concentration of illegitimate births, there lies a generational catastrophe,' says Murray. This is not because of morality or marriage, he cautions, rather it is a crisis because 'communities need families. Communities need fathers.' Despite his caveat that it is not morality and marriage that worry him, Murray challenges the efficacy of the extended family among American Afro-Caribbeans – the object of much theorising about the underclass. He insists that *marriage* is the family cement. Having said that, he lets his angst bleed across the argument: without marriage there is no father, he says, and furthermore, 'grandfathers and uncles, too, become scarce.' What is remarkable about Murray's thesis is the invisibility of women, mothers, grandmothers, aunts, as the real, live, operational carers. Having minimised their work, he minimises their strength. 'A child with a mother and no father, living in a neighbourhood of mothers with no fathers, judges by what he sees.' We can only speculate as to what Murray thinks they see. Shall we guess, dear reader, that what children see is their mothers making their world go round? Nope. Murray's thesis is that up to fifteen years ago every poor neighbourhood had 'plentiful examples of good fathers around them'. They did? But it seems they have been evicted, or allowed to abscond. He never asks himself the question which has vexed mothers for a millennium: what is it about cultures of masculinity that means men will not cooperate with women and take care of their children? He cannot explain modern men's resistance to the reform of domestic life. By situating himself on the side of fathers' rights he ignores the history of mothers' responsibilities.

The flight of the fathers has been reinterpreted by the underclass theorists as something new, as a purge orchestrated by the mothers. In the nostalgic appeal to the olden days when men were men and mothers were only mothers, they invoke the heyday of respectability as the proper regime of family life. However, in the respectable classes fatherhood was expressed in the wage packet. Among the rich it was expressed in the inheritance. Fathers were expected to be *providers*, not *parents*.

This was consummately shared with the nation by the most famous father of all, the aspiring King of the United Kingdom, Prince Charles. The future queen was handed over, by one of the great households in the country, to the future king, to marriage and motherhood. Unlike most of her generation – though consistent with the alleged mores of the so-called underclass – she was uneducated and unworldly, with no more earning potential than the lasses on the estates. She was assigned to an arranged marriage, to a family so preoccupied with the Prince's power and potential paternity that it failed to enlighten her during her engagement about the most important thing in her life – him, his past and his present. Until the publication of Andrew Morton's revelatory biography of Princess Diana, the Prince was projected to the nation as the model of modern man.[5] According to Morton, however, he behaved, not like a modern man but as an old-fashioned paterfamilias, both selfish

[5] Andrew Morton, *Princess Diana: The True Story*, Michael O'Mara, London, 1992.

and sexist. Like the late and unlamented Andy Capp, the future king has been revealed by Andrew Morton's book as a shameless chauvinist with conservative passions and prejudices about modernity, who behaves towards his family as a quintessential patriarch. Having sired children he rarely sees them; indeed he seems to prefer sport to the company of his sons.

Among the underclass theorists, woman's economic dependence is dignified as the condition of active fatherhood; her independence as the *cause* of absent fatherhood. A woman's impoverished independence is deemed utterly unworthy. It might mean a movement from poverty, as a result of the inequality within marriage, to poverty, as a result of dependence on benefits – not from adequacy to penury.[6] Another cigarette might seem to the New Right and the respectable as extravagance, when to a woman managing a home and the wellbeing of all its inhabitants on less than the means of subsistance it might provide a moment to calm down, to find solitude, shrouded in a smokescreen. A cigarette might be all that she thinks she can give in return to a neighbour or sister who is relied upon for survival routines, for what Professor Hilary Graham has called 'funding respite'.

A candid though eccentric defence of women's dependence was published in the wake of the riots of the early Nineties and indeed purported to *explain* them.[7] In his introduction to *Families Without Fatherhood*, Professor A.H. Halsey explains that Norman Dennis and George Erdos push the boundaries of Charles Murray's inner-city underclass: 'For them, growing illegitimacy and family breakdown, the reduction in the work ethic and rising crime are signals of a general *malaise* affecting British culture.' Dennis' track record includes a text co-authored with Professor Halsey, *English Ethical Socialism*,

---

[6] Eileen Evason, *Just Me and the Kids: A Study of Single Parent Families in Northern Ireland*, Equal Opportunities Commission, Belfast, 1980. Hilary Graham, *Women, Health and the Family*, Harvester, Sussex, 1984.
[7] Norman Dennis and George Erdos, *Families Without Fatherhood*, Institute of Economic Affairs, London, 1992.

which claims to be 'in essence the moral view of the respectable working class, based on solid family life.' This was, of
course, the moral view of advertising's C2 man, whose socialism had no stomach for the new egalitarianism of the Seventies
and Eighties and who found his voice in the patriarchal 'family
values' of Thatcherism.

Respectability, which codified the settlement of the great
struggle over masculinity and femininity, was one of the
formative ideologies of modernity. That drama of domination
defined the way men, women and children occupied space
and created communities. When capital withdrew from the
industrial areas which were the cradle of the 'moral view of
the respectable working class' then the historic compromise
between capital and men, mediated by the Labour movement,
collapsed. The authority of the Labour-movement man, with
his National Service haircut, his Clubs and Institutes Union
card, his pride and his prejudice against women, was at an
end. Dennis and Erdos argue that it is foolish to look to
poverty to explain the 'resistible rise of the obnoxious
English man in the last generation' as if his antecedents were
otherwise. Their tract does not suggest that we look at men's
culture for an explanation. Rather the cause is to be found in
feminism and the cure in Catholicism: 'As the Marxist–
feminist attack on the family is the last fling of Marxism,
the Catholic family was the last bastion against what in
England (and indeed throughout the world) was in the 1980s
popularly thought of as Thatcherism.' Men were absconding
from fatherhood once women could survive without them.
Once the 'onerous tasks' of parenthood 'became avoidable'
then 'it was quite natural that fatherhood was increasingly
avoided' and a generation of 'egoists' was born. It led Dennis
and Erdos not to a critique of masculinity, but towards a
paranoid notion of the North East as a haven of Marxism.
Actually, the region was famously resistant to the allure of
Bolshevism. Boilermakers and miners, not revolutionary
socialism, defined the conservative Labourism for which it
was well known.

Dennis and Erdos are shamelessly old-fashioned in their advancement of a 'men are beasts' theory of human nature. Their fatalism finds echoes in a long tradition of snobbish English socialism, from George Orwell to Jeremy Seabrook, which found another angry young ally in Tony Parsons, *Arena* magazine's 'young fogey' columnist.[8] His splenetic rant on the 'tattooed jungle' conflates the working class with the lads he meets on the terraces. However, theirs is less a *class* culture than a *male* culture. These men have more in common with the men who represent the nation, the rowdy louts in the Palace of Westminster whose manners are modelled on an upper-class cult of conflict. The lads on the terraces behave more like MPs on the benches than school dinner ladies and secretaries, and the women who have to put up with them. There is a riposte to Parsons' diatribe in a tattooist's manifesto on Newcastle's Byker Bridge: 'The only difference between tattooed people and non-tattooed people . . . is that tattooed people don't care if you are not tattooed.'

The underclass theorists' moral panic about fathers was ignited not by their flight and failure – that, after all, was nothing new – but by their redundancy. Having failed to identify their refusal to cooperate with women and children, the underclass thesis redirects its rage against the women when they show that they will survive, just about, without them. To *reveal* the redundancy of the fathers is the crime of the mothers.

Since the hidden agenda of the underclass theory is an attack on mothers as practitioners of parenting and feminism as a theory of male domination, its exponents are paralysed by the problem of marauding masculinities in the cities. Like the men they criticise, however, they cannot imagine a political and cultural coalition with women. The underclass theorists refuse to address what the nineteenth-century socialist and

[8] Tony Parsons, 'The Tattooed Jungle: the decline of the working class' in *Arena*, Autumn 1991.

advocate in the cooperative movement, William Thompson, designated the 'sexual Toryism' of men.[9]

The theory of the underclass entered the vernacular together with the image of the *estate*. The two became synonymous in Britain and they found their bridge in Peter Hall's prestigious book, *Cities of Tomorrow: An Intellectual History of Urban Planning and Design in the Twentieth Century*.[10] This sees parallels of the black ghetto of the US in Britain's riots of the Eighties. Much of Hall's case is drawn from Patrick Moynihan's 1965 report, *The Negro Family: The Case for National Action*,[11] a mysogynist critique of the black mother in the United States. According to Moynihan, the black community had been 'forced into a matriarchal structure which, because it is so out of line with the rest of American society, seriously retards the progress of the group as a whole and imposes a crushing burden on the Negro male.' Moynihan conceded that the black female was burdened, too, but that was clearly *her* problem. Moynihan's report was overshadowed by the government-appointed – and hardly radical – Kerner Commission into the riots in American cities in the Sixties, which located the crisis of American blacks not in their mothers but in 'white racism' and in the cultures of the ghetto which created 'ruthless, exploitative relationships'. A decade later those cultures would be called sexism.

Moynihan was resurrected in the Eighties, when the economic recession and political regression of Reaganomics inaugurated a new era of decline in the American cities. Hall incorporated the British riots into his exposition of the 'city of the permanent underclass', and cited Broadwater Farm as

[9] Barbara Taylor, *Eve and the New Jerusalem*, Virago, London, 1983.
[10] Peter Hall, *Cities of Tomorrow: An Intellectual History of Urban Planning and Design in the Twentieth Century*, Basil Blackwell, Oxford, 1991.
[11] Patrick Moynihan, *The Negro Family: The Case for National Action*, report for the US Department of Labor, 1965.

an exemplar of 'indefensible space'. The theory of 'defensible space' derived from Oscar Newman's exhaustive and influential study of New York municipal housing, *Defensible Space*.[12] The resonance of Newman's study lay in its scrutiny of the design detail that attracted danger in public housing. He believed that safety was secured by the casual surveillance of the neighbourhood by the neighbours. Unsafe spaces were those where vigilance was designed out by the creation of blind corners, blank corridors and blank decks. Racism and horrible council housing came together to produce what Hall predicted was a British story, 'the same or worse' than the US.

Britain had its own home-grown exponent of defensible space, the geographer Alice Coleman, who deployed blunt statistics which, following Oscar Newman, mapped an assault on nasty municipal modernism in the tower blocks and deck walkways of high-rise estates.[13]

Formidable in her critique of the municipal high-rise and the unmanaged, unprotected, unspecified and unused – though much abused – nooks and crannies of cheap public housing, she adopted the postwar moral panic about 'stranger danger'.

Coleman had a passion for suburbia; indeed she went so far as to suggest that 'the redemption of the semi's reputation is only the first stop in encouraging a housing revolution.' Coleman offered no critique of the withdrawal of management services from the municipal estates. She had nothing to say about the *social* pleasures of public space, since she celebrated only the privacy of the family home. Nor did she offer economics as a variable in the prevalence of crime in neighbourhoods.

Coleman became a star in the Eighties, employed by the

[12] Oscar Newman, *Defensible Space: Crime Prevention and Urban Design*, Macmillan, London, 1972.
[13] Alice Coleman, *Utopia on Trial: Vision and Reality in Planned Housing*, Hilary Shipman, London, 1985.

Conservative Westminster Council to rehabilitate the massive and troubled Mozart estate, and well resourced in her research by the Government. The riot territories of the Eighties, particularly Broadwater Farm, appeared to vindicate her 'design creates crime' thesis. But the estates which combusted in the Nineties devasted her suburban premise: they happened on essentially suburban, greenfield estates. She had studied Blackbird Leys, which had few high-rise blocks, and exempted it from her wrath. But a later study of the estate showed that tenants' problems were not manifest in buildings but in social relations, not shown in vandalism and litter – but in stress. Their problem was not design so much as management – the endless battle over repairs and their difficulty in engaging the attention of their landlord. 'The need to battle for repairs to be attended to undermined their self-respect.' Their sense of a reciprocal relationship with the council was unrewarded – they paid their rent but the housing departent did not do their repairs. Only ten per cent of households were managed by a lone parent, but the problem facing all young mothers was the absence of childcare, the lack of waged work, and the absence of a social life other than visiting each other. Contrary to the notion of wanton dependence, these women were struggling single-handledly, without seeking help, 'lest they be thought unable to manage.'[14] It was not physical arrangement of their estate that was their problem, it was the lack of a social infrastructure.

The crisis of Scotswood's society did not conform to the 'design creates crime' prediction. All the riot estates exemplified suburban patterns, but none more than Scotswood where the dwellings were a monument to the Coleman model of defensible space: a front garden, front-facing door facing the residents opposite, back gardens meeting the back gardens of the next street. The design did create vigilance – residents could at least see burglars climbing the drainpipes opposite or,

[14] F. Reynolds, *A Problem Estate: An Account of Omega and its People*, Gower, London, 1986.

from their kitchen windows, racing across the back gardens. But by the time of the 1991 riots nearly four hundred households had fled Scotswood within a couple of years because they felt endangered.

Crime was *spatialised* in the Nineties. The collective gaze was directed at localities rather than, for example, the grandiose corporate frauds which vexed, and ultimately exhausted, the judicial system. The 'symbolic locations' shifted from the *frisson* of chaos and cosmopolitanism in the inner city – the *interior* of the celebrated metropolis – to the edge of the city, archipelago, out there, anywhere. These were places that were part of a mass landscape in Britain, *estates* were everywhere. But in the Nineties estates came to mean crime.

David Harvey's influential text, *The Condition of Post-Modernity, An Enquiry into the Origins of Cultural Change*, has been subjected to a robust critique by the feminist scholar, Professor Doreen Massey, as an exemplar of the resistance to feminism's scrutiny of sexual difference in social space.[15] His rumination that the working class is better at organising 'place' than social or national 'space' typically effaces the conflict *within* the working class to control local place and social space, between men and women, which so disabled the democratic ambitions of working-class politics.

Harvey follows a long tradition in localising and parochialising working-class culture – the dynamic between globalism and localism in the cultural consumption of the young, urban working class in the Eighties and Nineties escapes him. He misses the geography of gender and space: a millennial struggle between the sexes over space, from the region of the body to

[15] David Harvey, *The Condition of Post-Modernity, An Enquiry into the Origins of Cultural Change*, Basil Blackwell, Oxford, 1989. Doreen Massey, 'Flexible Sexism' in *Society and Space, Environment and Planning* D, vol. 9, pp. 31-57, 1991.

the neighbourhood to the space of society.

Within the estates, the space of the street, the chip shop, the kitchen, the club, are all shaped by solidarities that show the communities' social system. Social space, argues Henri Lefebvre, 'is encounter, assembly, simultaneity, either through conflict or cooperation.'[16] These peripheral locales reveal something larger than themselves about the 'spacialisation' of conflict and cooperation within communities. Everyday comings and goings are the labyrinths of local intercourse, the 'space of enunciation'.[17]

The crisis of the estates is spatialised when the young men assert their dominance by flooding the public domain, primarily the streets, with their own, exclusive, coteries. Bill Hillier and Julienne Hanson have mapped this spatialisation of solidarities and discovered stark differences between how men and women move across the social landscape.

Control over space is used to dominate – to confine and fragment the social space of the dominated. The character of women's encounters emphasises movements from the local to the larger space, which are non-exclusive, easy-access, and expansionist. Men's movement emphasises exclusiveness, restriction, symbolic ordering and control over access. Women's encounters tend to proceed from the local to the wider networks beyond, men's imply membership of more contrived associations which may or may not be lived locally.

For Hillier and Hanson the relationship between men and women's solidarities 'is perhaps the dominant force in shaping space.'[18]

These typical spatial expressions of social organisation are manifest in the stark distinction between the way men and women deal with distress and manage their troubles in

[16] Henri Lefebvre, *The Production of Space*, Basil Blackwell, Oxford 1991.
[17] M. de Certeau, *The Practice of Everyday Life*, Berkeley, California, 1984.
[18] Bill Hillier and Julienne Hanson, *The Social Logic of Space*, Cambridge University Press, Cambridge, 1984.

neighbourhoods living on the edge of emergency. The criminal fraternity is, typically, exclusive, secretive, coercive, destructive. Its pay-off is that it yields to impoverished places access to basic material provisions and the commodities for cultural consumption that connect them to the world they live in. Their challenge, however, is not to the systems surrounding the neighbourhood that produce economic and political crisis, but to the community itself. The criminal fraternity is nothing if not about the means by which coteries of men constitute their dominance. The price is that the neighbourhood is thus endangered by a fraternity with which it is also economically engaged.

Solidarity and self-help are sustained by networks that are, by contrast, open, expansive, egalitarian and incipiently democratic. Their challenge is to the systems which bear upon their local life.

Crime and coercion are sustained by men. Solidarity and self-help are sustained by women. It is as stark as that.

The word that embraced everything feared and loathed by the new orthodoxy about class and crime was *estate*: what was once the emblem of respectability, what once evoked the dignity and clamour of a powerful social constituency, part of the body politic, but which now described only the edge of a class and the end of the city. 'Estate' evoked rookery, slum, ghetto – without the exotic energy of urbanity.

Estates were once the *ordinary* manifestation of modernity. The agent was the municipality and mass housing was the form in which late modernism rearranged the landscape of most British cities. Those were the days when working-class homesteads dominated the housing market, before and after the Second World War, when *estate* cultures held the rough and the respectable in eternal and exhilarating tension. But those days were to disappear with the ascent of Thatcherism and the decline of *public* housing as *popular* housing.

And so, the modern, the municipal and the masses found

themselves cramped together into a failed concept. But estates
were a contradiction: whether they were a retreat to the rustic,
a celebration of functionalism, or a whim of brutalism, they
repudiated the modern metropolis as an emporia of *public*
pleasures. Apart from the odd church, shop or hall, they were
stripped of urban services and of the means of congregation.

Estates were space but not place – only the recidivism
of the popular classes in their determination to gather survived the suburbanisation of the working class, usually to
the irritation of those who prided privacy above all. People,
young and old, discover corners, paths, hedges, shops and bus
shelters, junctions, gates and conters around which to meet.
But estates do not make it easy – they meant it when they
were designated *housing estates*; they are warehouses of the
working class, primarily on the periphery of the cities, where
they were supposed to benefit from the air, cleansed of the
naughty but nice entertainments of the city.

The crisis of public space on the estates was not caused
by people's congress, but the extinction of their economy and
the erosion of *cooperative* use of public space, its tyrannical
appropriation and degradation by the lads who terrorised the
men, women and children with whom they shared space. This
is the problem with no name.

Men, of course, were the traditional model for this capture
of sociable spaces – they met in bars, pubs and clubs designed
for their exclusive enjoyment. They were never very good at
sharing space. Men's relationship to estates tended to be like
their relationship to home – not exactly a place to live so
much as a place to leave, to return: to come and go. Work
and pleasure were expected to be located somewhere else.
Their social behaviour appeared in the contours of their
spatial relations, and they provided the model for their lads.
Mass unemployment changed the men's relationship to space
because when their means of making a legitimate living was
destroyed, then their licensed means of episodic escape – waged
work – was withdrawn. They were stuck at home. The lads, on
the other hand, stuck to the streets.

However, the potency of gender in shaping society and the cultures of classes has been reasserted. When unemployment brought men back home, nothing changed except the terrain where the drama of difference was played out. Meadowell exemplified men's enforcement of the sexual division of labour in space, in its politics and in its streets: one of the defendants in a Meadowell riot trial offered a piquant instance of the way that men moved in a different orbit from women. When asked whether he hated the Asian shopkeepers in Avon Avenue because he hated 'Pakis', a mature man, whose name and extended family were 'well known' on the estate, offered this as his alibi: he told the court that he never went to the shops because his wife did all the shopping, he only went to the club and the bookies. When men were asked why they didn't take part in the practical politics the women had generated they said all that was women's work.

Crudely, the underclass theorists target planners, single mothers and children as the detonators of order, discipline, community. Single mothers become represented as a contagion, their children become aliens, their neighbourhoods become colonies contained in the imagery of big dogs, smoking women, wall-to-wall TV, snotty children who learn to say 'fuck off' before they can say 'please'. But the theorists' real lament is the loss of *respectability*.

Of course, respectability was only a way of regulating the domestication of women and the discipline of men. It was a way of making sure that women did not wander, that they managed men while the men were assured of their public power and their personal irresponsibility.

The death of respectability has meant that the movement of women across both public and private space is no longer constrained: that boundary is burned out, women are anywhere. All the riot territories testify to that – it was the women who sustained the personal, public and political lives of these neighbourhoods.

But the death of respectability also meant that there was no personal or political context, culture, institution, rhetoric or discipline to make men cooperate with women, children, or community. When their patrons – the owners of private capital – walked away and left them without their one guarantee of their power and privilege – work and wages – they were left to the company of the *other* within their own class, the women. They refused to cooperate, however; they became the refuseniks of the community. Meanwhile, so did everyone else. That was the prehistory to the riots.

Meadowell's roofless houses, every tile stripped from scores of evacuated homes, bore witness to a vigorous and destructive illegal economy. You knew you were entering Scotswood because you suddenly sighted burglar alarms on council houses, the bright yellow boxes telling their own story of a neighbourhood besieged and doing its legal best to defend itself. Men, it seemed, were everywhere unmanned, their identity as men put into crisis because they were poor. It did not occur to the orthodoxies to suggest that women were unwomanned by their poverty. Certainly, the economic crisis gendered an identity crisis – for men and boys. However, it was not that they *lost* their identity, but the way that they *asserted* it, that was the problem.

The heralds of defensible space and underclass theory in Britain were, consciously or not, lamenting the lost respectability of the estates. They were grieving over the wrong corpse. Their mourning turned vicious because they did not know how to read the estates, and because they refused to disclose their own disposition – they themselves were *situated* in an ideology saturated with piety and respectability. Exponents of the underclass thesis scapegoated mothers, not masculinity. The effect of economic crisis was, of course, *gendered* but mothers were culpable for the lads' culture of predation that tyrannised the places of the poor. The *Sunday Times*, fizzling with moral panic about children as killers in early 1993, floated the mantra of Charles Murray and mother-blaming.

'Consider the plight of today's child of the underclass,' the *Sunday Times* editorialised on 21 February. In sink estates where 'illegitimacy' is more than fifty per cent, the 'disastrous consequences of being without fathers from birth can be seen in the uncontrollable behaviour of today's sink-estate male teenagers.'

The alleged absence of role models, as we have seen, came not from the absence of men and masculinities in their lives – the lads were surrounded by a macho propaganda more potent in its penetration of young men's hearts and minds than at any other time in history – they were soaked in globally transmitted images and ideologies of butch and brutal solutions to life's difficulties.

In the Nineties young men were schooled in unprecedented displays of personal and public force. In the prelude to the Nineties, with the demise of the Cold War, real war, real killing, became, once again, one of the world's ways of doing things. Going to war was what nations did to each other – they recruited their young men to kill and they rounded up women to be raped.

The lads on the estates were not estranged from those cultural reference points: they, like journalists and judges, consumed as well as created those images and ideologies. The lads' problem was not that they were starved of male role models, it was that they were saturated with them. That was the problem with no name that set the estates on fire in 1991.

There is nothing in the political economy of Britain that will make any difference to the people living in a state of emergency on the edges of the cities. The restoration of respectability is no more an option for the poor than it is for the worldly working class, still the majority class in Britain, or for the metropolitan middle class.

It is hard to imagine anything in *fin de siècle* Britain that will change the conditions of existence among the poor people. By the end of the century the children who entered society when they started school during the riots will be entering their dangerous years when they become teenagers. Among them will be these five-year-olds, who talk about their life and times in Meadowell with an enlightening realism. They reveal how far their identities as boys and girls are assigned to the tasks of taking *from* and taking *care*. Their futures are already ancient history. When asked what she wanted to be, a girl insisted, 'I want to be a mam.' Her playmates agreed, they wanted to be mams and dads. Then a boy dissented: 'I don't want to be a dad, I want to be a robber.'